TORT LAW

TORT LAW

A COMPARATIVE INTRODUCTION

ERIC TJONG TJIN TAI

Professor of Private Law, Tilburg Law School, Tilburg University, the Netherlands

Edward Elgar
PUBLISHING

Cheltenham, UK • Northampton, MA, USA

Published by
Edward Elgar Publishing Limited
The Lypiatts
15 Lansdown Road
Cheltenham
Glos GL50 2JA
UK

Edward Elgar Publishing, Inc.
William Pratt House
9 Dewey Court
Northampton
Massachusetts 01060
USA

A catalogue record for this book
is available from the British Library

Library of Congress Control Number: 2022941181

ISBN 978 1 80392 435 9 (cased)
ISBN 978 1 80392 437 3 (paperback)
ISBN 978 1 80392 436 6 (eBook)

Printed and bound in Great Britain by TJ Books Limited, Padstow, Cornwall

CONTENTS

FIGURES

PREFACE

The following text comprises an introduction to comparative tort law. It is based on tort law research in recent decades, where there is growing support for a reconstruction of tort law that transcends national details and finds a broadly similar basic structure underlying national differences. I believe that it is feasible and useful to teach students national tort law rules on the basis of such a fundamental structure. An immediate advantage of such an approach is that it facilitates practical comparative legal research on a functional basis. Without such a fundament, the study of concrete tort law systems would quickly confuse the beginning student who is faced with a host of conflicting and seemingly incommensurable concepts and doctrines. Admittedly, some degree of simplification is unavoidable, given the limitations of an introductory text.

This introduction therefore does not aim at perfect comparative correctness. Instead the aim is a first-order approximation, as is the term in exact science: an approximation which is formally incorrect in detail but correct in outline and allows further, better refinements that approximate reality continually closer. At an introductory level we cannot expect students to fully understand all the details and nuances of legal culture and practice. Just like you don't expect beginners in a language to speak fluently and are already happy if they can make themselves understood, we should be satisfied if beginning students can already follow legal reasoning in tort law in many jurisdictions, even if they will need to do additional work to get the details right. Indeed, as practising lawyers well know, most law graduates brought up in a single system still need to catch up with the full amount of detail of that system that is required in practice. The practice of law is eternal learning.

The knowledge that the student obtains is therefore less detailed for a specific system than would be acquired when studying a single jurisdiction. That is unavoidable, as the student needs to look at three national systems simultaneously, instead of only a single one. Nonetheless this broader perspective does have advantages. Young children who are raised in a multi-lingual environment may take longer to speak each language well, and may in the beginning make mix-ups, but eventually they learn all these languages faster and at a much higher level of proficiency than students who have started out with a single language.

The basic structure of tort law is complemented with more detailed knowledge in three key jurisdictions: France, Germany and England (and Wales). These details are necessary to give body to the actual structure: herein the present text differs from more abstract treatments in the philosophy of tort law. Tort law only comes to life when we examine the actual compromises and dilemmas of law, as exemplified in the actual choices that legal systems make when dealing with real-life cases. The three jurisdictions that are discussed here are exemplary for a large number of jurisdictions around the world: common law and various kinds of civil law systems.

The text furthermore provides guidelines and examples to help the student find their way in a legal environment that is not restricted to a single jurisdiction. There are numerous examples of different solutions and terminology from all around the world to get a feel of how tort law is implemented in other jurisdictions besides the three that are the focus of this text. A brief characterization of other tort law systems in the world rounds off the comparative approach.

After studying this text, the reader should not be afraid to approach an unfamiliar tort law system, rather they should feel challenged to do the research that is required, aided by the basic tools and knowledge of this introduction.

While this text can be read on its own, it is highly recommended to also use supplementary materials. The concepts discussed in this text really only come to life when discussing them in the context of a specific court case or a detailed analysis of case law in a specific legal system. Similarly it is highly recommended to examine the codes quoted here as an entire system instead of the bits and pieces that are discussed and quoted here.

The quotations from codes and statutes in this text support the content of this introduction. The reader has to learn how to analyse provisions from a code, and what kind of provisions and instruments are generally available. The translations have been made by the author to facilitate access to the systems of French and German law in particular. They deviate from translations found elsewhere particularly in that they aim to match more closely the conceptual framework set out in this text.[1] That can occasionally lead to terminological choices that may be controversial due to debates among national legal scholars. Also, the translations are on occasion somewhat stiff and clunky in order to keep the logical structure of the original provision. These translations are only provided as an aid for the discussion, the reader is encouraged to consult other translations elsewhere.[2] The text also liberally refers to other codes and cases all over the world. These references are added mostly to illustrate the idea that the fundamental structure of tort law is indeed applicable in most jurisdictions.

At this place I would like to express my gratitude to Paul Verbruggen, Marc Loth and Kasia Kryla-Cudna who commented on an earlier version of this text. The department of Private Law, Business Law and Labour Law of Tilburg Law School has been a friendly and stimulating environment for developing my thoughts, and the course of Global Tort Law that I have taught as part of the Tilburg Global Law Bachelor program has provided a fertile ground for testing out the presentation of comparative tort law. I'm grateful for the insightful questions and comments from my students who helped to pinpoint the more difficult concepts and find a way to make these more tractable. I feel privileged in being able to help you take your first steps into the world of global law. Furthermore my warm thanks to Ben Booth and Amber Watts for supporting this project. Finally I wish to thank Karlijn, for keeping me grounded in actual legal practice, and Christiaan and Jonathan, for helping me to see the novice's perspective to expert issues.

Dear reader, please note that there is also a companion website which shows some supplementary materials and these can be found at: https://www.e-elgar.com/textbooks/tjong-tjin-tai.

---

[1]   Such as the distinction between harm and damage.

[2]   For instance, S. Hardy & N. Kornet (eds.), *The Maastricht Collection: Selected National, European and International Provisions from Public and Private Law*, 6th ed., Groningen: Europa Law Publishing 2019, volume IV: Comparative Private Law, or the translations of German law on www.gesetze-im-internet.de/Teilliste_translations .html and the partial translation of the French Code civil on www.textes.justice.gouv.fr/art_pix/Translationrevise d2018final.pdf.

ABBREVIATIONS

AC	Appeal Cases
AIR	All India Reporters
All ER	All England Reports
art	article
BGB	Bürgerliches Gesetzbuch
BGH	Bundesgerichtshof
BGHZ	Entscheidungen des Bundesgerichtshofes in Zivilsachen
Bull.civ.	Bulletin des arrêts de la Cour de cassation, chambres civiles
BVerfGE	Entscheidungen des Bundesverfassungsgerichtes
BW	Burgerlijk Wetboek (Dutch Civil Code)
Cass.	Cour de cassation
Cc	Code civil
Ch	Chapter
civ	civile (the civil chamber of the Cour de cassation)
CLR	Commonwealth Law Reports
D	Receuil Dalloz et Sirey
DC	Recueil critique Dalloz
DP	Recueil périodique et critique Dalloz
eds	editors
ECnHR	European Convention on Human Rights
ECtHR	European Court of Human Rights
EGLR	Estates Gazette Law Reports
Eng.Rep.	English Reports
ERPL	European Review of Private Law
EWCA	England and Wales Court of Appeal
EWHC	England and Wales High Court
Ex.Ch.	Court of The Exchequer Chamber
ff	and further
Gaz.Pal.	Gazette du Palais
HCA	High Court of Australia
HR	Hoge Raad (Dutch Supreme Court)
IR	Irish Reports
ISO	International Organization for Standardization
KB	King's Bench

NIQB	Northern Island Queen's Bench
NJ	Nederlandse Jurisprudentie
NJW	Neue Juristische Wochenschrift
no	number
p	page
para	paragraph
plén	pléniere (the full chamber of the Cour de cassation)
QB	Queen's Bench
RGZ	Entscheidungen des Reichsgerichtes
s	section
SCC	Supreme Court of Canada
SCR	Supreme Court Reports (India)
SGCA	Singapore Court of Appeal
SLR	Singapore Law Reports
StGB	Strafgesetzbuch (German Criminal code)
UKHL	UK House of Lords
UKPC	UK Privy Council
UKSC	UK Supreme Court
WLR	Weekly Law Reports
ZPO	Zivilprozessordnung (German Code of civil procedure)

1
Introduction to private law terminology

1.1   INTRODUCTION

This textbook provides an introduction to comparative tort law for students who may never have studied tort law before. Before being able to do so, the reader needs to become acquainted with a few basic concepts that are presumed in tort law. That is the purpose of the present chapter. I will conclude with a brief explanation of the approach of this text.

An overview of fundamental concepts is even more relevant as this textbook does not take the perspective of a single national system. Due to the lack of a generally accepted terminology and conceptual framework there is not a single vocabulary that we can rely on. As the present text is in English, it is tempting to apply the terminology of English tort law. Such an approach would, however, defeat the purpose of this text. Even if we wish to avoid preferential treatment to the common law approach, the English language unavoidably biases legal expressions towards the terminology of English tort law which may be ill suited for a discussion of other legal systems. However, the alternative would be to use artificial terms that are too far removed from the actual language of tort law in national systems.

As a compromise I will in the present text mix both approaches. I will use words that may have specific meaning in English law, but may employ them in a slightly different manner where necessary given the aims of this text. For example, 'harm' and 'damage' are defined here more strictly than is common in English law. On other occasions I will use translations of civil law concepts that are not part of the English legal tradition. Furthermore, I will also note the equivalent words in German and French. This approach hopefully helps the reader to find the way in national doctrinal literature. Simultaneously it may serve as a brief introduction to law and legal research.

1.2   GOING TO COURT

Historically speaking, tort law has grown out of the practice of courts that decided cases where individuals sued others. The court procedure in civil proceedings[1] is still relevant for a full understanding of tort law, wherefore we will start with a condensed overview.

Let's start with a simple example. If your car is damaged by a cyclist who slipped on an icy road, you will probably want to be compensated for the costs of repair of your car. Cases like this are often settled amicably, out of court: the cyclist feels responsible and reimburses you voluntarily, or, more realistically, refers you to their insurer (§ 11.5). But what if the persons involved do not reach agreement? In that event the aggrieved party may start a court procedure to get what they claim from the other party.

Courts are one of the principal instruments by which a state resolves disputes among citizens. Court decisions are usually obeyed by the parties to the dispute and by third parties that help in effectuating the decision (such as banks). If necessary, court decisions can be enforced with the help of the state's officials and institutions, such as the police, bailiffs, land registries. As litigation before the court is fundamental to the operation of law, we need to go over its main aspects.

A court procedure usually involves two parties. The parties may be individuals (natural persons, meaning human beings), but they can also be corporations or more generally what are called 'corporate bodies' in common law, or in civil law 'legal persons'. A common example are incorporated companies.[2] The state is also a legal person. While the rules of the law apply to legal persons and natural persons alike, there are also special rules to take into account. For instance, under certain conditions corporations can be liable for actions of directors and subsidiaries (§ 14.7). The state has a special position in tort law: there are particular rules for state liability (§ 7.6).

The court procedure is started by one party, called the *claimant*.[3] In tort law this is often the victim, the person who actually suffered the harm.[4] The claimant wants something from the other party, such as an award of damages or an injunction. The thing that the claimant wants is in tort law generally called a *remedy* (§ 2.8, Ch. 11). The claimant starts the procedure by filing a *claim*[5] with the court. There are particular rules for doing so, such as first summoning the other party by using a process server. The rules that govern procedures between private parties are part of the *law of civil procedure*.

The claimant has to state the facts that support the claim. The claimant does so in a *statement of claim*,[6] a document that the claimant files with the court that explains the claim. The

---

[1]   Which is distinguished from criminal prosecution and administrative courts.

[2]   Usually designated, depending on the legal system and the kind of company, by abbreviations such as Ltd, PLC, Inc., S.A., GmbH, A.G., B.V., N.V.

[3]   In German *Kläger*, in French *demandeur*. In older English cases you may encounter 'plaintiff'.

[4]   Later we shall encounter exceptions, such as liability for other persons.

[5]   German: *Klage*, French: *demande*.

[6]   German: *Klageschrift*, French: *demande*.

facts support the claim if they fulfil the legal requirements for granting the claim. For instance, to obtain damages, the facts have to match all elements of the tort that the claimant invokes, and have to support the amount of damage that is claimed. The applicable legal rules determine the applicable requirements. If one or more of the requirements are not fulfilled, there is no ground for liability and the claim will be dismissed.

The other party, the *defendant*,[7] opposes the claim by putting forward a defence. The claimant and the defendant have opposing positions: whereas the claimant tries to build up the case, the defendant attempts to destroy it. In order to get the claim dismissed the defendant will usually focus the attack on the weakest link in the claimant's argument: positing that this or that requirement is not fulfilled. The defendant may argue for example that the facts as described by the claimant are different and/or have not been proven, or that the law has to be interpreted differently than claimant holds. Alternatively, the defendant may claim that an exception[8] to the general tort applies or may invoke a defence, and prove that the criteria for these exceptions and defences are fulfilled.

Insofar as parties are in disagreement about certain facts, the court has to decide who bears the *burden of proof*. For instance, the claimant may state that the defendant was texting while driving and is therefore liable for negligence. This may be supported by testimony from a witness near the accident, a passenger in the car, records from the telephone company. But if there are no such materials, the court may conclude that there are insufficient evidentiary materials and therefore find that the fact is not proven. Consequentially the claimant may lose the case as the breach of a duty of care cannot be established. The claim is then rejected. The claimant bears the burden of proof of that fact: if the claimant does not convince the court, the fact as stated by that party is not established. The claimant usually bears the burden of the proof for the facts that support the elements of the claim, while the defendant bears the burden of proof for the facts that support the exceptions and defences invoked. The court may in certain situations *reverse the burden of proof*, which means that the burden of proof rests on the other party than the party who normally would have to prove the fact. Certain legal rules amount to a reversed burden of proof. We will encounter some examples later on.

In the end the court will assess which facts can be established, either because parties agree on them or because they have been proven. The court then applies the relevant rules to the facts and considers whether they support the claim or not. The court usually provides a written judgment.

Incidentally, the costs of litigation are often substantial. They are generally not fully compensated, even if you win the case. The procedural costs can be a major disincentive against victims going to court, as may the duration of a court procedure. As a consequence, the legal system is perceived by many scholars as an inefficient system for compensation. Be that as it

---

[7]   German: *Beklagten*, French: *defendeur*. In tort law we also use the term 'tortfeasor' for the person who committed the tort. However, the defendant is not always the tortfeasor, as will become clear when discussing vicarious liability.

[8]   Such as the exception in German law to liability for employees, that the employer took sufficient care in selection and management of the employee (§ 14.3).

may, there is still a need for tort law to provide compensation to aggrieved parties, even if the court procedure is too costly for most minor injuries. The law was never intended to resolve all disputes: it is a measure of last resort, but no less important for that matter.

1.3   SOURCES OF LAW

In the description of how courts operate I referred in passing to the legal rules. Courts in the Western approach to law have to base their decisions on the law. This model is nowadays adopted all over the world, even though there is also evidence that the official description may not always match reality.[9] For the purposes of this book, we can provisionally define the law as the set of official rules that bind citizens (including corporate bodies) and officials (including the courts). In the context of tort law, we concentrate on the rules that determine under what conditions persons are liable outside contract.

The next question is: where do those rules come from? How do we find out what the law is? The rules of the law, are primarily[10] found in two sources:[11]

−   Legislation (also called statutory law), and
−   case law.

Legislation is the law as laid down in legislative acts or statutes.[12] If the act contains a compilation of rules for a large domain of the law, this is called a 'code'.

Case law is the body of law that consists of court decisions that have legal authority in the legal system. A complication in comparative law is that there is no consensus on the precise status of case law. In certain countries, particularly those with a common law system, the case law of the highest courts has formally the same status as statute law. In particular so-called *precedents* establish important rules and principles and cannot easily be overturned. Other countries, in particular civil law countries, do not formally accord case law legal authority. Case law may only show how statutes are to be interpreted. Nonetheless, in those countries the practice is usually that case law of the highest courts is followed nearly as strictly as statute law.[13] Sometimes lawyers speak of *persuasive authority*: a case may not have legal authority but may still persuade a court in its interpretation of statute law. Here we will gloss over these precise differences and simply assume that leading cases of the highest courts indicate what the law is, regardless of whether they actually constitute law or only have persuasive authority.

---

[9]   For instance, Bussani and Infantino 2021 at p. 12 point to the survival of traditional customary law and dispute resolution in Ethiopia despite the enactment of an official code.

[10]   There are other sources of law, in particular customary law. For practical purposes, however, we can focus on legislation and case law. Furthermore, there are other influences on the law. We will discuss some of those in § 6.2, as well as in Chapter 16.

[11]   The term of *sources of law* is mainly found in civil law systems.

[12]   French: *loi*, German: *Gesetz*. In this context legislation also comprises treaties and supranational legislation.

[13]   Hondius 2007.

The entire collection of rules from legislation and case law can be called 'the law'. Calling such rules 'law' is to distinguish them from other rules that may be relevant to court cases, but are not binding as law. Examples are rules of mathematics or physics, sports regulations, technical standards. Such rules may be applied in a specific legal case to resolve an issue about the facts, and in that way can influence the outcome of a court case. They are, however, not *law*.

The rules of law are *authoritative* in the sense that you are supposed to simply follow them, even if you do not agree with them. The fact that these rules have legal authority ends the discussion as to whether they must be followed. They are rules of *positive law*, rules that describe the law as it is, not how you might want the law to be. This distinguishes law from morality: as it can be objectively determined what the rules of positive law are, we can agree on these rules even if we disagree about what would be the most desirable rules.[14] The availability of objective statements on the law in turn allows courts to reach decisions in relatively short time that can be shown to be based on something else than purely personal preferences. In morality there is no such distinction between the rules which we think are correct and the rules that are valid, whereby moral debates may not be easy to resolve.

Rules only have value when there is also a broad consensus about their interpretation and application. As you will find when reading the following chapters, the rules of law are often not immediately clear to novice readers and may seem ambiguous. Even experienced lawyers may find it hard to make sense of a rule that they have not encountered before. In practice lawyers find support in what is called *doctrinal literature*, the body of legal scholarship (books and articles) that explains, systematizes and elaborates legislation and case law. Doctrinal literature has significant influence on the development of law and may influence the outcome of many court procedures, especially if the main authoritative legal scholars are in agreement. French lawyers refer to this general consensus as *la doctrine*, in Germany lawyers speak of the *herrschender Meinung* (dominant opinion) among lawyers. However, doctrine is not a source of law, even though doctrinal opinions may ultimately find acceptance in leading case law and new legislation, and thereby becomes law. Doctrinal literature is invaluable for practising lawyers, as it is usually the best way to obtain an overview of a body of law, describing the relevant statutory provisions and case law, thereby saving the lawyer from time-consuming research.

1.4   QUALIFICATION AND CAUSE OF ACTION

An unavoidable bit of jargon relates to a particular task of lawyers, namely the need to combine facts and legal rules to reach conclusions, in particular whether a claim succeeds. Lawyers generally reason as follows. They take the facts of the case and examine whether these facts fulfil the requirements of the relevant rules. As the rules often refer to somewhat vague concepts, such as 'wrongfulness' or 'foreseeability', lawyers have to do quite a bit of work to determine

---

[14]   Morality can indirectly influence legal rules: as regards content there is a large overlap (in particular in an area of tort law). However, the mere fact that a something is morally required does not in itself imply that it is legally required. A clear example is the moral obligation to rescue people in extreme peril, which does not always translate to a legal duty to rescue (§ 6.3).

whether the facts actually match these concepts. This labour is called *qualification*: the lawyer qualifies the facts to see whether a certain concept is fulfilled or not. Although legal rules purportedly are comprehensible for everyone, in actuality many legal concepts have a meaning that is not readily understood by lay persons. Considerable legal training and research may be required to ascertain whether a given set of facts actually fulfils what is required by a given legal rule.

In English law this process of qualification is implied in the phrase 'cause of action'. This derives from the ancient so-called forms of action.[15] The law used to be organized around forms of action (listing the requirements for each action) instead of more theoretical concepts like rights and obligations. In practice, the cause of action is still important to plead your case before the court. The claimant has to show that the facts of the case constitute the tort that the claimant invokes: if that is so, the claimant has an 'actionable' case.

In civil law systems the general legal analysis may use concepts like duties and wrongfulness, but when it comes to a court procedure the process is not too dissimilar from the English cause of action. German law works with the notion of *Tatbestand* (§ 4.2). This concept refers the set of facts required to fulfil a specific legal norm. The *Tatbestand* resembles the cause of action in English law. French law refers to the *cause de la demande*.

A noticeable difference is that the English cause of action is usually built up from words that are current in common parlance, while the *Tatbestand* often uses abstract legal concepts. Another difference is that the cause of action, when its elements are fulfilled, more or less directly leads to the consequence that the action or remedy that was claimed can be awarded, while the *Tatbestand* (in private law cases) only leads to the interim conclusion that the defendant may be liable, after which it must be determined what remedies may be awarded. The intermediate step is that there is an *obligation* on the side of the claimant to provide reparation. The use of the concept of obligations as intermediate step in a legal argument is typical of civil law and distinguishes civil law reasoning from common law argumentation.

1.5   SOURCES OF OBLIGATIONS

Central to civil law reasoning is the concept of *obligation*. An obligation in the legal sense is similar to obligation in common parlance: it means that you have to do (or refrain from doing) something. In law we are only concerned with *legal* obligations, which means obligations that are legally recognized, will have some legal effect.

The principal consequence of the presence of an obligation is that performance of the obligation can be enforced, either by claiming specific performance or indirectly through a claim of damages when the obligation is not performed. Obligations chiefly arise from a *contract* or from a *tort*. These are the most important sources of obligations. There are other sources as well, in particular *negotiorum gestio* (taking charge of another's affairs, for instance during unconsciousness), *solutio indebiti* (obligation to return a good or payment that you obtained without justification, such as after an erroneous bank transfer) and *unjust enrichment*.

---

[15]   Samuel 2013, pp. 50–56.

The set of rules that constitute a coherent part of law is called a *doctrine*,[16] not to be confused with doctrine in the sense of 'doctrinal literature'. An example is the doctrine of vicarious liability which regulates under what conditions an employer is liable for torts committed by his employees. An important part of private law reasoning is the ability to determine the relevant doctrine for a given set of facts. A good lawyer quickly identifies all possibly relevant doctrines and then examines each of these doctrines in turn to see whether it actually applies or not.

As stated, the two principal sources of obligations are contracts and torts. Contracts are well understood: they are voluntary agreements between parties whereby they mutually accept obligations towards each other. Contracts are often put in writing, but oral contracts are usually valid as well. If a contractual party does not do what they promised, they may be in *breach of contract*, and therefore is liable to the other party.

Torts are another source of obligations. This begs the question, what are torts? A tort, simply put, is a certain set of events that gives rise to liability *without any basis in* contract. Tort law can be defined as the part of private law concerned with non-contractual liability. An example is the tort of trespass to goods, liability incurred by tampering with or damaging a movable good without the owner's consent.

As we will explain later, the name 'tort law' derives from common law systems. Civil law systems refer to the same area under different names, such as the law of delict, the law of extra-contractual liability. However, in comparative literature the use of 'tort law' in a more general sense is well established. We will use this term as well in this broader sense.

1.6   CONCURRENCE

The fact that there are several sources of obligations may give rise to the question whether one source has precedence over another, or whether several sources may apply simultaneously. This is the question of *concurrence*. Generally speaking, most legal systems allow a claimant to invoke multiple sources of obligations simultaneously: claimant can invoke several causes of action or grounds for a given set of facts. Even though the court will usually base its decision on only one of those grounds, it is possible that several grounds are applicable.

It is usually possible to sue a contract partner on the basis of breach of contract and at the same time on the basis of a specific tort, as long as the requirements for each action are fulfilled. This is explicated in common law precedents.[17] In Germany there are no general provisions

---

[16]   The term 'doctrine' therefore (unfortunately) has two distinct meanings: the complete body of legal scholarship (§ 1.3), and a specific coherent set of rules regulating a certain issue. The context usually makes clear which meaning is intended.

[17]   For English law see *Henderson v Merrett Syndicates Ltd.* [1995] 2 AC 145, as well as the speech by Lord Macmillan in *Donoghue v Stevenson* [1932] AC 562; in the USA see for example the Californian case *Comunale v Traders & General Insurance Co.*, 50 Cal. 2d 654 (1958): 'where a case sounds both in contract and tort the plaintiff will ordinarily have freedom of election between an action of tort and one of contract'.

on concurrence; it follows from case law that concurrent claims are in principle allowed.[18] It is also generally possible to sue someone on the basis of several different torts. If several grounds apply, it depends on the possible consequences which basis the claimant will want to use. Complications in proving necessary elements may also be a reason not to limit oneself to a single cause of action. An example is a claim based on battery and negligence: the claimant may be unsure whether he can prove the requisite intention for battery, and to remain on the safe side alternatively grounds his claim on negligence.

However, this approach is not accepted always and everywhere. For example, French law does not allow a claim based on contract and on tort at the same time (the rule of *non-cumul*, from which it follows that you cannot claim under tort law if the facts principally point to breach of contract as the proper frame of assessment). Furthermore, even if the general rule is that concurrence is allowed, there may be exceptions to that rule.

If a rule has been created specifically for a certain set of cases, the specific rule usually prevails over the more general rule (following the Latin maxim *lex specialis derogat legi generali*).[19] An example is the existence of a specific rule for liability for motorized vehicles: such a rule presumably implies that a general rule of liability for movable objects does not apply if the object is a car. But this maxim doesn't apply everywhere or in all situations. A strict liability rule for motorized vehicles does not mean that the owner cannot also be sued on the basis of negligence. As another example: in English law the tort of breach of statutory duty can be applied concurrently with the tort of negligence, even though a statutory duty seems to be more specific than the general liability for negligence.

1.7   AIMS OF THE PRESENT TEXT

This book is premised on the assumption that it is possible for beginning students to gain a basic understanding of tort law in the principal varieties found around the globe. Thereby students may approach other jurisdictions more easily than if they would have solely learned the tort law of a single country. As this is a different approach than is customary in textbooks on tort law, a few additional remarks may be useful to dispel any misconceptions.

The knowledge you may obtain from studying this text does not equal the in-depth knowledge that is required of a practising lawyer, who is capable of quickly providing the precise state of the law. This also does not amount to having detailed knowledge of all or most tort law systems in the world.[20] Indeed, compared to a student who only studied a single system you

---

[18]   Wolf and Neuner 2012, § 21, nr. 8 (*Anspruchskonkurrenz*), refering to BGH 19 September 2008, V ZR 28/08, BGHZ 178, 90, also see BGH 24 May 1976, BGHZ 66, 315 (quoted in Van Gerven, Lever and Larouche 2000, pp. 38–40.

[19]   A codification of this maxim can be found in the Chinese Tort Liability Law (2010), art. 5.

[20]   There are many comparative studies of tort law which provide valuable insights, but even these cannot provide a complete overview. Relevant materials are: Von Bar 1998 and 2000, Zweigert and Kötz 1998, chapters 39–42, Van Dam 2013, Bussani and Sebok 2021.

will have less knowledge of the details of a specific system. Instead, the present text aims at the following:

1. comprehension of the instruments and doctrines in tort law,
2. knowledge of the tort law systems of three key jurisdictions,
3. basic knowledge of variations in tort law found around the world.

The present text focuses on the first two goals, while also giving you an impression of the variety of rules that is found in different legal systems. We discuss tort law in English common law, French and German civil law. These represent the three dominant traditions in tort law around the world.

You will learn the basics of these systems, and thereby also become familiar with the main doctrines, concepts and kinds of rules in tort law found around the world. Local variations can be understood by way of variation of these systems.[21]

Hereby you will be armed with a sizeable amount of knowledge. However, you have to be aware that you have only achieved an understanding of the broad outlines of the law: further research is needed to reconstruct the actual law, including the institutional context and practice. The approach here is similar to what exact sciences call a first-order approximation: the description is close to reality but is not exact and needs further refinement. An approximation is valuable as long as you remain aware of its limitations: surely a sketch is better than not having any description at all.

In an analogy: the approach of this text is a tourist guide rather than an extensive language course plus study of local history and anthropology: it helps you get around, but won't prevent you from misunderstandings and errors if you forget to be careful. In particular our approach focuses on the main two sources of law, statute and case law, at the expense of other sources and influences. While it is certainly useful to understand what the code in a certain country says, it is only the starting point of actually reconstructing the law. Statute and case law are the surface of the law, important as they provide the basis (the first-order approximation), but insufficient for the complete picture. They need to be supplemented with other sources (depending on the jurisdiction), and influences that determine how the law is actually applied in practice.

For determining the actual state of the law, you will need, as always, to put in the necessary work to ensure that you have not overlooked relevant legal sources (for example newer precedents, authoritative re-interpretations of codified rules). In Chapter 16 a few pointers will be provided for further research.

As this is an introductory text, we cannot go into extensive debate on methods and approaches of comparative law. The approach taken in this text is mainly functional. The comparisons that are made are by necessity broad and ignore many details and nuances where the comparison falls flat. However, for an introduction it is preferable to have a broad

---

[21] Similarly Siems 2014, pp. 43–44, 68–70, argues that the differences between national systems are not as fundamental as they used to be presented by comparative scholars, and that English, French and German law are particularly influential.

overview that increases comprehension above an intractable extremely detailed comparison. Just as an introductory course into a foreign language provides translations that miss many of the nuances that experienced speakers and translators understand and apply, the reader of this text will only have gained a first footing in tort law. Hopefully this text does not promote over-confidence in the state of tort law in the world, but instead encourages the reader to take further steps in the exciting area of comparative tort law.

In line with the remarks in § 1.3, the description of the law in the following chapters will be supported by extensive references, to show that the law is found in relevant sources. References are primarily to statute and case law, supported with doctrinal literature for further reference and as authority for broader developments that cannot easily be traced back to a single source in statute or case law. Occasionally a doctrinal source will be used as authority for a reference to case law that I did not verify (as indicated by 'referring to', 'citing' and similar indicators).

2
Tort law and the structure of fault liability

2.1   INTRODUCTION

Let's start with an example case.

One fine Sunday morning in August 1924 Ms. Palsgraf, at the time 42 years old, entered a platform of East New York station in Brooklyn to board a train to Rockaway Beach, together with her two daughters Elizabeth and Lilian, of 15 and 12 years old. Lilian went away to buy a newspaper, while Elizabeth and her mother waited next to a large coin-operated scales, the kind on which a person stands to determine his weight. Meanwhile further along the platform a train was getting ready to pull out, when two men ran up to board the train. One of the men jumped in while the train had already started moving. The other man was a bit behind, because he was carrying a round package 18 inches in diameter, wrapped in newspaper. A guard on the train and the platform man helped him aboard, but accidentally hit the package which fell down between the train and the platform, where it got stuck and exploded. The package apparently contained fire-crackers.

The explosion, some three metres away, shattered the glass of the scales next to Ms. Palsgraf. She told her daughter Elizabeth quickly to turn her back against the explosion, and then the scales toppled over and hit Ms. Palsgraf on the left side of her body. Smoke filled the station, people were running, and Ms. Palsgraf heard Lilian somewhere crying 'I want my mama'. She tried to protect Elizabeth by hiding in a corner while the crowd was running past. After a while she was escorted by a policeman to the newsstand where Lilian was hiding. They exited the station. Outside the station a doctor examined Ms. Palsgraf and sent her home. Afterwards Ms. Palsgraf developed a stammer which caused her to lose her job as janitor and made her also unable to do housework. A doctor diagnosed her with traumatic hysteria. She sued the train company that employed the guard and the platform man to obtain compensation. The men carrying the package have never been identified.[1]

---

[1]   *Palsgraf v Long Island Railroad Co.*, 248 N.Y. 339, 162 N.E. 99 (1928). The facts can be determined from the court record of the case, at www.law.berkeley.edu/files/Palsgraf_Record.pdf.

Now the question is whether Ms. Palsgraf should be compensated by the railway company for her illness and its consequences, or as lawyers say, be awarded damages. Answering such a question is the job of tort law. If you approach the case of Palsgraf without any knowledge of the law, you may quickly get lost in the mass of details and the many possible perspectives to approach the case. It may seem obvious that the actual culprit is the man carrying the package – or did he not actually do something wrong? Does it matter that Ms. Palsgraf is suing the railway company and not the actual culprit? Why is she suing the company and not the employees who helped the man? Did the employees actually do something wrong: should they have expected that the package contained fire crackers? Is the whole chain of events so unlikely that the railway company doesn't deserve to be blamed for it? Does Ms. Palsgraf really deserve compensation, or is the trauma something that is simply her bad luck? Would she have developed traumatic hysteria anyway? Is it relevant whether persons generally develop traumatic hysteria in such circumstances, and if so, should the damages be reduced? And should all the details matter, or should we disregard the presence of her children and their anxiety during the chaos after the explosion?

Tort law provides a common vocabulary and conceptual framework to analyse cases and to streamline our discussions. The kind of intuitions that lay persons have about torts are mirrored in the legal vocabulary of tort law, but the legal terms are more precise to facilitate legal analysis. They have been developed to promote coherence in the law and to avoid mistakes in reasoning. Training as a lawyer means that you know the concepts of the law, and are able to translate (qualify) the facts of a case to the corresponding legal terms. When lawyers look at a concrete case they usually agree under which heading a specific issue must be discussed, which helps to focus their debates. Admittedly there are differences as well, such as the tendency of English tort law to start with the manner in which the harm or injury occurred in order to find the relevant torts versus the German approach focusing on the violated interest in itself, but these differences do not stand in the way of mutual comprehension.

As explained in § 1.7, we will approach tort law from a comparative perspective. To that end we will use a unified vocabulary and terminology. At the same time, we need the interface or dictionary to translate between the common vocabulary and the specific national approaches. To make this feasible we will use a two-pronged approach.

First of all, we will work with a model of tort law that describes its fundamental structure. It is submitted that this model is common to *all* systems of tort law around the world. I will use terms that are recognizable for most legal systems, and will point out where alternative terms are used in specific jurisdictions.

Secondly, we will zoom in on three specific jurisdictions: France, Germany and England. These jurisdictions are the three most influential models of tort law. By explaining how to connect the abstract structure of tort law to these specific legal systems you will learn to connect the model approach to the local details of most jurisdictions. The advantage from looking at specific systems is that this allows the reader to understand the intricate connections and nuances that may exist between and in various elements of tort law. The three legal systems also are models of differing approaches to analysing tort law cases. By going into some of the details of these systems, the general description of tort law remains grounded in positive law instead of becoming a mere theoretical exercise that may be correct in broad outlines, but is unhelpful for providing exact outcomes.

In this chapter we discuss the structure of fault liability. This serves as the basis of the comparative approach to tort law proposed here. First of all, we will discuss the notion of tort law (§ 2.2), followed by a discussion of the justification of tortious liability (§ 2.3). After that we will analyse fault liability in general (§ 2.4), going into its main elements one by one (§§ 2.5–2.8).

2.2 WHAT IS TORT LAW?

Tort law can be defined as the law of non-contractual liability.[2] This definition highlights two characteristics of tort law.

1. Tort law has to do with liability *outside* contract. If there is a contract, liability may simply follow from violation of the terms of the contract (breach of contract). In tort law we are concerned about liability that arises regardless of any contractual arrangement.
2. Secondly, tort law has to do with *liability*. The tortfeasor (the person who committed the tort) has to *compensate* the person who suffered damage as a consequence of the wrongful conduct. Compensation usually takes the form of damages (payment of money as compensation for losses).

The principal intuition of tort law is that the person who is liable has done something wrong, has committed a wrongful act. The rules of tort law build on this intuition. They may extend it or soften it, but at the core there remains the idea that something happened which should not have occurred. This intuition can be found in all societies. It is unthinkable that a society would not have prohibitions against injuring others. But this doesn't mean that there is always liability whenever someone suffers an injury. The injury on its own is insufficient reason to hold someone liable. Individual freedom would otherwise be curtailed to an unacceptable degree. Tort law is the result of the sustained attempt to draw the line between freedom and protection from harm.

2.3 JUSTIFICATION AND AIMS OF TORT LAW

An unavoidable fact of life is that accidents happen. This finds expression in notions such as bad luck. The consequences of such unfortunate occurrences are principally to be borne by the person who suffers these consequences. This is expressed in the Latin maxim *casum sentit dominus*, bad luck (chance) remains where it falls. You need a good reason to make someone else pay for your damage, or legally speaking: you must show that the other person has an *obligation* to provide compensation. Tort law provides grounds for such an obligation.

The central issue of tort law is the balance between *autonomy* and *protection against harm*. While it is generally accepted that individuals should be free to do as they wish, individual

---

[2]   Suggested reading: Weinrib 2012, Cane 2017.

liberty is limited where it threatens to harm the interests of others. Liability in tort law indicates where the exercise of individual liberty crosses over into prohibited harm. Not every harm gives rise to liability. For instance, if you host a party at your house, your neighbours will have to tolerate some amount of noise. A certain degree of harm is generally allowed if the volume remains within reasonable limits and the party does not continue deep into the night. The interests of individuals to act freely must be *balanced* against the interests of others not to be harmed. The need for finding a balance is an important theme in the following chapters.

As regards the aims of tort law, the primary aim of tort law was and is what is called *reparation*: repairing the consequences of the wrongful act. This is the notion of *restitutio in integro*, restoring the victim to the state of affairs that existed before (or would have existed in the absence of) the tortious conduct. In legal theory this is identified with *corrective justice*.[3] This is to be distinguished from distributive justice.

Reparation usually takes the form of an award of damages, that is payment of a sum of money that is supposed to compensate for the harm inflicted on the victim. Because of the dominance of damages, it is also said that tort law aims at compensation, even though that is just one kind of reparation. The remedy of damages allows tort law to redistribute risks: the risk of damage is financially transferred from the victim onto the tortfeasor.

An important secondary aim of tort law is *prevention*. The perspective of having to pay damages can provide a powerful incentive against harmful behaviour. More generally, it is argued that tort law serves the purpose of promotion of welfare. This position is usually associated with the field of Law and Economics, which posits the hypothesis that tort law can best be construed as rules for maximizing social welfare.[4] A related viewpoint is that tort law serves the goal of risk regulation. These approaches have in common that they tend to abstract from the individual perspective of tortfeasor and victim, and rather take the viewpoint of the state or legislator regarding the general effects of legal rules. While it is important to be aware of broader consequences of individual decisions and rules, you should not forget that the law also needs to promote justice, which it does by deciding in a way that is comprehensible and acceptable to individuals.

Other aims that tort law may serve are *satisfaction* or *recognition* of wrongdoing. A victim may obtain satisfaction and some form of immaterial relief from a court decision that recognizes that the tortfeasor acted wrongfully. Although the victim may primarily want compensation, the fact that the decision also acknowledges that the victim is correct in its position may be an additional benefit. The aim of satisfaction or recognition is an argument against wholesale adoption of a non-fault compensation scheme such as in New Zealand (see § 11.5).

---

[3]   Weinrib 2012.

[4]   Dari-Mattiacci and Parisi 2021. The two great scholars of this movement are Guido Calabresi and Richard Posner.

2.4   FAULT LIABILITY IN GENERAL

If we look at the cases in which courts hold a defendant liable in tort, there appear to be three elements that are always present:[5]

- fault
- harm, and
- a causal connection between fault and harm.

These elements make sense, considered together. You are only liable if you have indeed done something wrong, committed a 'fault'. But that on its own is not sufficient. For liability it is presumed that the fault also led to some kind of undesirable outcome, that there is 'harm'. This implies that there is what we call a causal connection: the fault caused the harm.

The three main elements – fault, harm and causality – function like three valves which you can turn in order to restrict or increase liability. For instance, in German law the notion of harm is restricted to protected interests. A similar result can be achieved in French law by using the combined requirements of fault and causality to reject a claim. The balance between autonomy and harm is achieved by the way in which each element is applied, and by the combination of these elements.

The elements for fault liability also function as *conditions* or *requirements*: there is only liability if all three requirements are fulfilled. If you need to determine whether a defendant is liable, you have to check each of these elements in turn. We will furthermore see that these elements can consist of several further, more detailed elements. The recommended approach is to check each element separately and explicitly by reference to the facts of the case. Note that certain facts may be relevant for more than one element. In the Palsgraf case, for example, the fact the accident was fairly far removed and unexpected from the alleged wrongful conduct could be relevant both for establishing fault and for causality.

Here we only discuss the elements in a fairly abstract manner. In actuality you will need to discuss the specific form each element takes in the legal system with which you are concerned. The facts of a case have to be qualified in light of the rules of the legal system. However, the framework presented here can be used to analyse cases in general. Such an analysis helps to pinpoint the areas of contention, regardless of the specific shape it may take in a particular system. For instance, a general analysis may show that the issue is not causality but rather whether the behaviour was wrongful.

Incidentally, even if the three elements are fulfilled, the defendant may raise a so-called *defence* (Chapter 12). That is an argument to the effect that he should not be liable. For instance, a demolition company argues that they were allowed to demolish the building because the claimant consented to it.

---

[5]   Similarly for English law: Cane 2017, and German law: Wagner 2021, paras 5.20, 5.39.

2.5   FAULT

A *fault* consists of wrongful conduct (acts or omissions) by a tortfeasor. If we take the Palsgraf case, claimant argued that the employees should have taken better care to ensure that the package would not have been dropped. Although 'behaviour' or 'conduct' is preferable as a general term, we often simply say that there is an act or action, thereby zooming in on a specific part of the broader conduct.

The concept of fault can be further analysed in two sub-elements that some systems (such as German and Dutch law) separate:

1. the *wrongfulness* of the act (objective fault),[6] and
2. The *accountability* or *culpability* of the act (subjective fault).[7]

The first sub-element is *wrongfulness* (also called unlawfulness). Wrongfulness means, loosely speaking, that the act should not have occurred. It constitutes the *objective* side of the fault: the behaviour that forms the basis for liability. For example: someone drives above the speed limit, is unable to brake in time when another car crosses the road, and collides with that car.

The 'should not have' means that it *legally* should not have occurred. While you may assert that a friend should not wait two days before responding to a message in WhatsApp, such behaviour is at most only socially undesirable but not prohibited by law, not wrongful.

There are various ways in which an act can be wrongful. In Chapters 6 and 7 we discuss this in more detail. Wrongfulness is the most important element of tort law, and is the hardest to determine.

The second sub-element is *subjective fault*. It is also important that the act is the 'fault' of the person, they can be blamed for it, the person is culpable, accountable. When looking at an individual's conduct, we can assume that the individual is to blame for it, but under specific circumstances this assumption may not be warranted. An example: a driver has a stroke while driving a car. During the stroke his foot slips on the accelerator, leading to an accident that damages another car.[8] Another example is an involuntary reaction out of surprise or fright.[9] In English law and German law individuals are generally not found liable for such actions.[10]

An important area where subjective fault may be in question is in the case of certain persons who as a group seem to lack capacity for mature judgement. Young children are a clear

---

6   In German law: *Rechtswidrigkeit.*

7   In German law: *Verschulden.*

8   In German law the driver would not be culpable, but might be held liable under the 'fairness correction' of § 829 BGB, see Deutsch and Ahrens 2014, para 4, referring to BGH 15 January 1957, VI ZR 135/56, BGHZ 23, 90.

9   In German law a pure reflex does not provide a ground for liability, see BGH VersR (Versicherungsrecht) 1968, 175 about a bowler striking someone with a bowling ball in a reflex after being hit in the stomach, mentioned in Deutsch and Ahrens 2014, para 3.

10   Wagner 2021, para 5.25, refering to *Mansfield v Weetabix* (1998) 1 WLR 1263 and BGH 1 July 1986, VI ZR 294/85, BGHZ 98, 135, NJW 1987, 121.

example, as are mentally disabled persons. The legal question is whether such individuals are still accountable for their actions (§ 8.3).

There is also another aspect to subjective fault: what did the tortfeasor want to happen?[11] Normally it suffices that the tortfeasor acted consciously even if they did not want the harm to occur. It is sufficient that the behaviour was *negligent*, careless. For some kinds of torts, however, we require a stronger degree: *intention*. This means that the tortfeasor deliberately, intentionally committed the tort. An example is the tort of battery in English law. If you accidentally push your elbow in someone's face, that may amount to negligence, but it is only battery if you wanted to do that. There are some further degrees of intentional action, which we will discuss in § 8.4. Here we will only mention a third category used in common law for certain torts: *malice*. Malice means the action was not only intentional, but actually aimed at causing harm to the victim. An illustration is that you are having a party with loud music solely to annoy your neighbour: that is malicious. If you had the party for your own enjoyment this would merely be intentional. The difference between malice and intention is similar to the difference in criminal law between murder and manslaughter.

Note that the boundary between objective and subjective fault is blurry. The concept of negligence, in particular, seems to point both at the conduct (careless behaviour) and at the frame of mind (being careless).[12] However, there is merit in the distinction as it allows us to explicate that the frame of mind of the tortfeasor may be relevant besides the observable conduct.

When analysing a tort, we look primarily at the wrongfulness of the action. Only rarely is there reason to consider whether there is actually subjective fault. The (lack of) accountability therefore functions more like a defence or an exception than as a requirement for liability: usually you only need to examine it if there is reason to doubt whether the tortfeasor is really accountable for his conduct.

The model of fault liability is not exhaustive for tort law. Besides the obvious category of risk-based forms of liability (strict liability),[13] there are other forms of liability that do not require fault. A well-known category is *liability for lawful acts*. An example is tearing down a house in the course of war, in order to prepare for a military defence. While it is clear that such an act is desirable from the perspective of the general society, and may be lawful (it may be based on specific statute), it seems unfair that the owner of the house should not receive any compensation. Other examples are appropriation of property on behalf of the national interest (eminent domain, expropriation), or having to suffer nuisance because of necessary constructions works at your neighbour's house.[14] A characteristic of this form of liability is that the victim only has a right to compensation, but cannot obtain an order to prohibit the

---

[11]　The technical term of the mental state towards the action is 'intention'. Confusingly, lawyers also use intention to denote a specific form (§ 8.4).

[12]　German law distinguishes between external and internal care (*außere/innere Sorgfalt*), but it is admitted that this distinction is mainly theoretical (Wagner 2021, para 5.26).

[13]　Introduced in Chapter 13.

[14]　In German law you cannot prohibit such works but may have a claim to compensation outside tort law (§ 906(2) BGB).

act.[15] Liability for lawful acts is found in many legal systems.[16] In France there is the doctrine of *égalité pour les charges publiques* (equality regarding public burdens), that is, the public burden must be shared and therefore is paid for by the collective. Another example of liability without fault is the equity-based liability in China, where in the absence of fault the judge may still hold the defendant liable for reasons of equity.[17]

2.6   HARM

Harm means injury to an interest.[18] Clear examples are harm to material interests, such as damage to a car or injury to a person. In Chapters 10 and 11 we will discuss the related concept of damage. At this point we can provisionally define damage as the losses that were caused by the injury. Lawyers employ specific categories of harms and damage, and you need to be able to translate the facts of a case into the appropriate categories. In the Palsgraf case the harm would consist of personal injury (the bodily harm to Ms. Palsgraf), which caused losses in the form of loss of income. Harm may also involve immaterial interests, such as slanderous statements, violation of privacy by publication of private photographs and other acts that are generally found undesirable but do not have a clearly definable material harm as result.

Harm is defined in reference to interests. In certain jurisdictions the notion of interests gives rise to a further limitation of liability, through the notion of *protected interests*. An example is the German BGB, which spells out in detail which interests are protected for certain grounds of liability. The interests that are not listed are not protected (i.e. harm to such interests does not lead to liability). The reason for such restrictions is to limit the extent of liability, for fear of exposing a defendant to a disproportionate burden of liability. This approach will be discussed in § 9.1.

2.7   CAUSALITY

The element of *causality* means that the harm is caused by the fault: the injury is a consequence of the wrongful conduct.

The need for this requirement is intuitively obvious. If we take the Palsgraf case, and assume that a tap in the apartment of Ms. Palsgraf broke just after the accident occurred, it is clear that the railway company would not liable at all for the resultant water damage, even if the company would have been liable for the bodily harm. The actions of the employees of the company and the malfunction of the tap are simply unrelated, or as lawyers say, there is no causal connection between the one and the other. If causality were not required, a tortfeasor

---

[15]   Such cases may also be decided on the basis of the defence of necessity (§ 12.3).

[16]   In German law see Deutsch and Ahrens 2014, nr. 9, citing the case of a hotel owner who suffered damage by works on the river Mosel which were required by international obligations of the German state.

[17]   Art. 24 Tort Liability Law, see Jiang 2021, pp. 418–22.

[18]   Bussani and Infantino 2021, pp. 19–22 discuss the cross-cultural notion of injury.

would be liable for everything that happened around or after the wrongful behaviour, which is clearly nonsensical.

A closer look at causality shows that it actually involves two different, cumulative conditions:[19]

– factual causation, for establishing a causal connection, and
– legal causation, for limiting the extent of liability.

Both are required in order to fulfil the requirement of a causal connection.

In Mali both conditions are explicated.

RÉGIME GÉNÉRAL DES OBLIGATIONS (1987)

ART. 114
Le dommage peut être matériel ou moral, actuel ou futur. Mais il doit toujours être certain et direct.

…

ART. 116
La responsabilité implique une relation de cause à effet entre le fait générateur et le dommage.

Art. 114.
The damage may be material or moral, actual or in the future. But it must always be certain and direct.

…

Art. 116.
Liability implies a relation of cause and effect between the original act and the damage.

At the very least we require *factual causation*. Lawyers often use the Latin phrase *condicio sine qua non* (c.s.q.n.),[20] the condition without which the event (harm) would not have happened. English lawyers refer to the 'but for' test of causality. In effect the criterion is what would have happened if the act would not have occurred: if the damage would have materialized anyway in that hypothetical situation, there is no factual causation, otherwise there is factual causality. Taking again the example of the Palsgraf case: what would have happened if the employees would have taken better care of the package? It seems likely that the package would not have dropped, therefore would not have exploded in the station, the scales would not have fallen on Ms. Palsgraf, and she would not have been injured. It appears obvious that there was factual causation, and indeed this was not disputed in the case.

---

[19]   Infantino 2021, pp. 280–82, also pointing out that French law is less clear on this distinction.

[20]   '[C]onditio sine qua non', with a 't', is also common.

While factual causation is a *necessary* condition, it is not sufficient for establishing causality. In particular there is a need to *limit* the consequences that the tortfeasor is liable for. It seems unfair to hold the tortfeasor liable for each and every consequence, regardless of how far removed and how unlikely it is.

Hence tort lawyers generally require a second form of causation as well: *legal causation*. The idea is that even if there is harm, not all consequences from the wrongful act are sufficiently related to the wrongful act to deserve compensation. Thus the extent of liability is limited by not awarding compensation to losses that are too far removed from the act. The precise criterion varies: remoteness (England), direct and immediate consequence (France), adequacy (Germany), proximate cause (USA). Another interpretation of legal causality is that it restricts compensation to the kind of harm and damage that pertains to the norm that was violated (§§ 9.1, 10.2).

In the Palsgraf case, it was indeed debated whether the injury of Ms. Palsgraf was not too far removed from the original accident. There were several steps between the explosion and the materialization of the psychic disorder. Ultimately the case was decided on another basis, the absence of wrongfulness on the part of the (employees of the) railway company.

2.8   REMEDIES

Once it is established that the tortfeasor is liable, the defendant has a duty to repair the harm, to provide reparation. The victim may want monetary compensation, or may wish that the tortfeasor repairs the harm in some other manner, such as by retracting a false statement, removing a tree that has fallen on his property, return a painting. The court can order the tortfeasor to provide reparation in various ways. Such a specific kind of order by the court for reparation is called a *remedy*.

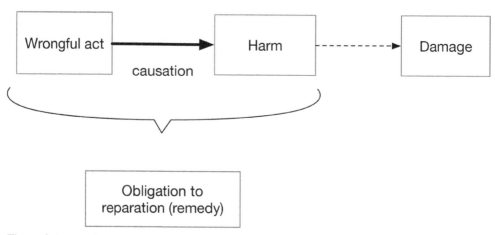

Figure 2.1   The relation between the elements of fault liability and the resulting remedy

The principal remedies are the following.[21]

- The most important remedy is the *award of damages*. This means that the defendant has to pay a sum of money to the claimant (which is awarded by the court to the claimant).
- It is also possible to obtain a *court order*. Common law speaks of an *injunction*, an order which requires the defendant to perform a specific action or refrain from certain conduct.[22] The court order is the general procedural instrument.
- A particular kind of remedy is the *declaration of rights*, which means that the court only declares that someone is liable, without awarding damages or any other remedy. A declaration can be useful as a basis for negotiation to obtain compensation without involvement of the courts, or because the mere pronouncement that defendant is liable may in itself provide moral satisfaction.
- Other, more specific, remedies are generally variations of those mentioned above. An example is an injunction to rectify a public statement, which is a species of a court order. In the case of infringement of a property right, there are specific remedies that restore the property to the owner or end an infringement.

The rules on remedies are often found in a different part of the code. In a system such as the BGB, remedies apply to all cases of breach of obligations, whether following from contract or from tort. It therefore makes sense to regulate remedies in the part of the code that deals with obligations in general.

---

[21] Bussani and Infantino 2021, at pp. 30–33, provide a broad overview of other ways of 'making good the loss'.

[22] The terminology varies among jurisdictions, as does the precise distinction between an order and an injunction.

3
Fault liability in French law

3.1   INTRODUCTION

After the conceptual introduction to tort law in the previous chapters, we can finally discuss actual systems of tort law. The following three chapters provide an outline of French, German and English tort law, considered from the framework discussed in Chapter 2. The discussion goes into some depth and presupposes several concepts that are only discussed in more detail later on. The reason for doing so is that it is preferable to discuss national tort law systems before treating the details of concepts like causality, while it is also useful that the descriptions of national systems are self-contained and provide a fairly comprehensive overview. The materials in these chapters thereby also overlap to some extent with the descriptions in Chapters 6 through 12. While reading Chapters 3 through 5 for the first time it is advisable to concentrate on the difference in structure, and not on the specific details: in later chapters it will become clear that a lot of the details are common to most countries or are of minor importance.

Chapters 3 and 4 describe French and German law. These are examples of so-called civil law systems. These systems are typically based on a comprehensive statute, called a code, covering a large area of private law. The cases of the highest court are often considered as interpreting the code but not an official source of law, although in practice they have practically the same authority as legislation. The highest court is not bound by its earlier decisions (there is no system of precedent law as in common law). There are other typical differences in civil law systems, which are described at some length in comparative literature.[1]

3.2   THE CODE CIVIL

French law is a codified system.[2] In 1804 the Code civil was established and was one of the first written codes for civil law. The highest French court for civil law is called the Cour de cassation (abbreviated as Cass. when referring to case law). Formally the Cour de cassation may only interpret the code, not change the law, and case law does not have a binding status in the way

---

[1]   As an introduction see Zweigert and Kötz 1998, Glenn 2010, Ch. 5, Chs 6–13 and 18, Merryman and Pérez-Perdomo 2019.

[2]   A good English introduction is Steiner 2018. Youngs 2014 is also useful, but predates the revision of the Code civil in 2016.

English precedents do. In practice, however, the case law of the Cour de cassation is used as a strong indication of the state of French law.

A brief note on the references to French case law. The Cour de cassation consists of several chambers (*chambres*) that are independent and may on occasion hold different opinions, whereby lawyers also mention the chamber that decided the case (in the form Cass. 1, or 1re (for 1st, première). The Cour de cassation may decide particular important issues by the entire court, called the full chambre (*chambre plénière*, abbreviated as 'plén.'). Also, sometimes the reference adds '(civ.)' to explicate that it is a civil chamber of the Cour de cassation that decided, instead of one of the criminal or commercial chambers. After the date of the decision, there is usually a docket number or a reference to publication in a case law journal. Here we observe the French conventions to facilitate research. However, the dates have been translated to English.

The general structure of French tort law closely resembles the fundamental structure that we discussed in the previous chapter. Originally a mere five articles sufficed for the whole of tort law. Later the section on torts in the Code civil has been extended to incorporate for instance product liability, while also occasional modifications were introduced. The system of the Code civil has been elaborated piecemeal by case law. In some instances a new development has been codified in a specific law.[3]

As of 1 October 2016 the Code civil has been revised, whereby contract law was changed significantly.[4] Tort law, however, has not materially changed; the relevant provisions were only renumbered. What is now art. 1240 used to be art. 1382 of the Code civil of 1804, 1241 was 1383, and so on. When you consult older literature and case law you will therefore need to mentally replace the old article numbers with the current numbers. The French government has subsequently started a project to reform tort law, which in 2021 is still ongoing.[5]

In French law, non-contractual liability (*responsabilité extracontractuelle*), often called delictual liability (*responsabilité delictuelle*), is treated as part of the general law of civil liability (*droit de la responsabilité civile*), which covers both contractual liability and non-contractual liability. The latter topic covers largely the same ground as tort law in common law systems.

3.3   THE GENERAL NORM OF ART. 1240 CC

The basic norm of French tort law is found in art. 1240 Cc.

---

[3]   Noteworthy is the *Loi Badinter*, covering liability for traffic accidents in a specific law outside private law.

[4]   Legislation can be found at www.legifrance.gouv.fr/. Case law of the Cour de cassation can be found at www .courdecassation.fr/ and also at www.legifrance.gouv.fr/. Some translations can be found at https://law.utexas.edu/ transnational/foreign-law-translations/.

[5]   See the current legislative proposal: www.assemblee-nationale.fr/dyn/15/dossiers/alt/DLR5L15N40255, www .senat.fr/dossier-legislatif/ppl19-678.html.

> *Art. 1240*
> *Tout fait quelconque de l'homme, qui cause à autrui un dommage, oblige celui par la faute duquel il est arrivé, à le réparer.*
>
> Art. 1240
> Any human act that causes damage to another obliges the person by whose fault it occurred to repair it.

This is followed by art. 1241 Cc, which provides further explanation:

> *Art. 1241*
> *Chacun est responsable du dommage qu'il a causé non seulement par son fait, mais encore par sa négligence ou par son imprudence.*
>
> Art. 1241
> Everyone is liable for the damage they have caused not only by intentional acts, but also by negligent conduct or by imprudence.[6]

Art. 1240 formulates the basic norm that damage caused by wrongful acts has to be compensated.[7] In order to avoid misunderstanding, it is explicitly stated in the next article that this comprises intentional as well as negligent acts (the latter are also called *quasi-délit*; intentional acts are also referred to as *delits*). In practice this distinction has no consequence.[8]

You may notice that the elements of these provisions, in particular the concepts of 'fault', 'cause' and 'damage' are not explained. It was left to the courts to determine how these articles had to be applied in specific cases. If you want to know the exact state of French law, it is therefore necessary to research case law. In practice you do so by consulting the doctrinal literature which provides analysis and references to relevant case law.[9] I will discuss some details in the following sections.

If we compare the basic rule of French law to the fundamental structure of fault liability described in Chapter 2, we can note that there is no explicit requirement of subjective fault: that is simply presumed to be present (§ 2.5). In French law, fault (*faute*) implies an 'objective' standard of wrongful behaviour.

---

[6] The translation expands slightly on the literal text to clarify some notions.

[7] This norm can be traced back to Grotius, who only partly based himself on the older Roman Law provisions of the Lex Aquilia. It was generally accepted in the French legal writings before the Code civil, in particular the works of Pothier and Domat.

[8] Fabre-Magnan 2021, p. 116.

[9] An extensive leading text is Viney, Jourdain and Carval 2013. More concise and clear is Fabre-Magnan 2021. A very extensive treatment with numerous distinctions and references to case law is Le Tourneau 2020. English texts are Van Dam 2013, Borghetti and Whittaker 2019.

The Code civil does not provide further subdivision in different kinds of wrongfulness. Case law and doctrine have suggested various ways to determine when there is a fault, which we will turn to now.

3.4 CATEGORIES OF FAULT

The general rule of art. 1240 Cc relies on the intuition that we can recognize when conduct is wrongful, which indeed we may often be able to do. However, there are also many boundary cases where our intuitions may not provide a clear answer. Lawyers therefore look for more detailed rules, and use case law to construct a categorization of cases. Unfortunately there is no general consensus on the appropriate classification of cases.

I find it instructive to borrow the categorization in a leading commentary on delictual liability, where the authors propose that liability implies the violation of a non-contractual duty.[10] These duties can be divided as follows.[11] You need to bear in mind, however, that the categorization is not strict: a breach of an unwritten duty can be influenced by the fact that there is also a relevant statutory rule.

3.4.1 Explicitly written duties

1. Written rules proscribing certain behaviour: these encompass statutes as well as other kinds of rules. This category resembles the English tort of breach of a statutory duty, except that it is broader than statutes.
2. Within the category of written rules there are the rules for the protection of subjective rights (rights of others), i.e. the fault consists of infringement of another's right. Such a right is to be found in a statute. This category overlaps with a number of English torts, in particular torts such as trespass that protect property rights and the right to personal integrity.

3.4.2 Unwritten duties

3. Unwritten non-contractual duties.[12] The courts have to determine when there is an unwritten non-contractual duty. This category is very similar to the English tort of negligence (§ 5.2).

---

[10] Viney, Jourdain and Carval 2013, p. 450. They also discuss contractual liability, but that is outside the scope of the present text.

[11] Viney, Jourdain and Carval 2013, p. 451ff. The proposed art. 1241 for the reform of French tort law similarly distinguishes between violation of a legal or reglementary command, and breach of the general duty of prudence or diligence (*devoir general de prudence ou de diligence*).

[12] Viney, Jourdain and Carval 2013, p. 457.

4. Finally, within the category of unwritten non-contractual duties, we can recognize a sub-category of *abuse of right* (*abus de droit*).[13] This covers intentional actions intended to harm another person. This category is important as it allows comparison to the English intentional torts and the German § 826 BGB.

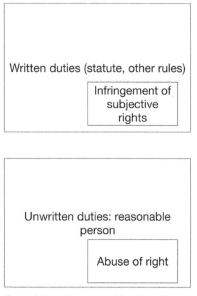

Written duties (statute, other rules)

Infringement of subjective rights

Unwritten duties: reasonable person

Abuse of right

Figure 3.1   A categorization of the element of fault in French law

To determine whether there is a fault, courts can therefore look in several directions. They may look at written rules, such as statutes, but also technical and professional standards and similar rules (§ 6.2).[14] In the absence of a written rule, lawyers assess whether there is an unwritten non-contractual duty in the circumstances of the specific case. The doctrine suggests that the general way to do so is to examine whether the tortfeasor's conduct is that of the reasonable person (*personne raisonnable*).[15] This is presumed to be a normally prudent and diligent person.[16] In older texts you may find alternative (gendered) formulations, such as the 'reasonable and informed man' (*l'homme raisonnable et avisé*), or the 'good father of the family' (*bon père de la famille*).[17]

---

[13]   Extensively Le Tourneau 2020, chapter 2213, also Viney, Jourdain and Carval 2013, p. 495, para. 475, Fabre-Magnan 2021, p. 105.

[14]   Viney, Jourdain and Carval 2013, pp. 474–8.

[15]   Fabre-Magnan 2021, p. 101.

[16]   Fabre-Magnan 2021, p. 102.

[17]   This phrase, going back to Roman law, was until 2014 used in some provisions in the Code civil and is nowadays still found in codes elsewhere, for example the Philippines Civil code, art. 1173 (which also applies to tort, see art. 2178).

The standard of the reasonable person is still not very informative. The case law on art. 1240 Cc is extensive and there is no generally recognized way of classification.[18] The case law may be divided according to a variety of fairly abstract obligations or duties following from reasons of social utility, such as duty to take precautions, to supervise persons and things that one controls, to take guard of dangers, a duty of diligence, a duty of competence, a duty of skill.[19] The broad outlines of the case law are recognizable and not too different from the case law in other countries.

For the area of commercial delicts (comparable to economic torts, see § 7.4) the courts have worked with an alternative, more specific standard, namely the demands of good faith, loyalty, honesty.[20] Examples where this standard was applied are cases concerning not informing the other party of information relevant to a contract, injuring the reputation of someone else by diffusing incomplete information, conspiracy to defraud someone of an advantage, profiting of someone else's investments in his reputation.[21] Other cases can be characterized as violating the respect due to others, examples are being complicit in a party violating a contractual obligation, or cases of treating others' interests too lightly, such as using the freedom of expression without sufficiently taking effort for being complete and correct, lightly breaking off contractual relations.[22] These cases show that you have to take the interests of others to heart.

You should also be aware that several kinds of wrongful acts are regulated outside the Code civil. In particular the *Code de la Consommation* (Consumer Act) covers torts towards consumers (which we shall not discuss in this introduction). The rules on defamation are found in the law on the freedom of the press (see § 7.5). Those laws explicate when there is a fault, but for other elements and consequences (such as assessment of damages) rely on the general rules of the Code civil.

3.5   INCOMPETENCE OF THE TORTFEASOR

As mentioned above, French law presumes that the tortfeasor is accountable for his actions. There is no requirement of subjective fault. French law recognizes the possibility that a person is not fully aware of the consequences of his actions, lacks full discernment (*la faculté de discernement*). But the rules for these persons are not overly protective.

For adults who are mentally disabled, the Code civil contains a specific rule.

Art. 414-3 Cc[23]
Celui qui a causé un dommage à autrui alors qu'il était sous l'empire d'un trouble mental

---

[18]   Viney, Jourdain and Carval 2013, pp. 489–91.

[19]   Viney, Jourdain and Carval 2013, pp. 499–505.

[20]   Viney, Jourdain and Carval 2013, p. 492, Le Tourneau 2020, chapter 2214. Further § 7.4.

[21]   Viney, Jourdain and Carval 2013, pp. 492–4.

[22]   Viney, Jourdain and Carval 2013, pp. 495–9.

[23]   The provision was originally numbered art. 489-2, but was renumbered in 2007.

> *n'en est pas moins obligé à réparation.*
>
> Art. 414-3
> He who has caused harm to someone else when he was under the influence of a mental disease is no less obliged to reparation.

Adults who are mentally disabled are therefore liable, without a correction for the fact that they may not have understood that they acted wrongfully. This specific rule does not apply to children in general.[24] It is not yet known whether the law also requires an objective approach to contributory negligence of such persons (when the victim also was at fault).[25]

For children there is no specific provision in the Code civil. The courts nowadays simply apply art. 1240 Cc directly to children, using an objective standard. When determining whether a child is liable, it is not necessary to determine whether the child actually understood its actions, the court merely looks at whether the behaviour would be wrongful for a normal adult.[26] For instance, a seven-year-old boy was found liable for pushing another child onto a bench, causing internal bleeding.[27] This objective approach to the faults of children is applied also when it comes to contributory negligence (when a child is the victim of a wrongful act, but also contributed to the accident). An example is a case of an eight-year-old girl, who was playing at a friend's house, who suddenly appeared from under a table and bumped into the friend who carried a bowl of hot water. The hot water spilled on her and caused serious burn wounds. While the father of the friend was held liable, the liability was reduced because of contributory negligence on the part of the child.[28] The approach of the Cour de cassation in these cases has been criticized as being overly harsh, although the effects are mitigated largely by the presence of mandatory insurance.[29]

3.6   CAUSALITY

Art. 1240 Cc requires a causal connection, but does not explicate what is meant by that. The case law established that two conditions need to be fulfilled.

- First of all the fault needs to stand in *condicio sine qua non* connection to the harm (factual causality).

---

[24]   Art. 414-3 Cc does apply to a child who acted under the influence of a mental condition, Cass (civ.) 1, 20 July 1976, Bull.civ. I., no 270.

[25]   Viney, Jourdain and Carval 2013, p. 700.

[26]   Cass. (plén.), 9 May 1984, no. 80-93031 (Lemaire), and other cases discussed by Le Tourneau 2020, paras 2111.21–2111.22, who also points to divergent case law of the Cour de cassation.

[27]   Cass. (civ.), 2, 12 December 1984, Bull.civ. II, no 193.

[28]   Cass. (civ.), 2, 28 February 1996, Bull.civ. II, no 54.

[29]   Viney, Jourdain and Carval 2013, pp. 702–05.

- Secondly, there is the additional requirement of legal causality. In French law the criterion is that the damage must be 'immediate and direct' (art. 1231-4 Cc) in order to be compensated. This criterion derives from contract law,[30] but is extended to tort law.[31] Doctrine also refers to 'certain and direct' damage.[32]

More difficult cases of causation, such as multiple causes and intervening causes have been decided in case law and are treated extensively in legal doctrine.[33] Such cases are mainly discussed under the heading of 'foreign cause' (*cause étrangère*). This covers

- causes attributable to the victim: these may give rise to contributory negligence or lead the court to find that the act was not wrongful,
- causes attributable to third parties (hence involving multiple tortfeasors), and
- causes that cannot be attributed to anyone (*cas fortuit*, chance events): force majeure, which may lead to a defence (§ 12.3).

When there are multiple tortfeasors, the solution is that these are solidary liable (i.e. jointly and severally liable). Each solidary debtor is liable for the whole obligation (art. 1313 Cc), while internally the debtors are only held to contribute for their share in the obligation, and may take recourse on each other when they have paid more than their share (art. 1317 Cc). The case law shows that solidary liability has broad application, on condition that the actions of the different parties have actually caused the harm and that the harm is indivisible (i.e. there are not two distinct kinds of harm).[34]

3.7   HARM, DAMAGE AND DAMAGES

French law does not clearly distinguish between harm and damage. The law requires the presence of 'dommage', damage. A synonym for 'dommage' is 'préjudice réparable',[35] compensable disadvantage. French doctrine has not developed a clear concept of what this involves, even though it is recognized that 'préjudice' means harm to an interest.[36] French law is rather liberal as to the kinds of interests that are protected.

---

[30]   Formerly found in art. 1151 Cc 1804. Furthermore art. 1231-3 Cc (art. 1150 Cc 1804) declares that the debtor need not compensate unforeseeable damage except in the case of gross negligence or intentional breach of contract.

[31]   Fabre-Magnan 2021, pp. 245–52 (speaking of 'cause adequate'), Viney, Jourdain and Carval 2013, p. 252–3, 266.

[32]   Le Tourneau 2020 chapter 2132. See also the proposed art. 1236: 'Le préjudice futur est réparable lorsqu'il est la prolongation certaine et directe d'un état de choses actuel' of the proposal to reform French tort law (www.justice .gouv.fr/publication/Projet_de_reforme_de_la_responsabilite_civile_13032017.pdf).

[33]   Viney, Jourdain and Carval 2013, pp. 317–436, Le Tourneau 2020, chapters 2141–2144.

[34]   Viney, Jourdain and Carval 2013, p. 374, Le Tourneau 2020, paras 2132.90–183.

[35]   Viney, Jourdain and Carval 2013, p. 17.

[36]   Viney, Jourdain and Carval 2013, pp. 17–25.

The amount of money to be awarded for reparation of damage (damages) is called 'dommages et intérêts', or more briefly 'dommage-intérêt'. In line with other civil law systems, damages are viewed as a particular form of reparation. There are no specific rules in the code for assessment of damages or the kind of damages that can be awarded.

French law does not have restrictions against compensation of pure economic loss: the concept is only a translation from English law and is not part of French law.[37]

3.8   OTHER REMEDIES

Besides damages, French law allows other actions to repair the loss suffered by the victim. This is called *reparation en nature*[38] and is based on an extensive interpretation of art. 1143 Code civil. In a court procedure such actions are awarded in the form of orders and injunctions. These may be further strengthened by a court-imposed fine (called *astreinte*) in case the defendant does not obey the order or injunction.[39]

For cases of defamation art. 32 of the Loi de 29 Juillet 1881 allows the court to order publication of the decision of the court,[40] by way of rectifying a defamatory statement.

---

[37]   Fabre-Magnan 2021, p. 136, Viney, Jourdain and Carval 2013, p. 43.

[38]   Fabre-Magnan 2021, p. 517.

[39]   Notice that the fine is due to the claimant.

[40]   'L'affichage ou la diffusion de la décision prononcée dans les conditions prévues par l'article 131-35 du code penal.'

4
The German law of delict

While a general rule for fault-based liability like the French art. 1240 Cc has the advantage of apparent simplicity, it cannot avoid the principal problem of non-contractual liability, namely to distinguish wrongful behaviour from actions that are allowed, in an extremely varied set of cases. A single rule is conceptually clear, but it provides no guidance how to deal with a multitude of cases, except by appealing to our intuitions as to what should be considered wrongful. Legal practice stands in need of more detailed distinctions. These are provided amply by German law.[1]

German legal writing usually refers to case law solely by reference to the publication in a case law journal, particularly the BGHZ or the NJW. This has the advantage of saving space and allowing German scholars to compile long lists of case law in a highly condensed format. Here we deviate from this practice and principally explicate the court and date of the decision, docket number, and only then list the publication reference. This makes it easier to find the decisions and place them chronologically.

4.1   THE PLACE OF THE LAW OF DELICT IN THE GERMAN BGB

The drafters of the German *Bürgerliches Gesetzbuch* (BGB), when drafting the part on what the Germans call law of delict (*Deliktsrecht*), attempted to provide further guidance in two ways, and thereby restrict the power of the courts to develop the law on their own. First of all, they provided not a single general rule, but rather three general norms which together cover most of the cases where liability might be in order. Secondly, they used the concept of protected interests to narrow down the scope of those general rules. The result of these choices is unfortunately a rather complicated system. Nonetheless the innovations of the German code have been influential, and particularly the 'protected interests' approach can be found in several modern codes. One thing you need to bear in mind: the BGB follows a logical structure wherein rules are placed at the corresponding level of generality. In particular rules that are

---

[1]   An excellent English treatise is Markesinis, Bell and Janssen 2019. German textbooks are Deutsch and Ahrens 2014, Kötz and Wagner 2016, Geigel 2020. Legislation can be found at www.gesetze-im-internet.de, where also another translation of the BGB is available. Case law can be found at www.rechtsprechung-im-internet.de/. Some translations are offered at https://law.utexas.edu/transnational/foreign-law-translations/. A general introduction in German law, with a brief section on the law of delict, can be found in Youngs 2014.

common to contractual and non-contractual obligations are not placed in the title on tort law, but are placed in the part on obligations in general.

The BGB is based on a division of the various prohibited acts (*Unerlaubte Handlungen*) in so-called *Deliktstatbestände* or simply *Tatbestände* (plural). 'Tatbestand' (singular) means a set of facts that give rise to a legal consequence, which in this context is liability. 'Tatbestand' may be translated as 'factual ground' or 'set of facts' and serves a role similar to the English 'cause of action'. In this context, however, 'ground of liability' is more suitable to explicate the link to liability. The various *Tatbestände* provide a categorization rather like the way in which English torts function. German law distinguishes between the three main grounds of liability (*Grundtatbestände*) and the specific grounds of liability (*Einzeltatbestände*).

In the following I will give an abridged presentation of the German system.[2] If you consult the German literature you will quickly find that there are numerous concepts, theories and distinctions, but that unfortunately there is no general agreement about their interpretation. It is impossible to describe the diversity in opinions and retain the clarity required of an introduction. Hence the following description is based on choices between competing theories, it strives to present German tort law in relation to the framework of Chapter 2, while simultaneously introducing the major concepts of German law. Thereby you will be able to engage in a discussion on German tort law, even though you should be aware that the description given here may be disputed by German lawyers who adhere to alternative theories.

4.2   § 823 I BGB: PROTECTED INTERESTS

The first two main grounds are found in § 823 BGB, a general provision consisting of two parts. We will start with the first. Unfortunately, as we shall see, a discussion of this part leads to a complicated discussion of legal concepts in German law. You should not despair but rather soldier on, even if you do not immediately understand everything that is said. At the end I will try to summarize what we have discussed. Now on to the text of § 823 I BGB.

---

§ *823 BGB*
§ *(1) Wer vorsätzlich oder fahrlässig das Leben, den Körper, die Gesundheit, die*
§ *Freiheit, das Eigentum oder ein sonstiges Recht eines anderen widerrechtlich verletzt, ist*
dem anderen zum Ersatz des daraus entstehenden Schadens verpflichtet.
§ *...*

§ § 823 BGB
§ I . Whoever intentionally or negligently unlawfully injures the life, body, health, freedom, property or some other right of another person is obliged to compensation to the other for the damage arising out of it.

---

[2]   I feel emboldened in doing so by the example of Wagner 2021, paras 5.14–20, 5.37–39, who – with admittedly vastly superior knowledge – attempts to simplify the system of German law in a way more aligned with comparative research.

The text suggests five requirements for liability:

- *Verschulden*, meaning culpability/fault. This is inferred from the phrase 'intentional or negligent'
- Unlawfulness
- Injury (infringement) to certain protected rights or interests (life, body etc.)
- Damage
- Causal connection between the act and the damage ('arising from it').[3]

The element of causal connection does not require further discussion at this point, as it is simply the general element of causality. The element of damage partly overlaps with the general element of harm. Strictly speaking, the requirement of harm is fulfilled by the third element (injury to interests) as we shall see. The reason that § 823 I BGB requires damage and not harm is that it also explicates the remedy of an award of damages (see § 10.1).

The first and second element together constitute the requirement of fault. We will return there in a moment, but first we need to discuss the third requirement.

The requirement of injury to certain interests was an innovation at the time of enactment. It can be contrasted to the French approach where in principle harm to any interest may give rise to liability. § 823 I BGB only provides a ground for liability for injury to specific protected interests. This limits the kinds of harm for which the tortfeasor is liable: liability on the basis of § 823 I only arises if the wrongful act consists of an injury to one of these interests.

This provision limitatively specifies which interests are covered: life, body, health, freedom, property, or 'ein sonstiges recht', some other kind of right. This latter category has been interpreted by the German Supreme Court (*Bundesgerichtshof*, BGH) to include (besides real rights[4] and intellectual property rights) also the personality right,[5] privacy and an 'established and operating business' (*eingerichteten und ausgeübten Gewerbebetrieb*).[6] The explicitly named interests appear quite clear. In that respect the provision is indeed successful: it provides the reader with an indication of the kinds of injury that might lead to liability. Nonetheless there remains ample scope for discussion as there are numerous boundary cases that require elucidation by the courts. For example, does the right to health and body also protect against the shock of hearing about the death of a beloved close relative? Furthermore, the 'other rights' are not as intuitive and need explanation.[7]

---

[3]   The German phrase is 'daraus entstehenden Schaden' which can be translated as 'damage caused by'. The English translation above is more literal to make clear that the German original does not use the word 'cause' (noun: *Ursache*, verb: *verursachen*).

[4]   These are rights related to the use of land, for instance, a right of way or a restrictive covenant preventing development of the land.

[5]   Markesinis, Bell and Janssen 2019, pp. 43–9. See § 7.5.

[6]   Wagner 2021, para 5.68, Markesinis, Bell and Janssen 2019, pp. 39–43. See § 7.4.

[7]   See §§ 7.4 and 7.5.

The interests stated in the text of § 823 I BGB do not include patrimony,[8] therefore pure economic loss (*reiner Vermogensschaden*)[9] is in principle not recoverable on the basis of this provision. However, the damage of injury to the right to an established and operative commercial enterprise typically amounts to pure economic loss, and is therefore an exception to the rule that § 823 I BGB does not protect pure economic loss.

Returning to the requirements of unlawfulness and *Verschulden*: the precise application of these elements is the subject of a complicated theoretical debate in German law. For purposes of this introduction, I will simplify by presenting one view in abbreviated manner, while briefly explaining the alternative approach.[10]

In the model introduced in Chapter 2, we distinguished between objective and subjective fault as elements within the general element of fault. § 823 I BGB requires that there is an infringement or injury to a protected interest. The question is whether this already suffices to assume the presence of objective fault, or whether there is an additional requirement.

We can understand the notion of unlawfulness as the requisite additional requirement on top of injury to an interest. However, if one of the protected interests was *directly* violated by the action, the unlawfulness can be presumed. In such a case the defendant would need to explain why the action was justified; he would raise a defence (Chapter 12). If, on the other hand, the infringement occurred indirectly, the unlawfulness of the act is not evident and needs to be established. This approach can be supported by way of example. A direct action such as what the English call battery is indeed of such a nature that it is hard to see why it should not be unlawful. But there are many actions that may ultimately cause infringement of an interest while not clearly being wrongful. For instance, you order a pizza from a courier, and the courier is hit by a car while coming to your house. This causes infringement of the courier's bodily integrity. If unlawfulness would be given from the mere injury, you would only escape liability by successfully invoking a defence (Chapter 12) or arguing for lack of *Verschulden* (which we will discuss shortly). While it is certainly possible to work with such a system of liability, it seems needlessly complicated and removed from the intuitive perception that ordering a pizza is completely normal behaviour. Calling that 'unlawful' stretches the meaning of that word.

In this view, how do we decide on unlawfulness for indirect actions? The answer is, by using what is called an objective negligence standard (*objektiver Fahrlässigkeitsmaßstab*) in the action. Doctrine relates this test to § 276 II BGB, which states a general principle for all relationships (contract and extra-contractual).

---

[8]   Patrimony (*Vermögen* in German) means the entire set of assets of an individual: goods, money, anything of value. In this context is it meant that patrimony as such is not protected, although specific assets (in particular tangible goods) are.

[9]   See § 10.4 for this concept.

[10]   See also Markesinis, Bell and Janssen 2019, pp. 49–53.

> **§ 276 BGB**
> *(2) Fahrlässig handelt, wer die im Verkehr erforderliche Sorgfalt außer Acht lässt.*
>
> **§ 276 BGB**
> (2) Conduct is negligent when a person behaves without observing the care required in society.

As this is still a rather broad formulation, the norm for what constitutes negligent behaviour (objective carelessness, *objektive Fahrlässigkeit*) is usually found in a more precise standard, the conduct of a normal person.[11] In this interpretation the element of objective carelessness is subsumed under unlawfulness, whereby *Verschulden* is reduced to a test of capacity and culpability in the sense of subjective fault.

The alternative view is that the infringement of one of the protected interests automatically satisfies the requirement of unlawfulness, even though the text of § 823 I BGB suggests that this is an additional element. In this view the approach for direct infringement is also applied to indirect infringement. The brunt for the assessment of the conduct will lie on the element of *Verschulden*, which then comprises both objective carelessness and subjective fault. In the end this interpretation will normally lead to the same result as the first interpretation, hence this is mostly a theoretical debate.

As stated above, § 823 I BGB also requires that the injury or infringement was done intentionally or negligently. This element is interpreted as the requirement of *Verschulden*, literally culpability, but also translated as fault.[12] Here we may translate it as culpability as long as we realize that the concept also may cover part of objective fault. The German concepts do not neatly match up with the general framework of Chapter 2.

In German doctrine you may find the position (implied in the alternative view discussed above) that *Verschulden* can be analysed in external carefulness and internal carefulness (*äußere Sorgfalt/innere Sorgfalt*).[13] The former is the objective negligence standard, the external carefulness, as is described in other jurisdictions (and in th first interpretation discussed above would be part of unlawfulness). The objective negligence standard is determined by considering how a normal person would behave.[14] The *innere Sorgfalt* (internal carefulness, subjective carefulness) is roughly equivalent with subjective fault. It covers both the possibility that culpability is lacking for certain groups (about which § 4.7) and the degree of culpability.

German law recognizes several degrees of culpability. For introductory purposes we need only look at the most important ones, negligence or carelessness (*Fahrlässigkeit*), gross negli-

---

[11] Wagner 2021, para 5.80 refers to the standard of the normally developed reasonable person of average competence (*normal veranlagten vernünftigen Menschen von durchschnittlicher Tüchtigkeit*). Also Deutsch and Ahrens 2014, paras 143–4.

[12] See Markesinis, Bell and Janssen p. 53.

[13] Geigel 2020, para 1-69.

[14] See above, footnote 11, citing Wagner 2021, para 5.22.

gence, and intention (*Vorsatz*). Intention and negligence are similar to how they are defined in English law, see further § 8.4. § 276 II BGB further defines what negligent conduct involves. Gross negligence (*grobe Fahrlässigkeit*) is extreme carelessness that borders on intention. In the law gross negligence and intention are often lumped together and treated with the same severity; courts may establish gross negligence simply because they are not entirely sure whether there was actually intention in the mind of the tortfeasor but the behaviour strongly suggests intention. For liability under § 823 I BGB the presence of culpable negligence suffices, as explicated in § 276 I BGB (which, insofar as relevant here, states that 'The debtor is responsible for intention as well as negligence …'[15]).

At this point you probably begin to understand why German law has a reputation for complex conceptual distinctions. For the application of § 823 I BGB you can use the five elements listed above, with the help of the explanation given here. To simplify matters, we can position the elements and concepts we encountered up to now relative to the abstract model we introduced in Chapter 2.

Notice that, compared to the general framework of Chapter 2, there is an additional element in that there must also be infringement of one of the protected interests. This imposes restrictions on the harm. The two requirements of unlawfulness and *Verschulden* cover the general concept of fault, while they appear to overlap to some extent: either may – dependent on the interpretation of German law that you follow – require an assessment of the lack of care of the tortfeasor. In practice, lawyers will simply apply the objective negligence standard, whereby both requirements will be fulfilled simultaneously (as we can presume that in such a case there is also subjective intention/negligence). *Verschulden* only requires additional attention where the capacity of the tortfeasor is in question.

4.3   *VERKEHRSPFLICHTEN*

§ 823 I BGB applies when someone 'injures' (*verletzt*) or infringes a protected interest: this presumes an *act* that directly or indirectly infringes the interest. Strictly speaking it does not seem to cover cases where someone is responsible for a certain location and does not remove a risk that arose by outside force. To remedy this, a separate category has been accepted by the highest German court: the so called *Verkehrspflichten*.[16] These have been translated as 'safety duties';[17] or 'duties of care';[18] the first translation seems preferable as that does not have a prior meaning. In the following we will usually keep the German term. The two cases in which

---

[15]   *Der Schuldner hat Vorsatz und Fahrlässigkeit zu vertreten ….*

[16]   Von Bar 1998, paras 104–05, Markesinis, Bell and Janssen 2019, pp. 55–60, Wagner 2021, paras 5.29–5.33. In the past these were called *Verkehrssicherungspflichten*. *Verkehr* means traffic, but also public interaction and contacts, dealings, circulation. In this context the meaning is close to traffic and public spaces. The concept derives from its use in § 367 *Strafgesetzbuch* where it referred to places where people interact/circulate, see Deutsch and Ahrens 2014, para 328.

[17]   Van Dam 2013, para 403.

[18]   Markesinis, Bell and Janssen 2019, p. 55.

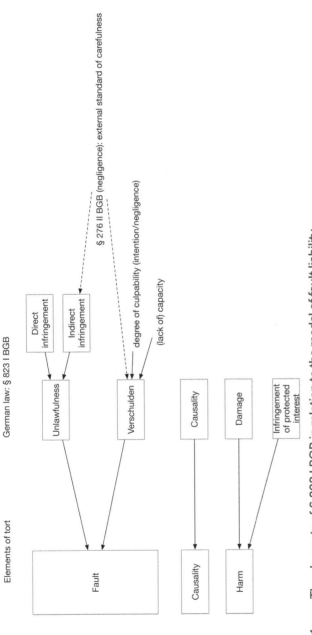

Figure 4.1   The elements of § 823 I BGB in relation to the model of fault liability

Verkehrspflichten (safety duties) as a ground for liability were accepted involved liability for neglecting to clean a snow-covered stairway and liability for neglecting to remove a rotten tree which subsequently fell on the street and hurt a passer-by.[19] Clearly the harm in these cases was only an indirect consequence of the negligent omission.

In later case law this concept has been extended to cover other cases where a risk was created or allowed to persist. A general norm from the case law is 'that everyone is liable for the damage caused by his things, insofar as he could have avoided this with fair and just consideration of the interest of others'.[20]

At this point you may wonder whether *Verkehrspflichten* are a specific category based on § 823 I BGB or rather a distinct, independent ground of liability. Unfortunately, German doctrine is not entirely clear on this issue. Formally, the doctrine of *Verkehrspflichten* is based on § 823 I BGB, but the specific requirements for *Verkehrspflichten* deviate from the text of § 823 I BGB.[21] Lawyers are divided over this issue and the German Bundesgerichtshof has not decided this. Here we can ignore the details of this debate. For practical purposes *Verkehrspflichten* are to be assessed as an additional category or ground besides the general rule of § 823 I BGB, since they have their own criteria. Whether they are ultimately based on § 823 I BGB is not relevant for the practical application.

In contrast to the literal scope of § 823 I BGB, the *Verkehrspflichten* can also protect other rights than those listed in that provision. Pure economic loss (§ 10.4), however, is not covered by *Verkehrspflichten*. They only provide ground for compensation of physical injury and property damage. An advantage of *Verkehrspflichten* over the rule of § 823 I BGB is that these also cover cases in which the infringement of the right occurred indirectly.[22]

The case law involves mostly cases related to public places or traffic on roads and similar semi-public areas like staircases and shops, sports centres. Examples are accidents that happened because the roads were not kept in proper order, neglecting to throw salt or sand on the roads after heavy snow-fall (to make them less slippery). Incidentally, the duty of the local authorities to keep public roads safe is nowadays mostly laid down in specific statutes, and violation of those gives rise to state liability hence is outside the area of *Verkehrspflichten*.[23] Nonetheless these cases give a good idea about the kind of duties that are *Verkehrspflichten*.

More generally, this doctrine covers cases where the defendant creates a certain danger or is required to supervise a specific *object* or location that may cause some dangers, and takes insufficient action to contain those dangers.[24] Examples are the duty to prevent trees near a road from falling down as much as feasible, keep the floor of a supermarket free from fruit

---

[19]　Reichsgericht 30 Oktober 1902, RGZ 52, 573, Reichsgericht 23 February 1903, RGZ 54, 53.

[20]　Reichsgericht 30 Oktober 1902, RGZ 52, 373: 'ein jeder für die Beschädigung durch seine Sachen insoweit aufkommen solle, als er dieselbe bei billiger Rücksichtnahme auf die Interessen des anderen hätte verhüten können'. Quoted by Wagner 2021, para 5.30.

[21]　Deutsch and Ahrens 2014, para 329, Wagner 2021, para 5.29.

[22]　See Van Dam 2013, para 402-2.

[23]　Wagner 2021, para 5.73.

[24]　Geigel 2020, para 14–28, Wagner 2021, paras 5.75–5.76. This partially overlaps with strict liability rules.

and vegetables in order to avoid customers from slipping, maintain a safe distance between a billiard table and a couch in order to avoid injury to guests by sudden movements by the billiard players, keep firearms secure, keep your car secure to prohibit a thief or joyrider from drive it and causing accidents.[25]

Finally, *Verkehrspflichten* are sometimes used for risky activities.[26] This applies not only to driving, but also in sports such as football or skiing.

The category of *Verkehrspflichten* has thus been used to assume liability in a large and diverse group of cases.[27] Nowadays this is considered to be the most important kind of delict, akin to the tort of negligence in English law. In the context of the German system the *Verkehrspflichten* are a category of last resort, which applies only when no other head of liability applies. Nonetheless it is invoked frequently.

Verkehrspflichten do not require the defendant to avoid or prevent all risks,[28] nor does the concept generally require active duties to protect against risks that the defendant did not create himself.[29]

- An example of the former is the case of an automatic bank door, where the victim's fingers were caught in the door.[30] The BGH considered that even though operating a dangerous installation requires taking safety measures, it is not required to exclude all risk of injury. In the present case the doors followed the relevant safety standards at the time of installation, and the doors did not have to be upgraded immediately when the safety standards became stricter a few years later. This is in line with the four factor approach discussed in § 6.2.
- An example of the latter is a judgment where the BGH declared that the owner of a forest does not owe a *Verkehrspflicht* to protect visitors from falling branches or other danger characteristic of forests.[31] The BGH in one decision stated that a person is required to take the measures 'that a sensible, circumspect, and within reason careful human being finds necessary and sufficient, to keep others safe from harm'.[32]

The applicable standard of behaviour is based on the notion of *Verschulden*, discussed in the previous section. For *Verkehrspflichten* the standard has been said to consist of the preventive measures 'that a prudent and circumspect, within rational boundaries careful person finds

25 Deutsch and Ahrens 2014, paras 338–47, Wagner 2021, para 5.75, referring to various cases.
26 Kötz and Wagner 2016, para 5.77.
27 See Van Dam 2013, para 403, Deutsch and Ahrens 2014, § 17, paras 328–61, Geigel 2020, chapter 14.
28 Wagner 2021, para 5.81. See also § 6.2.
29 Wagner 2021, para 5.78.
30 BGH 2 March 2010, VI ZR 223/09, NJW 2010, 1967.
31 BGH 2 October 2012, VI ZR 311/11.
32 '[D]ie ein verständiger und umsichtiger, in vernünftigen Grenzen vorsichtiger Mensch für notwendig und ausreichend hält, um andere vor Schaden zu bewahren'. Wagner 2021, para 5.80, refering to BGH 22 November 1990, NJW 1990, 1236.

necessary and sufficient, to avoid harming others'.[33] That can be viewed as a further application of the general standard of the reasonable person (§ 4.2).

4.4   § 823 II BGB: VIOLATION OF A STATUTORY NORM

The second main ground of liability is found in § 823 II BGB:

---

§ 823 BGB
(2) Die gleiche Verpflichtung trifft denjenigen, welcher gegen ein den Schutz eines anderen bezweckendes Gesetz verstößt. Ist nach dem Inhalt des Gesetzes ein Verstoß gegen dieses auch ohne Verschulden möglich, so tritt die Ersatzpflicht nur im Falle des Verschuldens ein.

§ 823 BGB
II. The person who commits a breach of a statute that aims to protect another person is held to the same obligation [=*the obligation to compensate damage, as stated in § 823 I*]. If it is possible according to the contents of the statute that it may also be breached without fault, then the obligation to compensation only exists in the case of fault.

This provision provides a ground for liability for violation of a statutory norm that protects a specific personal interest (*Schutzgesetzverstoß*). It is the equivalent of the common law tort of breach of statutory duty, or what in French law is called the violation of a legal duty (*devoir légal*). The general requirements of this ground of liability are as follows.[34]

1. A statute that states a certain legal norm (Rechtsnorm).
2. The legal norm protects specific individuals.
3. Violation of that protective norm.
4. If the violated statute requires a certain level of culpability, in particular intention (*Vorsatz*), then that is required as well for application of § 823 II BGB. If no particular level is mentioned, only negligence (*Fahrlässigkeit*) is required.[35]

Of course there also need to be causality and damage to have a right to an award of damages. These additional elements are often not mentioned separately for each ground of liability in German textbooks[36] because these are general elements of any action in German tort law.

The 'legal norm' means that it is a rule deriving from a legal authority competent to enact legal norms, such as the central legislator, or local authorities.[37] Rules from the European

---

[33]   Wagner 2021, para 5.80, citing BGH 22 November 1990, NJW 1990, 1236.

[34]   Wagner 2021, paras 5.109–5.125.

[35]   Deutsch and Ahrens 2014, paras 289–90, Kötz and Wagner 2016, paras 5.122–5.125.

[36]   For instance Wagner 2021, p. 92 (above par 5.110).

[37]   Wagner 2021, para 5.110.

Union also apply. Norms from case law (in particular the *Verkehrspflichten*) are not included in this ground of liability.[38]

Liability on this ground is restricted to the 'scope of the rule' (§ 9.1), in German law called *Schutzzweck* (protective purpose). The norm should not just aim at the general interest, but rather the interest of a specific group of individuals. For instance, the BGH decided that the norm of § 267 StGB[39] that prohibited falsification of certificates (*Urkunde*) is so weak and unclear that it cannot be assumed that it also directly aims at the protection of economic interests (*Vermogen*) of the individuals who were duped by the falsified certificates.[40]

In order to determine whether the harm is within the protective purpose, the court has to determine the legislative intent behind the norm (since the norm usually only states the kind of conduct, not the purpose behind the norm).[41] This requires determining

- the personal scope,
- the scope of interest.

In short, the victims and the injured interests must be within the protective purpose of the norm. An example of personal scope (*persönlicher Schutzbereich*) is whether a prohibition of stopping a car for more than three minutes (to keep traffic moving) also aims to protect pedestrians for a better view of the road, whether violation of a rule to avoid damaging electricity cables protects also customers deprived of electricity.[42] An example of the scope of interest (*sachlicher Schutzbereich*) is the director of an investment fund who manages the firm with gross negligence: this is a violation of his duty of diligent management towards the firm, but does not protect the losses of creditors of the firm.[43] If the norm protects property, body or health, the presumption is that it does not protect pure economic interests.

Finally, there is a third restriction which excludes certain cases: the norm should also protect against the manner in which the harm has been caused (*modaler Schutzbereich*). An example is a bowling alley who employed a child younger than 14 after 20:00 hours, which violated the child labour protection act. The child got injured by a visitor who accidently threw a bowling ball while the child was busy setting up the bowling pins. The norm lacked protective purpose in this case, as it did not aim at protecting against such a labour accident that could have occurred as well before 20:00 hours, but only against exhaustion of children.[44] On the other hand, operating a bank without licence does make the bank liable for damage of customers

---

[38] Wagner 2021, para 5.111.

[39] *Strafgesetzbuch*, the German Criminal code.

[40] BGH 3 February 1987, VI ZR 32/86, BGHZ 100, 13, also BGH 2 February 2004, VI ZR 105/03.

[41] Deutsch and Ahrens 2014, paras 280–81, Markesinis, Bell and Janssen 2019, pp. 74–7, Wagner 2021, paras 5.113–5.120.

[42] Wagner 2021, para 5.118.

[43] Wagner 2021, para 5.119.

[44] Wagner 2021, para 5.120.

losing their money because of lack of liquidity of the bank, as the applicable Act on credit companies (*Kreditwesengesetz*) does not aim to limit the compensation of these customers.[45]

Examples of application of this ground of liability are rules from traffic law, safety rules,[46] and of course criminal law. As a specific example we can point to the liability for failing to rescue someone in peril.[47]

The advantages of this ground of liability compared to § 823 I BGB are that it is not limited to a violation of one of the interests of 823 I BGB, and that it may allow compensation of pure economic loss if such loss is within the scope of the protective norm.

4.5   § 826 BGB: INTENTIONAL HARM

The third general ground of liability can be found in § 826 BGB, which states that causing intentional harm, in a manner contrary to public policy (*sittenwidrig*),[48] also gives rise to liability.

---

§ 826 BGB
Wer in einer gegen die guten Sitten verstoßenden Weise einem anderen vorsätzlich Schaden zufügt, ist dem anderen zum Ersatz des Schadens verpflichtet.

§ 826 BGB
Whoever intentionally inflicts damage unto another in a way that is contrary to public policy, is obligated to compensate the other for the damage.

The elements for application of this ground of liability are:[49]

- damage[50]
- conduct contrary to public policy
- intentional conduct

---

[45]   BGH 7 July 2015, VI ZR 372/14, see Wagner 2021, para 5.120.

[46]   Such as the *Gesetz über technische Arbeidsmittel und Verbraucherprodukte* (Act regarding labour equipment and consumer products). Geigel 2020, para 15-5 provides an extensive list.

[47]   BGH 14 May 2013, VI ZR 255/11, BGHZ 197, 225, for violation of § 323c *Strafgesetzbuch*. The case involved a father living with his mentally ill son, who obtained a court order to have the son evicted from his house. The bailiff who effected the eviction was shot by the son: the father should have prevented this or warned the bailiff as he had seen the gun and could foresee the action of the son. See also § 6.4 on pure omissions.

[48]   Literally 'sittenwidrig' means against (public) morality, but in its content can better be translated as against public policy.

[49]   Wagner 2021, p. 101 (above para 5.128).

[50]   Wagner 2021, p. 101 (above para 5.128) narrows this element to pure economic loss, which can be explained by the fact that cases of intentionally causing personal injury or property damage can already be litigated on the basis of § 823 I BGB.

Causality is also required (implied in 'inflict'),[51] but the literature does not always explicate this element and rather appears to leave it implicit.

This provision is used mostly when § 823 I BGB or 823 II BGB do not apply, as the requirements of those earlier provisions are easier to prove (negligence instead of intention, or violation of a legal norm without intention). It is mainly used for cases involving pure economic loss.

This article is particularly important for economic delicts (see § 7.4). It covers intentional actions that amount to unfair corporate behaviour, unfair commercial practices. As explicated in § 7.4, a free market requires that companies may cause economic loss to competitors. The notion of 'sittenwidrig' activity is meant to separate allowed behaviour from the kind of actions that are not allowed. § 826 BGB is potentially a powerful instrument in regulating economic life. This ground of liability has been used for holding shareholders liable for debts of the company in which they held shares ('piercing the corporate veil' as it is called in business law),[52] holding board members liable for misleading information that induced investors to buy shares in the company which subsequently was declared bankrupt.[53]

The case law is primarily concerned with economic torts (see § 7.4). Besides cases involving defrauding creditors such as those mentioned above, there is liability for intentionally (or with gross negligence) giving incorrect advice.[54] Furthermore § 826 is sometimes used in areas of family law.[55] It may also be used in case of unlawful prosecution[56] or unlawful execution of court judgements.[57] This serves a similar purpose as the English tort of malicious prosecution.

Cases of abuse of right will usually be litigated on the basis of § 826 BGB. Although § 226 BGB prohibits *abuse of right*, it does not specify a remedy.

---

§ 226 BGB
Die Ausübung eines Rechts ist unzulässig, wenn sie nur den Zweck haben kann, einem anderen Schaden zuzufügen.

§ 226 BGB
The exercise of a right is not allowed when it can only have the aim of harming another.

---

[51] I chose to translate 'zufugt' as 'inflict'. Although it can also be translated as 'cause', the meaning of technical causation is normally expressed with 'verursacht', and I wanted to make clear that the German text does not overtly express the technical requirement of causality.

[52] BGH 20 September 2004, II ZR 302/02, NJW 2005, 145: the majority shareholder had deliberately stripped the company of all assets to the detriment of creditors.

[53] BGH 19 July 2004, II ZR 402/02, NJW 2004, 2971, Wagner 2021, para 5.126.

[54] Bamberger Kommentar 2019, § 826, paras 75–6, Wagner 2021, para 7.98.

[55] Bamberger Kommentar 2019, § 826, para 92, Wagner 2021, para 5.133 and 5,64.

[56] Bamberger Kommentar 2019, § 826, paras 189–219, Wagner 2021, paras 7.67–7.70.

[57] Wagner 2021, para 5.133.

4.6 OTHER GROUNDS OF FAULT LIABILITY

Besides the three main grounds of liability, the BGB lists four other *Einzeltatbestände* ('specific factual grounds' of liability):

- § 824: statements endangering another's credit (see also § 7.4).
- § 825: unlawfully inducing someone to sexual acts.[58] The thrust of this provision is to explicitly provide victims of such a tort to a right to immaterial damages.
- § 839: breach of official duty (see also § 7.6).
- § 839a: liability of a court-appointed expert.

These four grounds bear some similarity to specific torts in common law in that they provide an explicit basis for a fairly limited category of wrongful acts.

 The list of grounds of liability in German law may be fairly restrictive, particularly as to the kind of damage that is compensated. German courts have found an alternative route to provide compensation, namely by interpreting the facts as if there were a contract intended to protect a third person (*Vertrag mit Schutzwirkung für Dritte*). This construct, nowadays codified in § 311 III BGB, is used for liability for information and as an additional ground for liability of employers where the German vicarious liability is too restrictive.[59]

4.7 CAPACITY OF THE TORTFEASOR

As mentioned above, German tort law requires culpability (*Verschulden*). This includes subjective fault. A person who lacks free exercise of will because of unconsciousness or mental disability is in principle not culpable (§ 827 BGB).

---

§ 827 BGB

Wer im Zustand der Bewusstlosigkeit oder in einem die freie Willensbestimmung ausschließenden Zustand krankhafter Störung der Geistestätigkeit einem anderen Schaden zufügt, ist für den Schaden nicht verantwortlich. Hat er sich durch geistige Getränke oder ähnliche Mittel in einen vorübergehenden Zustand dieser Art versetzt, so ist er für einen Schaden, den er in diesem Zustand widerrechtlich verursacht, in gleicher Weise verantwortlich, wie wenn ihm Fahrlässigkeit zur Last fiele; die Verantwortlichkeit tritt nicht ein, wenn er ohne Verschulden in den Zustand geraten ist.

§ 827 BGB

Whomever harms another in a state of unconsciousness or in a state of pathological mental disturbance that excludes the free exercise of will, is not responsible for th damage. If the person has brought that state on himself temporarily by alcoholic beverages or

---

[58] Originally this provision aimed at liability for seduction of married women, but in 2002 it has been modified to protect, *inter alia*, against obtaining sex by force or abuse of a dependency relationship.

[59] Wagner 2021, paras 6.47 and 7.100.

> similar means, he is responsible in the same way for damage that he unlawfully caused in this state as if he acted negligently; responsibility does not arise if he entered this state without fault.

This applies unless the tortfeasor was drunk or under the influence of drugs. That is understandable, since you are responsible for drinking alcohol or using drugs (except if someone else drugged you, which this provision also recognizes). Similarly, § 828 BGB provides an exception of liability for children, based on a categorization according to age where children become stepwise liable for more events.

---

§ 828 BGB
(1) Wer nicht das siebente Lebensjahr vollendet hat, ist für einen Schaden, den er einem anderen zufügt, nicht verantwortlich.
(2) Wer das siebente, aber nicht das zehnte Lebensjahr vollendet hat, ist für den Schaden, den er bei einem Unfall mit einem Kraftfahrzeug, einer Schienenbahn oder einer Schwebebahn einem anderen zufügt, nicht verantwortlich. Dies gilt nicht, wenn er die Verletzung vorsätzlich herbeigeführt hat.
(3) Wer das 18. Lebensjahr noch nicht vollendet hat, ist, sofern seine Verantwortlichkeit nicht nach Absatz 1 oder 2 ausgeschlossen ist, für den Schaden, den er einem anderen zufügt, nicht verantwortlich, wenn er bei der Begehung der schädigenden Handlung nicht die zur Erkenntnis der Verantwortlichkeit erforderliche Einsicht hat.

§ 828 BGB
(1) A person who has not reached the age of seven is not responsible for damage that he causes to another.
(2) A person who has reached the age of seven, but not the age of ten, is not responsible for the damage that he causes to another in an accident with a motorized vehicle, a railway or a suspension monorail. This does not apply when he intentionally caused the injury.
(3) A person who has not yet reached the age of eighteen is, insofar his responsibility is not excluded under subsection (1) or (2), not responsible for damage he causes to another if he, when committing the infringing act, did not have the insight required for recognition of responsibility.

The victim can in cases of § 827 and 828 BGB hold the guardian (including parent) or supervisor liable (§ 832 BGB). If there is no supervisor or guardian as meant in § 832 BGB, the court can make an equitable exception to § 827 and 828 BGB and hold the person liable anyway if certain specific conditions are also met (§ 829 BGB). An example is when someone causes an accident while having a stroke: it may be unfair to leave the victim without compensation, particularly if the tortfeasor can easily pay damages and the victim is in financial distress.

The liability of the guardian or supervisor of a child presumes that the child acted wrongfully. In assessing the behaviour of the child (and also for old persons!), courts make a subjective correction to the objective standard of the reasonable person, to account for the lesser capabilities of such persons.[60]

4.8   THE COMPLETE SYSTEM OF GROUNDS OF LIABILITY

If you feel confused by the system of German tort law, that is entirely natural. Even German lawyers find the resulting system of delict complicated.[61] Instead of the single overarching rule of French law, German law works with more or less specific grounds. However, as we have seen, French doctrine also found it necessary to make further distinctions in the general norm, which resemble some of the grounds of German tort law.

The different grounds of German law have to be applied by checking each ground against the facts of the case. Once you have identified the possibly relevant grounds, you can start the detailed assessment whereby you have to check the requirements for each relevant ground in detail. The elements of causality and harm/damage are always applicable but are not in each provision clearly explicated. The element of *Verschulden* (culpability) similarly applies for every ground of liability. In § 823 II BGB there is a specific rule about *Verschulden*, in § 826 BGB intention is required.

4.9   CAUSALITY

The German system for causality (*Kausalität*) consists of two phases:

- causality for establishing liability (*Haftungsbegrundende Kausalität*), and
- causality for determining the extent of liability (*Haftungsausfüllende Kausalität*).

The first phase essentially is factual causality. To determine whether there is a ground of liability, there needs to be a causal connection between the wrongful act and the infringement of the interest. This is determined in a manner similar to how other jurisdictions do this (see Chapter 8). It requires proof of factual causality between wrongful act and harm or as the Germans say infringement of a legally protected interest (*Rechtsgutverletzung*). The criterion used is the *Differenzhypothese*, which simply means that the courts compare the actual situation with the hypothetical situation in which there would not have been wrongful behaviour.

The second phase amounts to legal causality but also encompasses what in many other systems is considered as part of assessment of damages. Once the factual causality between act and infringement is determined, the extent of liability needs to be assessed. In this phase German law requires legal causality between the act and the heads of damage.[62] The name for legal causality is 'Adequanztheorie', adequacy theory. German doctrine is not clear as to what

---

60   Deutsch and Ahrens 2014, paras 168–70, Wagner 2021, para 5.25.
61   Wagner 2021, paras 5.17–5.18.
62   Cf. Deutsch and Ahrens 2014, para 57.

this really means: it seems to require that the act was in some way 'adequate', fit to cause the harm. Others argue that this is a requirement of reasonable foreseeability. In a 1951 case[63] the highest German court, the Bundesgerichtshof, declared that

> An event is adequate cause of a consequence when it has in a not insignificant way increased the objective possibility of a consequence of a kind similar to what has realized. In the assessment thereof only the following are to be taken into account:
> (a) all the circumstances that were discernable by an optimal observer at the time of the event,
> (b) in addition, the circumstances that were known by the person who caused event.

Recently German courts seem to have moved to an alternative approach to legal causality: scope of the rule, 'protective purpose of the rule' (*Schutzzweck der Norm*).[64] This is a technique which is applied explicitly for certain torts and can also be found in other legal systems, particularly in English law (§ 9.1). It can be argued that both approaches share a similar intuition in that the wrongful act in some way should match the kind of harm that was caused, it should be relevant to the wrongful act. Where the harm is too remote or insufficiently matched to the wrongful act, it is simply a general risk of life (*allgemeinen Lebensrisiko*) for which no compensation should be awarded.[65] To give an idea about where the boundaries of adequacy or scope of the rule are, consider an example.

Someone negligently crashed into a truck transporting money, whereby its driver was rendered unconscious and the door locks opened, and a third party stole the money from the truck. Is the tortfeasor also liable for the loss of money? Answer: yes.[66] Conversely, the owner of a Porsche did not succeed in a claim to compensation for money stolen from the locked glove compartment of the car after an accident.[67] The difference can be explained in that, in the first case the locks opened due to the crash, which facilitated the theft, while in the second case the car simply stood still after the crash and the theft was not more likely because of the accident, it was simply a normal risk.

---

[63] BGH 23 October 1951, BGHZ 3, 261, paras 11–13 (adopting a proposal by the lawyer Traeger): 'Eine Begebenheit ist adequate Bedingung eines Erfolges, wenn sie die objective Möglichkeit eines Erfolges von der Art des eingetretenen generell in nicht unerheblichen Weise erhöht hat. Bei der dahin zielenden Würdigung sind lediglich zu berücksichtigen: a) alle zur Zeit des Eintritts der Begebenheit dem optimalen Beobachter erkennbaren Umstände, b) die dem Urheber der Bedingung noch darüber hinaus bekannten Umstände.' See Deutsch and Ahrens 2014, para 52.

[64] Markesinis, Bell and Janssen 2019, p. 65. Wagner 2021, para 5.104 points out that under some interpretations the adequacy theory assimilates to the 'scope of the rule' approach. A similar position is defended by Deutsch and Ahrens 2014, para 56, where both approaches can support each other, as they are coming from different perspectives. Compare how in English law remoteness and scope of the rule are applied not to the exclusion of the other, but in conjunction.

[65] Wagner 2021, para 5.105.

[66] BGH 10 December 1996, NJW 1997, 865.

[67] Wagner 2021, para 5.106.

Another example: an army vehicle (for which the German State was liable) caused a traffic accident, causing a pile up. Other cars tried to get around the collision by driving on the bicycle path and pavement, thereby causing substantial damage to the path and pavement. The owner of the path and pavement could not hold the State liable, as that damage was not attributable to the violation of traffic rules by the army vehicle.[68]

In the literature one can find guidelines and rules of thumb. For instance, damage that is in line with the original harm is usually adequate, and in case of personal injury there is usually adequate causation.[69] Ultimately, though, the courts try to reach outcomes that are in line with what is just and fair,[70] which cannot be captured in hard and fast rules.

Finally, German law recognizes various forms of multiple causality involving multiple tortfeasors (we will discuss this topic in § 9.3). Such cases lead to joint and several liability of the tortfeasors (§ 830 BGB and § 840 BGB).[71]

4.10 REMEDIES

The remedies in German law follow the general pattern for civil law systems (§ 2.8; Chapter 10). A few details may suffice.

The remedies are covered in the part of the code dealing with all obligations, they are therefore common to contract and tort. The basic rule for damages is § 249 BGB, obliging the tortfeasor to pay full compensation. There are further rules on personal injury damages in §§ 842–847, and property damage in §§ 848–851 BGB. There is the possibility of immaterial damages (§ 253 II BGB). Furthermore the surviving family members may have a claim for loss of consortium when the income provider has died (§ 844 BGB).

Reparation may be achieved in a form other than damages: *Naturalrestitution*. This is implied in § 251(1) BGB which specifies that reparation may occur in the form of money when actual reparation is not possibly or insufficient. The claimant obtains reparation in 'nature' (in kind) by demanding specific performance (*Klage auf künftige Leistung*).[72] The court may order an action (*Handlungsgebot*) or may award an injunction to refrain from certain actions (*Unterlassungsgebot*). An injunction may be enforced by means of § 890 Code of civil procedure (*Zivilprozessordnung*), whereby the defendant has to pay a kind of fine (*Ordnungsgeld*) if they violates the injunction (similar to the French *astreinte*). A third remedy is the declaration of rights,[73] whereby the court declares that the defendant is liable. Such a declaration may be useful for moral satisfaction, but can also serve to initiate negotiation about the amount of compensation to be paid.

---

[68] BGH 16 February 1972, VI ZR 128/70, BGHZ 58, 162.

[69] Deutsch and Ahrens 2014, paras 54–5.

[70] Markesinis, Bell and Janssen 2019, p. 65, referring inter alia to BGH 23 October 1951, BGHZ 3, 261.

[71] Deutsch and Ahrens 2014, paras 60–63.

[72] § 258 ZPO, see Geigel 2020, Ch 38 para 8.

[73] The claimant submits a *Feststellungsklage* as claim, § 256 ZPO, to obtain a decision (*Entscheidung*) containing such a declaration (*Feststellung*).

For specific kinds of torts there are a few more specific remedies. Infringement of personality right may lead to an injunction (*Unterlassungsanspruch*) against publication, or a rectification/retraction (*Widerruf*).[74] As another example, there is a form of protection for the reputation of the deceased.[75] This includes the use of the image of the deceased (§ 22 S. 3 Copyright Act (*KunstUrhG, Gesetz betreffend das Urheberrecht an Werken der bildenden Künste und der Photographie*)).

---

[74]   Deutsch and Ahrens 2014, paras 427–9, Wagner 2021, paras 7.38–7.41.

[75]   Wagner 2021, paras 7.53–7.56, see § 189 StGB (Criminal Code).

5
Torts in English law[1]

5.1   INTRODUCTION

The English approach at first sight looks nothing like codified systems. The collection of torts appears haphazard, and devoid of any system. Indeed, the apparent lack of system is rooted deep in the English mentality. The highest English court[2] steadfastly resists the pressure to formulate general rules.[3] The general sentiment is well captured by one of the foremost tort law scholars: 'The search for "general principles of liability" based on types of conduct is at best a waste of time and at worst a potential source of serious confusion; and the broader the principle, the more is this so.'[4] After encountering the complicated theoretical debates in German law you may feel that there is some merit to this position, even though the result is also a lack of structure.

As this is not an introduction to legal systems as such, I will only briefly describe what is meant by 'common law'.[5] By common law we particularly mean the system of legal rules that has been developed mainly in case law in England and Wales, and in other countries that derived their legal system from English common law.[6] Confusingly, 'common law' also is used in a more restricted sense, indicating the body of rules established by the courts, to be contrasted to statute law. Hence it can be said that a certain rule holds 'at common law'.[7]

English tort law consists of a number of torts, each having its own characteristics and scope. The torts have developed over the course of centuries, extending liability steadily to

---

[1]   See generally Van Dam 2013, chapter 5. Detailed treatises are Clerk & Lindsell 2020, Winfield & Jolowicz 2020. Case law can in particular be found at www.baiili.org. Legislation can be found at www.legislation.gov.uk/.

[2]   Formerly the House of Lords, nowadays the Supreme Court.

[3]   Witness the recent *Robinson* case (§ 5.2), as well as the decision in *OBG v Allan* (§ 5.7).

[4]   Cane 2000, p. 552, cited in *OBG v Allan* [2007] UKHL 21, at 32.

[5]   See further Zweigert and Kötz 1998, chapters 14–18, Glenn 2010, chapter 7, Samuel 2013, Van Dam 2013, para 501.

[6]   For the sake of brevity I will hereafter speak of English law, where it would be more precise to speak of the law of England and Wales.

[7]   For example, Winfield and Jolowicz 2020, para 21-038: 'the employer … can in some cases recover damages from his employee at common law'.

new ways in which a victim could be harmed and where compensation would be in order.[8] A claimant will have to state and prove that the facts of the case meet the requirements of one of these torts. These requirements are referred to as the elements of a 'cause of action' (§ 1.4). To understand the various torts, you need to learn their respective elements. As the elements themselves may appear abstract, the following description also provides illustrations from case law or fictitious examples that may help to understand what kind of cases are covered within a specific tort. It is also important to know the boundaries of a tort and its relation to similar torts. Here we will discuss the torts and their main characteristics on their own. In later chapters we will discuss these torts again from a more systematic point of view, comparing them to approaches in civil law systems.

A few brief notes are needed beforehand. In civil law the principal basis for finding the elements of a tort is the text of the code. In common law, the main torts are usually not codified. So how do you determine the rules applying to a tort? The answer is that these are based on a reconstruction of the entire applicable case law. Fortunately, you do not actually need to read all cases yourself, rather you can, like many lawyers, rely on authoritative textbooks for a first impression of the main outlines and the relevant precedents. Subsequently you extend and deepen your knowledge on a specific tort by reading the main relevant precedents yourself (to form your own opinion) and do independent research of further precedents and literature. That process is not too dissimilar to what you do in civil law, except in civil law you start with the text of the code.

Quite often the current state of a tort is based on a specific precedent, the landmark decision which provides the most recent formulation of the tort.[9] The precedent would provide the main rules and criteria for the tort. Further precedents add more details and restrictions. There are also cases where the various elements have to be collected from several precedents. In some instances the tort is regulated by a specific act. An example is the Protection from Harassment Act 1997. English lawyers distinguish between the legal basis of a tort by speaking of a 'common law tort'[10] (or 'tort at common law'), based on precedent, versus a 'statutory tort'. Sometimes a tort that has developed in case law is modified by statute. An example is the tort of defamation that was modified extensively by the Defamation Act 1996 and Defamation Act 2013. You will always need check later case law for precedents that have changed details in the general rules set out by the leading precedent or relevant statute.

In textbooks you may encounter the category of intentional torts. These are torts that require the presence of intention. Here we do not use that categorization as it is not helpful for our discussion: the intentional torts are too varied and are better grouped according to other characteristics.

---

[8]   Historically this was connected to the so-called forms of action. See for an explanation Samuel 2013, pp. 50–56.

[9]   This need not be the latest decision on that tort. Rather it is the decision that is authoritative, to which all later cases about this tort refer. Lawyers also speak of the 'leading' case or precedent.

[10] For example, Clerk and Lindsell 2020, paras 14–18 on 'a common law tort of harassment'.

Incidentally, English tort law also covers areas that in civil law are discussed under contractual liability. An example is professional liability. Here we will limit our overview to non-contractual liability.

5.2   NEGLIGENCE

Negligence has become the most important tort in English law, a development that is mirrored by other jurisdictions. Since the nineteenth century this tort has seen an enormous breadth of application, as it may function as a catch-all for everything that is not covered by other torts.

The classic precedent of *Blyth* defines the tort of negligence as follows:

> Negligence is the omission to do something which a reasonable man, guided upon those considerations which ordinarily regulate the conduct of human affairs, would do, or doing something which a prudent and reasonable man would not do.[11]

For purposes of this introduction we can list the elements of an action for negligence:[12]

1. the existence of a duty of care owed by defendant to claimant,
2. a breach of that duty,
3. damage suffered by the claimant,
4. a sufficient causal connection between the breach and the damage.

These elements follow the fundamental structure of fault liability: the existence and breach of a duty of care are the equivalent of fault,[13] while the third and fourth element correspond by and large to the requirements of harm and causality.

You may have noticed that the tort of negligence establishes fault in a two stage process: first you need to establish whether there was a duty of care, and only subsequently you determine whether there has been a breach of that duty. In civil law, the focus typically is on the wrongful conduct: it suffices to determine whether the conduct is wrongful in the given circumstances, which implies that the first two elements of the English tort of negligence have been fulfilled.

The first element allows the courts to create new duties, as the duty of care is found in the circumstances of the case and does not require the infringement of a right or the breach of

---

[11]   *Blyth v Company Proprietors of the Birmingham Water Works* (1856), 11 Ex. Ch. 781. Nowadays 'man' is read as 'person'.

[12]   Winfield and Jolowicz 2020, para 5-002. Other texts often combine the last two elements into a single element, an approach that is also found in case law, for instance *Blyth v Company Proprietors of the Birmingham Water Works* (1856), 11 Ex. Ch. 781.

[13]   See in particular the category of 'violation of a pre-existing obligation' in French law: a pre-existing obligation is conceptually very similar to a duty of care.

a contractual obligation towards the victim.[14] The liberal use of the duty of care was inaugurated by the celebrated case of *Donoghue v Stevenson* where Lord Atkins held:[15]

> You must take reasonable care to avoid acts or omissions which you can reasonably foresee would be likely to injure your neighbour. Who, then, in the law is my neighbour? The answer seems to be – persons who are so closely and directly affected by my act that I ought reasonably to have them in contemplation as being so affected when I am directing my mind to the acts or omissions which are called in question.

Over the next decades, the tort of negligence found rapid expansion on the basis of this ruling. In principle anyone could be a neighbour. It became clear that there was a need to set boundaries. For almost 20 years English lawyers presumed that you should determine whether there is a duty of care by applying the so-called Caparo-test, referring to the case of *Caparo v Dickman:*[16]

> What emerges is that, in addition to the foreseeability of damage, necessary ingredients in any situation giving rise to a duty of care are that there should exist between the party owing the duty and the party to whom it is owed a relationship characterized by the law as one of 'proximity' or 'neighbourhood' and that the situation should be one in which the court considers it fair, just and reasonable that the law should impose a duty of a given scope upon the one party for the benefit of the other.[17]

This consideration indeed appears to suggest that there are three requirements that have to be satisfied in order for a court to assume a duty of care:

1. foreseeability of damage
2. proximity
3. the situation should be one in which the court considers it fair, just and reasonable that the law should impose a duty of care.

However, this reading of *Caparo v Dickman* has recently been rejected by the UK Supreme Court in *Robinson v Chief Constable of West Yorkshire Police:*[18]

> 26. … Where the existence or non-existence of a duty of care has been established, a consideration of justice and reasonableness forms part of the basis on which the law has arrived at the relevant principles. It is therefore unnecessary and inappropriate to reconsider whether the existence of the duty is fair, just and reasonable (subject to the possibility that this court may be invited to depart from an established line of authority).

---

[14]   It fulfils a role similar to the German *Verkehrspflichten* or the French category of violation of unwritten duties.

[15]   *Donoghue v Stevenson* [1932] AC 562, 580.

[16]   *Caparo Industries Plc. v Dickman* [1990] 1 All ER 568.

[17]   *Caparo Industries Plc. v Dickman* [1990] 1 All ER 568, 574.

[18]   *Robinson v Chief Constable of West Yorkshire Police (Rev 1)* [2018] UKSC 4.

27. It is normally only in a novel type of case, where established principles do not provide an answer, that the courts need to go beyond those principles in order to decide whether a duty of care should be recognized. Following *Caparo,* the characteristic approach of the common law in such situations is to develop incrementally and by analogy with established authority. The drawing of an analogy depends on identifying the legally significant features of the situations with which the earlier authorities were concerned. The courts also have to exercise judgement when deciding whether a duty of care should be recognized in a novel type of case. It is the exercise of judgement in those circumstances that involves consideration of what is 'fair, just and reasonable ...'

   ...

29. Properly understood, *Caparo* thus achieves a balance between legal certainty and justice. In the ordinary run of cases, courts consider what has been decided previously and follow the precedents (unless it is necessary to consider whether the precedents should be departed from). In cases where the question whether a duty of care arises has not previously been decided, the courts will consider the closest analogies in the existing law, with a view to maintaining the coherence of the law and the avoidance of inappropriate distinctions. They will also weigh up the reasons for and against imposing liability, in order to decide whether the existence of a duty of care would be just and reasonable. In the present case, however, the court is not required to consider an extension of the law of negligence. All that is required is the application to particular circumstances of established principles governing liability for personal injuries.

30. Addressing, then, the first of the issues identified in para 20 above, the existence of a duty of care does not depend on the application of a '*Caparo* test' to the facts of the particular case. In the present case, it depends on the application of established principles of the law of negligence.

So what does this mean for the application of negligence? In order to determine whether there is a duty of care in a specific situation, you first and foremost need to check the voluminous case law to find out whether there is a precedent that covers your case. If there is, that precedent plainly decides the issue (either that there is or there is not a duty of care). If there is no directly applicable precedent, chances are that there is a precedent that can be applied by way of analogy. This is simply how English lawyers need to determine the applicable law in general, so there is nothing particular about negligence. In very rare cases you may encounter a case for which the second approach doesn't work. Only then can the three-step Caparo 'test' be applied.

Although the Caparo test has been discredited as a general rule, there is a general rule for negligence: the standard of conduct is the conduct of a reasonable person.[19] As we shall see in § 6.2 it can be argued that there are several factors that help to decide what is or is not reasonable conduct. A few examples may give an idea of the kind of cases where the courts held that there was or was not a duty of care and a breach of that duty.

---

[19]   *Blyth v Company Proprietors of the Birmingham Water Works* (1856), 11 Ex. Ch. 781.

- Discharging oil into the water of a harbour, ultimately leading to a fire due to the (small) risk that the oil would ignite.[20]
- Digging a hole in the pavement for construction work without taking precautions against blind individuals falling into the hole.[21]
- Driving at a speed of 50 mph next to a school bus without taking account of the possibility that a careless child will suddenly cross the road from behind the bus.[22]

No breach was found in cases such as the following:

- Not closing a factory where the floor had become slippery due to exceptionally heavy rainfall, when only part of the floor had been treated with sawdust against slippage.[23]
- Playing cricket in a fenced area near public streets.[24]

5.3   BREACH OF STATUTORY DUTY

The tort of breach of statutory duty provides a ground for a claim of damages if the tortfeasor violated a statutory duty that is not a tort. Examples of such statutory rules are rules from criminal law, regulatory statutes such as an administrative requirement to have a licence for a certain activity. Note that this tort does not find application where the statute itself provides a ground for private liability, such as the Protection from Harassment Act 1997. The tort of breach of statutory duty may apply only where the statutory duty does not provide for liability (in particular damages).

The three principal elements for a claim on the basis of the tort are:[25]

1. A statutory duty on the defendant;
2. A breach of that duty;
3. Damage suffered by the victim, caused by that breach.

---

[20]   *Wagon Mound (No. 2), Overseas Tankship (UK) Ltd v The Miller Steamship Co* [1966] UKPC 10, [1967] 1 AC 617. The same facts had given rise to an earlier decision, *Wagon Mound (No. 1)* [1961] UKPC 2, [1961] AC 388, about the remoteness requirement in causality (§ 5.10).

[21]   *Haley v London Electricity Board* [1964] UKHL 3, in which the blind victim subsequently became deaf.

[22]   *Jackson v Murray* [2015] UKSC 5. In § 8.3 we will discuss that the court did find contributory negligence on the side of the victim.

[23]   *Latimer v AEC Ltd* [1953] AC 643. It was found that closing down the factory would have been disproportionate, while the owners had taken sufficient care with the available sawdust.

[24]   *Bolton v Stone* [1951] AC 850, [1951] UKHL 2. It was relevant that there had been very few accidents; the top of the fence was 17 feet (almost 6 metres) above the cricket pitch, the fence was almost 78 yards (70 metres) from the striker and the victim was standing some 100 yards removed from the striker.

[25]   *X and others (minors) v Bedfordshire County Council* [1995] 3 All ER 353. *Campbell v Gordon* [2016] UKSC 38 confirms that *X v Bedforshire* is still good law as regards breach of a statutory duty.

These elements are similar to the requirements for negligence: duty, breach of the duty, damage caused by the breach. However, not every breach of a statutory duty can provide a basis for a claim for damages. An additional requirement must be met:

4. Parliament (i.e. the legislator) intended to confer a private right of action for breach of this duty.

This final requirement requires interpretation of legislative intent. Sometimes there is an *explicit* private right of action: the statute says so. In the absence of an explicit statement, there are various indicators for an *implicit* private right of action:

-   If the statute does provide a criminal remedy, this indicates that there is *no* private right of action intended by Parliament. An exception to this rule applies if the statute shows that the duty 'was imposed for the benefit of a particular class of individuals'.[26]
-   A private right is indicated if the statute provides no other remedy for its breach and it is shown that Parliament intended to protect a limited class ('that the statutory duty was imposed for the protection of a limited class of the public and that Parliament intended to confer on members of that class a private right of action').[27]

It is not necessary that the duty was performed carelessly,[28] nor is negligence sufficient for finding a breach of the duty. For a given set of facts it is possible to sue both on the basis of breach of statutory duty and negligence:[29] the claim of negligence is assessed on its own merits, following the rules of that tort.

Undoubtedly you have by now realized that it is not easy to assess whether the breach of a specific statute fulfils all elements, particularly the fourth one. In practice you would examine the case law to determine whether the issue has already been decided for the statutory duty in question. The tort of breach of statutory duty finds particular application in the area of liability for labour-related injuries.

5.4   INTENTIONAL INTERFERENCE WITH THE PERSON

Several torts relate to infringement of another's body or freedom. The principal category is trespass to the person, supplemented by several other torts. Trespass is a more general cate-

---

[26]   *Campbell v Gordon* [2016] UKSC 38, Lord Carnwath at 8, refers to *Lonrho Ltd v Shell Petroleum Co Ltd (No 2)* [1982] AC 173, at 185. His speech (at 11 and 12) makes clear that there is debate in the Supreme Court as to whether this exception still holds in general or is restricted to statutory duties imposed for the benefit of employees.

[27]   *X and others (minors) v Bedfordshire County Council* [1995] 3 All ER 353.

[28]   For this reason lawyers say that this tort may lead to strict liability.

[29]   For example, in *Dryden v Johnson Matthey Plc* [2018] UKSC 18 about employees health problems following violation of labour conditions by the employer. In the case of public authorities, *X and others (minors) v Bedfordshire County Council* [1995] 3 All ER 353 ruled out the application of negligence insofar the Children Act 1989 applied. This has been overruled in *Poole Borough Council v GN* [2019] UKSC 25, at 74.

gory of torts, defined as consisting of a direct and forcible injury. Three forms of trespass are generally distinguished: trespass to the person, trespass to land, and trespass to goods. We will discuss the latter two in § 5.5.

5.4.1   Trespass to the person

Trespass to the person is a category that covers several more specific torts, all of which require intention. These are battery, assault, and false imprisonment.

Battery is the intentional and direct application of force to another person.[30] This implies the following elements:

- – an act
- – making intentional contact with another's body
- – direct contact
- – hostile contact
- – absence of consent with the contact.

The act need not involve contact of the tortfeasor: shooting a bullet may constitute battery since the bullet does contact the victim's body directly. If the shot was not aimed at the victim, there would only be an action for negligence: battery presumes the intent to hit the victim. The contact is presumed to be physical, forcible in nature, although there is discussion whether heat or light could constitute battery.[31]

The element of 'direct' contact is interpreted broadly. If an act was intended to lead to contact with some intermediate steps, it could still constitute battery. Examples are putting acid in a dryer so that it injures the next user, or planting a bomb set to go off.[32] The element of hostility is intended to demarcate battery from innocent forms of contact, such as tapping a person on the shoulder to get his attention. Courts have ruled that contact that is generally acceptable in the ordinary conduct of everyday life should not be actionable,[33] and that battery requires 'hostile' touching.[34] A proper interpretation of this element does need to take into account the specifics of a case, such as the relationship between parties and the kind of behaviour. Between friends a certain amount of touching may be appropriate which among strangers would be considered hostile.

The last element, absence of consent, is needed to exclude cases such as boxing. In other legal systems the presence of consent would simply constitute a defence (§ 12.2); here the absence of consent is a requisite element of the tort.

---

[30]   Winfield and Jolowicz 2020, para 4-006.

[31]   Winfield and Jolowicz 2020, para 4-009.

[32]   Winfield and Jolowicz 2020, para 4-010, referring to *DPP v K* [1990] WLR 1067 respectively *Breslin v McKenna* [2009] NIQB 50.

[33]   *Collins v Wilcock* [1984] 1 WLR 1172.

[34]   *Wilson v Pringle* [1987] QB 237.

Assault is an act by the defendant which causes the claimant reasonable apprehension of the infliction of a battery on him by the defendant.[35] By definition there is no contact in the case of assault, which distinguishes it from battery. Assault may, however, precede battery: the assault often occurs just before battery. Making a punching movement but stopping short of making contact with the victim's face is clearly assault. But threats of physical violence can also constitute assault. Conditional threats, such as a warning that trespassers will be forcibly removed, are no assault.[36] This is not an absolute rule: a robber who threatens to shoot you if you do not hand over your wallet is obviously liable for assault.

A third form of trespass to the person is false imprisonment. *False imprisonment* is described as the infliction of bodily restraint which is not expressly or impliedly authorized by law.[37] This consists of two elements: imprisonment, and absence of lawful authority for the imprisonment. Imprisonment can occur with physical restraints (like being locked in a room) or by being imprisoned by guards, or by threats and legal means (such as an electronic curfew that turns out to be illegally imposed). Partially blocking someone's movement (as in the case of a blocked road or defect elevator) does not constitute imprisonment. It is not relevant that the tortfeasor knew about the absence of lawful authority.[38] It is, however, necessary that the tortfeasor intended to detain the victim: an employee who locks a room, unaware that there is still someone inside, is not liable for false imprisonment. Similarly, there is no false imprisonment where someone places reasonable restrictions on leaving, such as a prohibition to exit an airplane during flight.

The advantage of trespass as a cause of action is that the mere infringement suffices, there is no need to prove damage. Trespass is *actionable per se*, damage is not an element of the tort. However, as trespass requires intention, lawyers often prefer to litigate on the basis of negligence if they fear that they may be unable to prove intention on the tortfeasor's side. In case of trespass to the person, there can be a further obstacle if there is no actual damage, as that will preclude an award of material damages. Hence one would usually only sue in trespass to the person where there actually is substantial damage, or if claimant wants nominal damages or another kind of damages that can be awarded in the absence of actual damage (§ 5.11).

5.4.2   Other torts involving interference with the person

Two other torts that do not constitute trespass also concern interference with the person. First of all there is the tort that started with the case of *Wilkinson v Downton*[39] and is nowadays usually referred to as *intentional infliction of injury*.[40] The case involved a practical joke: Downton, a customer of a pub, told the wife of a fellow customer, Wilkinson, that her husband

---

[35]   Winfield and Jolowicz 2020, para 4-017.

[36]   Winfield and Jolowicz 2020, para 4-020.

[37]   Clerk and Lindsell 2020, para 14-23, referring to *Collins v Wilcock* [1984] 1 WLR 1172, at 1178.

[38]   Many cases therefore involve police officers who arrested a person on insufficient grounds or in a procedurally incorrect manner.

[39]   [1897] 2 QB 57.

[40]   Clerk and Lindsell 2020, para 14-14.

had been seriously injured in an accident. Mrs. Wilkinson suffered a serious shock as a consequence of this information. As the case does not fulfil the conditions of battery or assault, there was no ground for trespass to the person. The court, however, found Downton liable because he had 'wilfully done an act calculated to cause harm – that is to say, to infringe … [a] right to personal safety and has in fact thereby caused physical harm'. As the act had undeniably been intended to cause some effect, there was intention. The precedent was useful to cover cases that did not fulfil the requirements of battery or assault, such as poisoning a drink.

In the recent case of *Rhodes v OPO*[41] the principle was extended to a case where the publication of a memoir was alleged to cause severe distress to the son of the author.[42] The Supreme Court held that the action for intentional infliction of injury consists of three elements: a conduct element, a mental element, and a consequence element. As regards the conduct, the court explicated that it must consist of words or conduct directed at the victim for which there is no justification or reasonable excuse. The consequences that are actionable are physical harm or a recognized psychiatric illness. The mental element implies intention to cause these consequences (in the sense that the likelihood of this harm was such that the tortfeasor cannot deny that they meant to cause this).

The second tort to discuss here is harassment. *Harassment* is nowadays a statutory tort, established with the Protection from Harassment Act 1997. Before that, harassment conceivable would be actionable under the tort of intentional infliction of injury. The Act does not provide a definition of harassment, instead it simply states that a person must not pursue a course of conduct which amounts to harassment of another (s.1(1)).[43] The Act provides the victim with the remedies of an injunction or damages (s. 3(A) and s. 3(2)). As the Act not only formulates the duty to refrain from harassment, but also specifies which civil remedies the victim can claim, this constitutes an independent tort and is not invoked on the basis of the tort of breach of a statutory duty.

5.5 TRESPASS TO GOODS AND LAND, AND RELATED TORTS

Another group of torts involves interference with land and goods. In § 7.3 we will go deeper into the definition of various kinds of goods.

This part of tort law is rather complicated due to its historical roots. Trespass and several actions to recover goods are based on ancient actions that survive in name but have been modified also through the intervention of the courts and by the Torts (Interference with Goods) Act 1977. Here we can only give a brief outline that allows you to recognize the torts, and understand to what kind of cases they are applicable. The torts we will discuss are trespass to goods, conversion, trespass to lands, and private nuisance.

---

[41] [2015] UKSC 32.

[42] The ex-wife of the author sued the author on behalf of their son.

[43] Some further forms of prohibited conduct are defined in s. 1(1A), but these do not give a right to damages.

Trespass to goods is defined as wrongful physical interference with goods.[44] An alternative description is that trespass to goods consists of interference with the possession of goods. Goods can be defined provisionally as tangible objects that are not land. Trespass is primarily used when the trespass is due to an intentional act. It is not necessary that the defendant intended the trespass, only that they acted intentionally (even if they didn't know they were trespassing), as in the case of someone innocently taking someone else's car from a garage.[45]

In the case of unintended interference, the appropriate action would be negligence. If unintentional trespass to goods is litigated, the defendant may invoke a defence of inevitable accident which may come close to proving they didn't act negligently.[46] Therefore the claimant might just as well base their action directly on negligence; the difference is only slight as to the burden of proof of the absence or presence of negligent behaviour. For this reason it is argued that trespass to goods requires intentional interference.

Trespass requires in principle a direct interference. This can occur by taking an object such as a backpack out of someone else's possession, but can also take the form of damage to a vase or killing an animal. Indirect interference, such as poisoning a pet, is not trespass but negligence. As was the case with trespass to the person, any interference, even mere touching, does constitute trespass.[47]

Trespass to goods is actionable per se (as explained in § 5.4.1). The claimant can therefore obtain damages for the mere touching of an object in their possession, even if there is no discernible damage. Although in such cases the claimant would usually only obtain nominal damages, in some instances a substantial award of damages could be appropriate.[48]

Conversion consists of 'dealing with the goods of a person in such a way as to deprive him of the use or possession of them',[49] This definition implies at least three elements:

- deliberate interference with a chattel (tangible, movable good, see § 7.3),
- which is inconsistent with another's right,
- thereby depriving the other of its use and possession.

It is crucial that the tortfeasor *intended* to deprive the possessor: if you take someone's cap just to tease him, it is trespass but not conversion, if you take the cap to claim it as your own it is

---

[44] Winfield and Jolowicz 2020, para 1-007.

[45] *Wilson v Lombank Ltd* [1963] 1 WLR 1294.

[46] It is also argued that this defence has no longer any place. This is true if negligence is required for unintentional trespass to goods.

[47] Again, trivial interference would not be actionable (Winfield and Jolowicz 2020, para 18-007), but touching a painting could be trespass due to the importance of keeping a work of art in pristine condition.

[48] An example is consequential loss without material damage to the good, where someone accidentally turned off a stopcock leading to gas outage of the customers of the gas company (*Transco Plc v United Utilities Water Plc* [2005] EWHC 2784 (QB)).

[49] Winfield and Jolowicz 2020, para 18-011, also Clerk and Lindsell 2020 para 16-07, referring to *Kuwait Airways Corporation v Iraqi Airways Company and Others (Nos 4 and 5)* [2002] UKHL 19.

conversion (and also trespass). Trespass and conversion can overlap. Temporary deprivation without intent to assert rights over the good is no conversion.

As conversion can take many forms, it is a difficult tort to understand in all its ramifications. The main forms of conversion are nonetheless fairly clear:[50] these consist of taking or abusing possession, or refusing to return goods. Taking another person's bag is conversion. Abuse of possession amounts to conversion: for instance, borrowing a car and using it to smuggle drugs, which leads to the forfeiture of the car to the state. The owner of the car has a claim of conversion against the borrower. Refusing to return goods occurs if you borrow a car from a friend and don't return it. This does not apply if there is a ground for refusal (for example a bailee may refuse return if the bill for bailment has not been paid). Other examples can be given. Keeping goods that have been involuntarily received is conversion, but not if you took reasonable efforts to return the goods. Wrongfully disallowing the owner access to a good is also conversion, such as when a former employer does not give the employee permission to pick up personal belongings left at their old desk. Destruction or alteration of goods constitutes conversion.

Trespass to goods and conversion are partly governed by the Torts (Interference with Goods) Act 1977, which changed some rules set by earlier precedents. These torts apply to corporeal (tangible), movable property (chattels).[51] They therefore do not apply to intangible 'goods' such as contractual rights, software or data (also called 'choses in action').[52] The remedies associated with these torts are specific to property, such as retaking of goods (by yourself), an order for delivery of goods, as well as the general remedy of an award for damages.[53]

An important difference between conversion and trespass to goods has to do with damages. Trespass to goods – like all forms of trespass – does not require the presence of damage, and if there is damage there is no foreseeability limitation. For conversion, damages are assessed in principle at the value of the goods that have been converted, regardless of actual damage. However, it can be presumed that if the goods are ultimately returned, their value may be deducted again from the damages.[54] Trespass seems more appropriate in cases of damage to or tampering with goods, while conversion is more useful where the goods have been destroyed or lost permanently.

Trespass to land consists of unjustifiable interference with the possession of land.[55] 'Land' means areas of land, including the objects that are more or less permanently affixed to the land (such as buildings, trees, fences). Classic examples of trespass to land are unauthorized entry to another's property, squatting, building on your neighbour's land. Setting foot on a lawn, throwing rubbish on a field, boring a tunnel under land, building a shed slightly over

---

[50]   Winfield and Jolowicz 2020, para 18-013 through 18-022 for these examples. A more fine-grained categorization can be found in Clerk and Lindsell 2020, para 16-08 through 16-34.

[51]   See § 7.3 for an explanation of these terms.

[52]   For conversion see *OBG v Allan* [2007] UKHL 21, at 94-106.

[53]   See s. 3(2) Torts (Interference with Goods) Act 1977.

[54]   Winfield and Jollowicz 2020, para 18-014.

[55]   Winfield and Jolowicz 2020, para 14-001.

the boundary are further examples. It is also possible to commit trespass by passing over land without setting foot on it: it is held in several cases that there can be trespass if an object is jutting out above another's land.[56] However, an aircraft does not trespass if the aircraft flies at a reasonable height given the circumstances.[57]

It requires an intentional act, which means simply that the interference is intentional, not that the trespass was intended: the trespasser may have been under a mistaken belief about the owner of the land. If you are flung out of a car by accident, or thrown out of a car, you do not trespass on the land where you end up.[58] The interference must be direct: if it is indirect it may constitute nuisance but not trespass. The claimant is principally the person having a legal interest in the land, such as a lessor or tenant.[59]

Trespass to land is actionable per se, as are all kinds of trespass. This can be explained partly by the fact that the property interest in land is absolute and should not need to be supported by objectively proven damage, while furthermore there is an immaterial interest of the possessor in enjoying privacy on their own land. On the more practical side, the reason that damage is not necessary can be explained in that the usual aim of an action for trespass to land is not to obtain damages, but rather to restore the possessor in their rights, such as ejectment of land (of the trespasser) and re-entry (of the rightful possessor). That said, it is possible to obtain an award of damages too, but that would usually only lead to an award of nominal damages (§ 11.2).

The remedies for trespass to land are principally intended to stop the interference, such as injunctions to refrain from future trespass, or to remove trespassers or trespassing buildings (ejectment). Nominal damages may also be awarded. Trespass to land may on occasion serve the protection of privacy as well, for instance where newspaper photographers enter the estate of a movie star without authorization.

Closely related to trespass to land is the tort of *nuisance*, which is divided in private nuisance and public nuisance.

Private nuisance is unlawful interference with a person's use or enjoyment of land, or some right over or in connection with it.[60] 'Unlawful' in this context means 'unreasonable'. The interference is to the value of the property, not to the person. An example is making loud noises, thereby disturbing the sleep of your neighbour, or emitting noxious fumes. Trespass

---

[56]   *Laiqat v Majid* [2005] EWHC 1305 (QB) about an extractor fan protruding 75 centimetres at a height of 4.5 metres, *Anchor Brewhouse Developments Ltd v Berkley House* [1987] 2 EGLR 173 about a crane swinging above neighbour's property.

[57]   See s. 76(1) Civil Aviation Act 1982. This is an example of a specific act influencing general tort law.

[58]   The classic precedent is *Smith v Stone* 82 Eng. Rep. 533 (KB 1647) where the defendant was carried by force and against his will unto the land of the plaintiff.

[59]   A peculiarity of English land law is that formally there is no normal owner of landed property: all land is owned by the Crown. The person who in civil law systems would be called 'owner' is in English land law a lessor or tenant. We will in the following text avoid the term 'owner', but bear in mind that where it says 'possessor', 'lessor' or 'tenant' this may be equivalent to what in civil law or other common law systems is the owner.

[60]   Winfield and Jolowicz 2020, para 15-10.

therefore relates to interference with possession, nuisance involves interference with the use or enjoyment.

The protection offered by the tort of private nuisance is more restricted than in civil law systems by tort law and neighbour law:[61] there is no right to an unobstructed view, the neighbour is not limited in what he may build on his land, an owner or occupier may divert water running over his land. Such actions, even if done with malicious intent, may be lawful. There is also no right not to be overlooked.[62] For other kinds of interference, the presence of intent may nonetheless lead the court to find that the behaviour constitutes nuisance, even if the behaviour might have been reasonable in the absence of intent to harm.[63]

Claims for damage only extend to chattel if this is consequential to damage to the land, and claims for personal injury cannot be awarded on the basis private nuisance at all. Examples of private nuisance are encroachment on a neighbour's land, direct physical injury to land, interference of enjoyment of the land. The interference must not be trivial. An occupier may also be required to abate (take reasonable measures against) a natural nuisance, such as land moving itself onto adjoining land.[64]

There is also a tort of *public nuisance*. In brief this involves a nuisance to the general public, where a private individual may in specific circumstances also have a claim. Examples of public nuisance are obstructing public roads, selling food unfit for human consumption.[65]

Environmental protection also falls under this heading. In this text we will not go into the details of this tort. The usual approach for citizens is to complain to the local authorities who can enforce environmental regulations and stop the nuisance. An action for public nuisance would be necessary if you would want to obtain damages.

Finally, the Occupiers' Liability Act 1957 and Occupiers' Liability Act 1984 establish liability for landed property. However, as these relates not to infringement of property but rather provides a ground of liability for the possessor of land to injured visitors, they will be discussed under the heading of liability for land (§ 15.3).

5.6   TORTS INVOLVING WRONGFUL STATEMENTS

Several torts concern wrongful statements. *Deceit* is a wilfully false statement of fact, made with the intention to have the victim act upon it. It requires a fraudulent misstatement.[66]

If the misstatement was merely negligent, this falls under the tort of *liability for negligent misstatement.*[67] An example is if a bank voluntarily provides information about a client's

---

[61]   Winfield and Jolowicz 2020, para 15-12.

[62]   *Fearne and ors v Tate Gallery* [2020] EWCA Civ 104, about an extension to the Tate Modern whereby visitors could look into the appartements of a neighbouring flat.

[63]   Winfield and Jolowicz 2020, para 15-25.

[64]   *Leakey v National Trust* [1980] QB 485.

[65]   Public nuisance is a crime, and such conduct would usually also violate specific statutory rules.

[66]   Winfield and Jolowicz 2020, para 12-002 through 024.

[67]   Winfield and Jolowicz 2020, para 12-026.

financial health to a third party, without any disclaimer, and the client subsequently turns out to be in financial bad shape and goes bankrupt.[68] Arguably this is a subcategory within the tort of negligence, but it has specific characteristics[69] whereby it begins to take shape as an independent tort.

Defamation means publication of a statement that has caused or is likely to cause serious harm to the reputation of the claimant.[70] This tort developed in case law but has been significantly modified by the Defamation Act 1996 and the Defamation Act 2013. An example is falsely accusing a person on a blog of having defrauded his employer. Defamation implies that the statement is untrue; truth is a defence to the tort (s. 2). There are also other defences, such as whether the statement is published in a scientific research article (s. 6), or is in the public interest (s. 4). Defamation is further discussed in comparative perspective in § 7.5.

Malicious falsehood, also called *injurious falsehood*, is similar to defamation and may overlap with it, but need not involve harm to reputation. This tort consists of a false statement that causes damage to the claimant by influencing the behaviour of third parties. The latter element is what distinguishes this tort from deceit: deceit involves a reliance by the victim on the false statement, while in the case of malicious falsehood the damage is caused indirectly by the reliance of others on the statement. The elements of the tort are a false statement directed to a third party, made maliciously leading to damage suffered by the claimant.[71] Malice here means simply that the defendant knew of the falsehood or did not care about its truth,[72] it does not mean intent to harm the victim,[73] only that the falsehood was intentional. A non-defamatory statement can still give rise to a claim for malicious falsehood. For instance, an incorrect claim that a shop will close for business can be a malicious falsehood, even though it is not defamatory. Since malicious falsehood does not require serious damage (as defamation does), it may be preferable as a cause of action in certain cases. A disadvantage is that this tort requires the presence of malice, while defamation does not.

5.7 ECONOMIC TORTS

Four torts are called 'economic torts', because they protect economic (commercial) interests. An action based on these torts can lead to recovery of pure economic loss.[74] They are also

---

[68]   This is in essence the case of *Hedley Byrne & Co. v Heller and Partners Ltd* [1964] AC 465, except in that case no liability was assumed as the bank had in fact put a disclaimer in its statement.

[69]   Such as that it allows for recovery of pure economic loss, which is exceptional for cases of negligence.

[70]   See s. 1(1) Defamation Act 2013.

[71]   Winfield and Jolowicz 2020, para 13-125.

[72]   An alternative is that the defendant believed that the statement was true but wanted to injure the claimant, Winfield and Jolowicz 2020, para 13-132.

[73]   Hence 'malice' in this context is more like intention than malice in other torts.

[74]   '[T]he economic torts are a major exception to the general rule that there is no duty in tort to avoid causing a purely economic loss unless it is parasitic upon some injury to person or property'. *JSC BTA Bank v Khrapunov* [2018] UKSC 19, at 6.

intentional torts, as they all require intention. The main problem for these torts is how to distinguish acceptable competitive behaviour from unlawful conduct. The outlines of these torts have been set out in the decision *OBG Ltd v Allan* [2007] UKHL 21.[75]

Interference with trade by unlawful means, also called the tort of *causing loss by unlawful means*,[76] or the tort of unlawful interference.[77]

'The gist of this tort is intentionally damaging another's business by unlawful means.'[78] It requires '(a) a wrongful interference with the actions of a third party in which the claimant has an economic interest and (b) an intention thereby to cause loss to the claimant'.[79] An example of this tort is threatening prospective customers of a competitor's shop in order to drive business away.[80] 'Unlawful means' would have to be means that are actionable by (i.e. wrongful towards) a third party and interfered with that party's freedom to do business with claimant.[81] Hence a record company having an exclusive contract with an artist would not have a claim against a seller of bootleg records of that artist: even though this infringes on the copyright of the artist, it does not interfere with the freedom of the artist to contract with the record company.[82]

Interference with a subsisting contract[83]

This requires that another person breached his contract, that the defendant induced that breach, that the defendant knew about this breach and knew that the defendant was inducing

---

[75] The validity of this precedent has been confirmed recently in *Secretary of State for Health v Servier Laboratories Ltd and Ors* [2021] UKSC 24.

[76] There has to be an independent ground on why the means were unlawful, for example violation of competition law.

[77] *OBG Ltd v Allan* [2007] UKHL 21, at 141.

[78] *OBG Ltd v Allan* [2007] UKHL 21, at 141.

[79] *OBG Ltd v Allan* [2007] UKHL 21, at 47.

[80] *OBG Ltd v Allan* [2007] UKHL 21, at 47.

[81] *OBG Ltd v Allan* [2007] UKHL 21, at 49, and at 51: 'Unlawful means therefore consists of acts intended to cause loss to the claimant by interfering with the freedom of a third party in a way which is unlawful as against that third party and which is intended to cause loss to the claimant. It does not in my opinion include acts which may be unlawful against a third party but which do not affect his freedom to deal with the claimant'. Lord Nichols defended a wider interpretation, but he held a minority position.

[82] *RCA Corporation v Pollard* [1982] 3 All ER 771, cited in *OBG Ltd v Allan* [2007] UKHL 21, at 52. The 'dealing' requirement, as it is called, was attacked but confirmed in *Secretary of State for Health v Servier Laboratories Ltd and Ors* [2021] UKSC 24 about a medical company attempting to patent a medicine without real ground, in order to keep competitors off the market and maintain high prices, to the detriment of the National Health Service.

[83] This means inducing someone to breach his contract, cf. *Lumley v Gye* (1853) 2 El & Bl 216. The tort may overlap with the tort of causing loss by unlawful means, but is different in several aspects: see *OBG Ltd v Allan* [2007] UKHL 21 at 8.

that person to breach the contract.[84] The classic case is *Lumley v Gye*,[85] about a theatre owner inducing a famous opera singer to break her contract with a competing theatre owner in order to hire her himself.

Intimidation

The tort of intimidation is established where (i) the defendant makes a demand backed by a coercive and unlawful threat; (ii) the claimant complies with that demand because of the coercive and unlawful threat; (iii) the defendant knows or should have known that compliance with its demand will cause loss and damage to the claimant and (iv) the defendant intends its demand to cause loss and damage to the defendant.[86]

An example involving three parties is that a company threatens to stop supplying materials to another company, unless that company fires a certain employee with which the first company has a dispute.[87] Cases of three-party intimidation could often also be subsumed under the tort of interference with trade by unlawful means.[88] Intimidation between two parties (such as a landlord forcing the tenant to agree with a higher rent by threatening to deliberately leave a leaky roof unrepaired) may also be actionable under economic duress or breach of contract.[89] The further intricacies of this tort are too complicated to discuss here.[90]

Conspiracy[91]

This may take two forms: '(i) conspiracy to injure, where the overt acts done pursuant to the conspiracy may be lawful but the predominant purpose is to injure the claimant; and (ii) conspiracy to do by unlawful means an act which may be lawful in itself, albeit that injury to the claimant is not the predominant purpose'.[92] The first form of this tort resembles the category of 'abuse of right' in civil law jurisdictions, where it is wrongful to exercise a right solely to harm someone else. However, English law does not recognize a general category of abuse of right or improper motive.[93] Conspiracy cases are rare and the case law is not easy to understand. An example of conspiracy by unlawful means is to conspire for contempt of court.[94]

---

[84] *OBG Ltd v Allan* [2007] UKHL 21, at 39, 42, 44.

[85] (1853) 2 El. & Bl. 216.

[86] *Kolmar Group AG v Traxpo Enterprises PVT Ltd* [2010] EWHC 113 (Comm) at 119.

[87] The example is inspired by the classic case *Rookes v Barnard* [1964] AC 1129 HL, which involved the threat of a strike to cause the company to fire an employee who was not a union member.

[88] Clerk and Lindsell 2020, para 23-63.

[89] Clerk and Lindsell 2020, para 23-75.

[90] See further Clerk and Lindsell 2020, para 23-62 through 23-77.

[91] *Meretz Investments N.V. & ASNR v ACP Limited & Ors* [2007] EWCA Civ 1303 and *JSC BTA Bank v Khrapunov* [2018] UKSC 19.

[92] *JSC BTA Bank v Khrapunov* [2018] UKSC 19, at 8.

[93] *OBG Ltd v Allan* [2007] UKHL 21, at 14.

[94] *JSC BTA Bank v Khrapunov* [2018] UKSC 19 about a business man helping a business associate to conceal assets against freezing and receivership orders.

Another important tort relevant to businesses, besides the four above economic torts, is *passing off*,[95] which involves a trader passing off (misrepresenting) their goods or services as those of associated with another trader, thereby profiting from the other's goodwill.[96] Required are goodwill owned by the trader, misrepresentation, and damage to the goodwill.[97] The tort of passing off may overlap with infringement of intellectual property rights such as copyright.[98]

5.8   MISCELLANEOUS TORTS

A few torts do not fit into any of the aforementioned categories.

First of all, there is what is called *invasion of privacy*. Presently there is not a single, all-encompassing tort of invasion of privacy.[99] The interests protected by the right to privacy are partly protected by other torts such as defamation and trespass to land, by actions such as breach of confidence, and by the Human Rights Act 1998 and the implementation of the General Data Protection Regulation.[100]

More specifically, there is an action in tort for the *misuse of private information*, as established in *Campbell v MGN Ltd*.[101] The case involved a supermodel who had denied that she was addicted to drugs, but was photographed when leaving a Narcotics Anonymous meeting. A journal printed the photographs with information on the meeting. Campbell successfully sued the journal, as the court found that the publication of the photographs and additional information were not necessary. The action for misuse of private information requires that

(1)   the defendant must have disclosed private information, and
(2)   the defendant's interest in publishing the information must be less important than the claimant's interest in the information remaining private.[102]

As you can see, this tort does cover some of the acts that would amount to violation of privacy.[103] It does not cover cases where no publication of information is involved, such as a neighbour spying on you.

---

[95]   There is also an extended form of passing off, which involves the quality of a similar product or the likeness of a celebrity.

[96]   The other trader may have a registered or unregistered trademark, but this is not necessary.

[97]   *Reckitt & Colman Ltd v Borden Inc* [1990] 1 All ER 873.

[98]   Infringement of intellectual property (IP) is also wrongful: IP rights are usually protected by specific acts, such as in the UK the Copyright, Designs and Patents Act 1988 and the Trademark Act 1994. It is possible that violation of trade mark also constitutes the tort of passing off.

[99]   *Wainwright v Home Office* [2004] 2 AC 406 [28]–[35].

[100]   In the Data Protection Act 2018, and later supporting rules enacted to maintain the high level of data protection after Brexit (colloquially referred to as the UK GDPR).

[101]   [2004] UKHL 22.

[102]   Winfield and Jolowicz 2020, para 13-144, referring to *McKennitt v Ash* [2006] EWCA Civ 1714 at [11].

[103]   A recent example is the publication of a letter of the Duchess of Sussex to her father (*Duchess of Sussex v Associated Newspapers Ltd* [2021] EWHC 273 (Ch)).

Secondly, the tort of *malicious prosecution* (also called *abuse of legal procedure*). For a long time this tort only covered criminal prosecution, not civil proceedings. The reasoning was that in civil proceedings there would not be any additional damage (as the English civil procedure awards the winner full recovery of legal costs, in contrast to many civil law countries that only award fixed or limited compensation for legal costs). However, there may also be additional damage from civil proceedings. The Supreme Court changed course in *Willers v Joyce*.[104] In cases where no actual proceedings started but there were other forms of abuse of the instruments available in and around litigation, there are supplementary torts such as *malicious proceedings* and *abuse of civil process*.[105] A detailed description of these torts (which may be considered simply as variants of malicious prosecution) is outside the scope of this text and would require an extensive discussion of the intricacies of the law of civil procedure.

The tort of malicious prosecution involves, simply put, instigating or causing a court case (or a criminal prosecution) intentionally, knowing that the case is entirely unfounded.[106] More precisely it requires (1) a prosecution by the tortfeasor, (2) the victim won the prosecution, (3) the prosecution lacked reasonable and probable cause, (4) the tortfeasor acted maliciously, and (5) the victim suffered damage. Prosecution may involve criminal and civil proceedings, and may also extend to other procedural instruments such as execution of a judgment.

Finally, the tort of *misfeasance in public office* is related to breach of a statutory duty. It applies to public officers, and requires (briefly put) that the officer intentionally or knowingly harmed the plaintiff by abusing their public power.[107] This tort is rarely applicable and is mostly discussed in conjunction with state liability.

5.9   ACCOUNTABILITY

A few general aspects of torts in English law can be discussed briefly. They will be covered in a comparative manner in Chapters 7 through 12.

Where civil law systems prefer to have general rules for accountability and causality that are applicable to all torts, in English law these issues are discussed for each tort individually, and there is resistance to discussing them as general concepts. Each tort has its own elements. Although the elements follow the broad outlines described in Chapter 2 for tort law in general, the specific content may differ. This applies both to the criteria for wrongfulness as to the other elements of a tort, in particular causality and harm. For example, the tort of conversion requires intention, while the causality requirement for this tort is that damage is compensated except where it is too remote. For negligence, the causality requirement is that damage must

---

[104]   *Willers v Joyce* [2016] UKSC 43, following the earlier decision of the Privy Council in *Crawford Adjusters v Sagicor General Insurance Ltd* [2013] UKPC 17.

[105]   Clerk and Lindsell 2020, para 15-66 through 15-80. Abuse of process is considered a distinct tort, although closely related to malicious prosecution: *Crawford Adjusters Ltd v Sagicor Insurance Ltd* [2013] UKPC 17, at 62.

[106]   Winfield and Jolowicz 2020, para 20-006

[107]   Paraphrasing Winfield and Jolowicz 2020, para 8-025.

have been foreseeable (which is more restrictive than that damage must not be too remote). Nonetheless a few general remarks may be in order.

As regards *accountability*, this is mostly discussed under the degree of intention. English tort law distinguishes between negligence, intention and malice. The degree of intention is therefore a principal element of specific torts. It may also be important for certain kinds of damages (§ 11.1).

With respect to persons lacking capacity, English law takes the mental capabilities of the tortfeasor into account. If the tortfeasor is a child, the standard for negligence is adapted to what can be objectively expected of a child of that age.[108] For persons of impaired judgement due to psychic issues the position is not entirely clear: courts in negligence cases appear to simply apply the objective standard of the reasonable person, unless the person's capacity for judgement was entirely removed (hence the actions where wholly involuntary).[109]

5.10   CAUSALITY

Although the specific requirements for causation are not the same for all torts, it is possible to discuss general principles of causation in tort.[110] English torts by and large require the presence of factual and legal causality.

Factual causation is established with the so-called 'but for'-test.[111] The main difference with civil law systems is the standard of proof, which rests on the 'balance of probabilities'. There are complications in establishing factual causality, in particular where there are possible other factors attributable to the claimant. We will return to this subject in Chapter 9.

Legal causality is referred to under the heading of remoteness of damage.[112] Different torts handle this requirement in different ways. Generally torts require remoteness,[113] but a few torts such as negligence restrict remoteness to foreseeable damage. If a consequence was intended, that consequence is never too remote.[114] If the damage is quite remote and may not be foreseeable, it makes sense to check whether you could sue on the basis of an intentional tort instead of only invoking negligence. The restriction to foreseeable damage in the case of negligence was established in the precedent *Wagon Mound (No. 1)*.[115] In that case the harm (fire) was not found to be foreseeable as a consequence of the negligent act (spilling furnace oil), as the causal chain was quite involved and not immediately obvious (the oil would normally not alight when floating on water, it only did so because it got mixed up with cotton in the water). There is

---

[108]   *Orchard v Lee* [2009] EWCA Civ 295, at 9.

[109]   *Dunnage v Randall* [2015] EWCA Civ 673, about a paranoid schizophrenic. See further § 8.2.

[110]   E.g. Clerk and Lindsell 2020, chapter 2.

[111]   Clerk and Lindsell 2020, para 2-09.

[112]   Clerk and Lindsell 2020, para 2-144ff.

[113]   Cf. *Kuwait Airways Corporation v Iraqi Airways Company and Others* [2002] UKHL 19, paras 103–04.

[114]   Clerk and Lindsell 2020, para 2-151.

[115]   [1961] UKPC 2, [1961] AC 388.

a further restriction on remoteness, namely the 'scope of the duty'. This will be discussed in § 9.1.

English law recognizes the problems arising when there are multiple causes. We will discuss such cases briefly in Ch. 9. Where there are multiple tortfeasors, the result is usually joint and several liability.[116] Nowadays such cases are principally governed by the Civil Liability (Contribution) Act 1978.

5.11   DAMAGES AND OTHER REMEDIES

The principal remedy in English law is an award of damages.[117] Several kinds of damages are distinguished, which may appear quite complicated from the outside. We will briefly look at the categories, and return to this issue in Chapter 11.

In common law the main category is *compensatory damages*. These aim at compensation of damage, loss and injury. These can be distinguished in two kinds:

- Damages for pecuniary loss. These are damages for financial and material losses, such as costs incurred, loss of value due to damage to property. Loss of profit is also a kind of pecuniary loss.
- Damages for non-pecuniary loss. These are damages for harm that does not consists of injury to financial or material interests. Examples are damages for pain and suffering, emotional distress, impairment of life.

There are also various kinds of non-compensatory damages. These will be discussed in § 11.1.3.

Besides damages, the main other remedy is *injunctive relief*, meaning that the court issues an injunction. An injunction is 'an order restraining the commission or continuance of some wrongful act, or the continuance of some wrongful omission'.[118] In other words, it is an order by the court that orders or prohibits certain behaviour by the defendant. Issuing an injunction is at the discretion of the court. Injunctions are commonly ordered for torts like nuisance or trespass to land.

Some torts are related to property and have specific remedies related to property law. In civil law systems, such remedies are not viewed as part of tort law. These property-related remedies in common law are quite specific and cannot be dealt with extensively here.[119] They mostly consist of specific injunctions or orders, but there are others as well. An example is abatement:

---

[116] There is a slight difference in meaning, see Winfield and Jolowicz 2020, para 22-005: joint means a common design of the tortfeasors.

[117] McGregor 2018.

[118] Winfield and Jolowicz 2020, para 23-124.

[119] Examples are ejectment, jus tertii, mesne profits, replevin.

a self-help remedy whereby the victim acts on their own to remedy the situation, in particular put a stop to nuisance.[120]

---

[120] For example, *Delaware v City of Westminster* [2001] UKHL 55 about cracks in a building caused by the roots of a neighbouring tree.

6
Categorizing fault (I): formal sources of rules

The previous chapters have introduced the various torts and grounds of liability in three legal systems. What isn't immediately apparent is how these torts and grounds are actually applied in practice. In particular it may be hard to apply a vague norm such as negligence. As we have seen, the general consensus is that a 'reasonable person' test is to be applied. Such a test is nonetheless not very descriptive. In practice courts tend to look at specific written rules to help decide cases and also to provide citizens a modicum of guidance on how torts like negligence will be adjudicated.

Furthermore, you may wonder how the various approaches we discussed map onto each other. The tort law approach of common law seems so different from French law that you may believe that they are incommensurable. However, on closer examination there are many points of overlap and broad similarities, despite the many differences in detail.

In this and the following chapter we focus on the first element, fault, more precisely objective fault or wrongfulness. Legal systems approach this in different ways.[1] In the present chapter we look at the formal categories of wrongfulness, distinguished by the source of the rules that determine wrongfulness. We will discuss how the doctrines and torts that were introduced before function as mechanisms to achieve a balance between the various influences, and how courts apply those rules. This broadens the focus on positive sources of law (statute law and case law) and shows how other normative influences are taken into account.

6.1   WRONGFULNESS AS A MATTER OF BALANCE

The principal question for tort law is how to distinguish permissible conduct from wrongful behaviour in a fairly predictable manner. As we discussed in § 2.3, this is a question of balance. On the one hand there is the need to be protected against injury caused by others, to which it would be hard or impossible to protect oneself. On the other hand, there is the social interest in that individual freedom or autonomy is not unnecessarily or unduly impaired. Liability, it could be argued, is the reaction of the law when the risks to others outweigh the interests of the tortfeasor. This applies to the rules of tort law in general, and more particularly to wrongfulness, as wrongfulness indicates what kind of conduct is allowed and what not.

---

[1]   From a historical viewpoint see Gordley 2021.

While the job of finding a proper balance may in theory seem clear, it is hard to give proper indications as to where the balance is or how to find it. Particularly for a novice approaching this subject, it may be difficult to give a definite assessment about a concrete case. Experienced lawyers are familiar with numerous cases from case law, which helps them to find their way around. In a comparative introduction it is hard to substitute for experience, as the cases in one jurisdiction do not necessarily translate well to other systems, particularly where it is not uncommon to find that a court in one country does find for the victim, while a court in another country rejects a similar claim.

In this chapter we will approach this question from the formal side. Who can determine the balance, and what tools do they have at their disposal in doing so? This relates to questions of distribution of power to establish the legal rules. At first sight the court may appear to be best situated to assess the case as it is cognisant of all the concrete circumstances of the case. That is what seems to occur when applying negligence. However, the court would be loath to make a completely individual assessment for each case, as that would be time consuming and could easily lead to unpredictable and inconsistent decisions. The courts themselves are therefore prone to rely on other instruments, rules from other sources, or relevant factors that may help to substantiate the decision on the proper balance (§§ 6.2 and 6.3).

Alternatively. it can be argued that the courts only have a subsidiary role vis a vis the legislator, hence if a statute decides on the permissibility of certain conduct, the courts are in principle bound by it (§ 6.4). However, the legislator can only provide general rules which are not always appropriate to specific cases. Hence it seems as if courts should take into account, to various degrees, the general rules and guidelines from other sources, but also require a certain amount of discretion in whether and how to apply these rules. There are various ways in which to find a proper combination of being bound and having discretion, depending on the kind of rules under discussion, and this explains the different rules we will encounter in this chapter.

An alternative approach that we will explore in the next chapter is to divide the possible cases into categories depending on the kind of conduct and the kind of interests that are injured. That approach has the advantage of being more expressive and intuitively easier to apply.

6.2 NEGLIGENCE AS GENERAL STANDARD FOR WRONGFUL CONDUCT

It appears that all jurisdictions recognize a tort similar to negligence: a ground of liability that uses a general standard or vague norm to determine what conduct is wrongful. Common law systems have the tort of negligence. Civil law systems typically have a general norm in line with French law, providing for compensation in case of fault, which includes negligent conduct. In German law, as we have seen, negligent infringement of protected interests falls under § 823 I BGB and cases of omissions towards obligations to remove risks where one is responsible for are covered by *Verkehrspflichten*. A sizable group of jurisdictions, in particular in East Asia, have a provision resembling § 823 I BGB whereby only negligence towards specific interests leads to liability.[2] In Nordic countries, the liability for negligent behaviour is accepted as a general rule.[3] In countries based on Islamic law, again, unintended negligent infringement gives rise to liability.[4]

A general norm for liability is indispensable to allow courts to keep up with new developments in society. Hereby courts are effectively empowered to create new forms of liability, new detailed rules within the general liability rules. You might think that this means courts can do whatever they want. A general norm would therefore simplify the court's job at the expense of predictability for lawyers and citizens. However, in actuality courts as well strive for predictability and are looking for guidance. There are three approaches commonly used to determine what is negligent conduct.

1. The first approach is to explicate the norm of negligence by referring to the conduct of a *reasonable person*. We have encountered this approach in English, French and German law, while it is also found all over the world, often in case law but sometimes explicitly in the code.[5]

The 'reasonable person' test implies an *objective* standard of wrongfulness. Legal systems differ as to how persons of limited intellectual capabilities are treated (§ 8.3). In France the objective standard is also applied to children and mentally disabled persons (§ 3.5). English and German courts, on the contrary, do take into account what can be expected of children, thereby using a subjective corrective to the reasonable person standard.[6]

When applying the reasonable person standard, courts need to take into account the situation: a doctor at an emergency post in a hospital is held to the professional standard of a doctor and not that of an ordinary person. This is fairly obvious. A further question is whether courts may hold a person to an even higher standard if he has actual knowledge and skill above the

---

[2] For example, Vietnam (art. 584(1) Bộ Luật), Thailand (s. 420 Civil and Commercial Code), Japan (art. 709 Civil Code).

[3] For Sweden art. 2(1) Skadeståndslagen (Tort Liability Act), for Finland art. 2(1) Vahingonkorvauslaki (Tort Liability Act). Further Von Bar 1998, pp. 264, 272 on Danish law.

[4] See for Jordan law, considered as a codification of an Islamic law concept, Al-Qasem 1989, at p. 192, who refers to the concept of *ta'adi* as an analogue to the duty of care. Basir Bin Mohamed 2021, p. 478 describes this concept as intentional act for indirect cause, and distinguishes this from unintentional act for indirect cause that he likens to negligence. At p. 490 he notes that *ta'adi* is like the subjective element of intention or negligence.

[5] For example, art. 152 of the Montenegro Law on obligations (2008).

[6] §§ 4.7 and 5.9.

reasonable person. In Germany and France, this is expected,[7] while in England it is at least accepted that actual knowledge needs to be taken into account.[8]

Implied in the notion of a reasonable person is a certain sociability which expresses itself in that a reasonable person also takes the interests of others into account, in particular those who might potentially be harmed by his actions. In short, the 'reasonable person standard' expresses the notion of balancing interests. The standard of the reasonable person does provide some guidance, as it suggests that you have to imagine a concrete reasonable person in the position of the tortfeasor. Nonetheless further support would be helpful to substantiate the 'reasonable person' standard. That is what the other two approaches provide.

2. The second approach is to look at rules external to tort law. By doing so, tort law can piggy-back on the decisions made by experts and authorities in other areas (including the legislator): this saves the court the effort of determining on its own what a reasonable person should do. It also supports the court decision: the authority of the drafter of the rule is mirrored in the court decision. One may presume that the drafter of the rule has undertaken the research to find an appropriate balance between opposed interests.

There are several kinds of external rules that can be used for assessing negligence. First of all, there are statutory rules. The breach of statutory duty may be an independent ground of liability (§ 6.4), but there are also systems that do not have a strict distinction, whereby breach of a statutory rule is merely a factor to take into account to assess conduct. We already encountered the example of France. In the US there is the doctrine of *negligence per se*, by which the violation of a statutory duty may lead to a finding of negligence.[9] Even in English law the breach of statutory rules may still be used as evidence of negligence in cases where the tort of breach of a statutory duty cannot be applied.[10]

For other official rules, such as local ordinances that are not statutes, negligence may be the only way to consider their violation as a ground for liability: it depends on the legal system whether they are covered in breach of official rules, or whether the court needs to take those into account when assessing whether behaviour is negligent.

Besides official rules, the assessment of negligent behaviour may reference other rules, even if these do not have official status. Examples of such rules are:

---

[7]   Wagner 2021, para 5.25, BGH 26 February 1987, NJW 1987, 1487, and BGH 24 June 1997, VI ZR 94/96; Viney, Jourdain and Carval 2013, p. 488: 'une appréciation plus sévère des devoirs de «compétence et d'habiliteté» que celle qui serait appliquée a un sujet n'ayant pas cet acquis', refering inter alia to Cass., 2, 8 July 1954, JCP 1954, I, p. 122, Cass., 3, 23 January 2003, no. 01-13875.

[8]   *Stokes v Guest, Keen & Nettlefold (Bolts & Nuts) Ltd* [1968] 1 WLR 1776, *Baker v Quantum Clothing Group* [2011] UKSC 17, see further Goudkamp 2004, Clerk and Lindsell 2020, para 7-163, Winfield and Jolowicz 2020, para 6-003.

[9]   Goldberg and Zipursky 2010, pp. 154–9. The tort of breach of a statutory duty is not accepted in US law.

[10]   Winfield and Jolowicz 2020, para 6-039.

- standards: product standards, safety standards, professional standards can be laid down in written rules,[11] or may be part of the professional diligence that is expected of professional service providers such as doctors and advocates.
- ethics: certain professions have ethical rules, the breach of which is often an indication of professional negligence.
- social rules and customary rules.[12] Customary rules are a general category of rules that find their origin in social acceptance in a society or social sub-group. Customary rules may regulate behaviour by creating social expectations, and such expectations are relevant when determining whether someone's conduct was negligent.

Nowadays the term 'private regulation' has come into vogue as a general term which includes standards and professional rules.[13] Private organizations may establish rules for regulating certain areas of human organization: the FIFA[14] may adopt rules for football (soccer), the International Olympic Committee may set rules regulating checks on doping, accountancy organizations may collaborate to draft standards such as the International Financial Reporting Standards.

Formally the aforementioned rules can only have effect through the sanctions and remedies within such an organization, but in practice courts also use such rules as an indication of what is proper behaviour, what can be expected of a 'reasonable person'. These rules can be considered as the embodiment of how a reasonable person would behave, or conversely it can be argued that a reasonable person will abide by reasonable rules that serve to protect others. In English law, for instance, the failure to adopt a common practice is strong evidence of carelessness, while conformity with a common practice is prima facie evidence that sufficient care was taken.[15] Hence the tort of negligence may serve as a portal through which outside norms may obtain legal effect. For instance, tackling an opponent in violation of the rules of soccer may lead a court to conclude that there is a negligent act, but acting within the rules will usually not be considered negligent.[16]

Another category is what is called *soft law*. These are rules that resemble legal rules but lack the binding force of law.[17] Examples are policy rules issued by a ministry on how a certain rule is actually applied, non-binding labour standards set by a UN organization. The main difference with private regulation is that soft law primarily emanates from the state or international organizations, while private regulation by definition is established by private parties. The boundaries can be fuzzy, such as in cases where the state adopted a set of non-binding rules or standards that have been drafted by a private organization.

---

[11] In particular standardization organizations such as ISO are important.

[12] See for example Le Tourneau, 2020, ch. 2212, p. 820ff.

[13] Cafaggi 2016, Verbruggen and Paiement 2017.

[14] Fédération Internationale de Football Association, International Federation of Association Football.

[15] Clerk and Lindsell 2020, para 7-194, also Giliker 2020, para 5-014, Winfield and Jolowicz 2020, para 6-026.

[16] See for French law in more detail, Cass., 2, 15 May 1972, D. 1972, p. 606.

[17] For a more detailed discussion see Senden 2005.

The violation of rules like the above can be taken as an indication or presumption that the defendant acted negligently. The courts are, however, not bound to use those rules, they can also decide that conduct in violation of such rules is not wrongful. Note that these rules need not be bound to a specific territory. They may therefore have a global reach.

3.   The third approach is to look at several factors to assess whether specific behaviour is negligent. This approach is merely a tool to help lawyers to apply the 'reasonable person' test. A set of factors serves as a lens, a heuristic device which helps to focus on relevant aspects in the facts. Courts in many jurisdictions use similar factors to argue about the wrongfulness of behaviour: these factors seem intuitively relevant to support their decisions. Famous is the so-called 'Learned Hand' formula.[18]

$$B < P * L$$

This means that the *Burden* of precautionary measures should be less than the *Probability* times the amount of *Loss*. According to this formula, the tortfeasor is liable if the cost of these measures does not exceed the expected harm (the amount of loss multiplied by the probability of that loss occurring). This formula has received considerable attention in the Law and Economics literature, following an article by Richard Posner who took this formula as a generally applicable instrument for bringing about an efficient level of accidents and safety.[19] However, there is doubt as to whether the formula actually lends itself to application in a mechanistic manner, while the underlying aim of maximizing social welfare is also found to be at tension with the aims of justice.[20] It seems preferable to use the formula merely as a heuristic device, an interpretative guideline to direct your attention to relevant aspects of a case.

For practical purposes we should not abide by the Learned Hand formula and its suggestion of mathematical precision, but rather work with a broader set of factors that serve as a guideline for assessing what may be expected of a reasonable person. In English law,[21] and in other systems as well, four factors are usually singled out as relevant.[22]

- seriousness of harm
- probability of harm
- burden of precautionary measures
- character and benefit of conduct

---

[18]   Named after the US judge and legal scholar Learned Hand, who suggested it in his decision in *United States v Carroll Towing Co.*, 159 F.2d 169 (2d Cir. 1947).

[19]   Posner 1972, see Wright 2003, Dari-Mattiacci and Parisi 2021.

[20]   Wright 2002, Wright 2003, Goldberg and Zipursky 2010, pp. 149–51.

[21]   Winfield and Jolowicz 2020, para 6-019, referring to the 'negligence calculus', Giliker 2020, para 5-005 (who substitutes foreseeability of harm for probability of harm, and lists as fifth factor 'common practice'), Clerk and Lindsell 2020, para 7-172 through 7-193.

[22]   Van Dam 2013, nr. 805-2, 806, 807 and 809. A theoretical discussion can be found in Wagner 2021, paras 4.4–4.34.

The fourth factor is an addition to the Learned Hand formula.

As an example we can again look at the Palsgraf case (§ 2.1). In that case, the harm suffered by the victim was rather serious, but the probability of its occurrence appeared to be quite low. It is not easy to estimate whether the employees could easily have taken precautionary measures (should they not have helped the men board the train? Should they have attempted to hold the package separately? And take into account that everything happened very quickly). Arguably the conduct in question was an innocent attempt to help individuals, but it can also be argued that the help provided was commercial in nature (by a company). These factors do not give a clear outcome, and indeed you may find yourself more inclined to conclude that the railway company should be liable. But the consideration of factors does help to highlight two weaknesses of the case: the probability of this kind of harm seems low, and it is not very clear that the employees could easily have taken preventive measures.

In the actual court procedure the claim was denied because the employees did not owe a duty of care to Ms. Palsgraf, meaning (as it is nowadays interpreted) that the duty of care that was breached (careful handling of the package to protect nearby individuals) did not cover Ms. Palsgraf. This is called the requirement of 'relationality of the breach' in US law,[23] similar to what we discuss here under 'scope of the rule' (§ 9.1).

Examples of cases in which some of those factors seem to be applied can be found in §§ 4.3 and 5.2. These factors can be found in court decisions all over the world, but they may not have legal status. Furthermore, even when similar factors are used, court in different jurisdictions may reach varying outcomes in similar cases, due to differences in culture and general expectations. You should therefore use these factors only as a guideline to determine which facts of a given case may be particularly relevant, and – pending further knowledge of the local case law – obtain a first impression of the outcome.

The three approaches can be applied in conjunction but also separately, partly depending on the legal system. In French case law, for example, a court may simply refer to the facts of the case and declare that the behaviour did not accord to what a reasonable person would have done, but a court could also specifically point out the lack of preventive measures, or the violation of a safety rule, in order to support its decision that the behaviour was not that of a reasonable person. If you are confronted with a case, you may similarly assess it first of all by reference to how a reasonable person would act, but might if needed support your assessment by specifically looking at the presence of the four factors in the case and/or by taking into account relevant external rules, particularly if such rules have already been applied by the courts in similar cases.

---

[23]   Goldberg and Zipursky 2010, p. 101.

6.3 OMISSIONS

A particular issue related to negligence, which may lead to some confusion, is liability for omissions.[24] Part of the confusion is due to the fact that omissions may refer to three different kinds of cases.

1. The tortfeasor was engaged in a permissible activity, but neglected to take sufficient precautions while doing so. This is simply a form of negligent conduct. Example: driving a car without paying attention to the road. The French call this *l'omission dans l'action*, the omission within an action. The action was incomplete as it didn't include sufficient precautions.
2. The tortfeasor has a specific duty to act in a certain way, and neglects to fulfil his duty. This is usually based on a form of responsibility for an object or area or person: the duty is to prevent individuals from harm by risks from that object of area. The German *Verkehrspflichten* principally cover such cases, while French and English law simply treat them under general negligence (in English law, by assessing whether there is a duty of care). An example is the owner of a house who may have the duty to keep the steps of their house from being slippery. This begs the question whether there is in fact such a duty or not. In German and English law the test is typically whether there is a (special) relationship to the risk in question.
3. The tortfeasor wasn't doing anything that impacted the victim, and did not have a specific duty regarding the object or area or victim. An example: someone has by their own carelessness fallen into a river and is in danger of drowning. If a passer-by doesn't do anything to help that person, this is a *pure omission*.

In common law the first category is also called misfeasance, while the last two categories are lumped under what is called nonfeasance.[25]

The first two categories are not actually problematic. The first category is simply covered by negligence. The second category is typically the violation of a duty brought forth by the relationship to the risk. The German *Verkehrspflichten* are a good example. Both categories may lead to liability in most legal systems. In France, the notion of fault is generally considered to cover acts as well as omissions. The case law mostly involves cases where there is a particular reason why the tortfeasor should have aided the victim. Arguably such a presumption is implied in the concept of a 'pre-existing obligation' in France, as well as in the common law approach where it is necessary that there should actually be a duty of care. Similarly for German law it is recognized that liability for omissions presumes the existence of an obligation to act.[26]

---

[24] For French law see Viney, Jourdain and Carval 2013, pp. 458–67.

[25] In the recent decision *Poole Borough Council v GN* [2019] UKSC 25, at [28] and [31], Lord Reed preferred the distinction between 'causing harm' versus 'failing to confer a benefit', which would be less confusing than the terms misfeasance and nonfeasance.

[26] Wagner 2021, para 5.16.

It is the third category, pure omissions, where there is a greater divide. Civil law systems are generally willing to accept a duty to aid strangers in peril, even in the absence of any prior relation to the stranger or the occurrence of the risk.[27] In France the concept of fault also covers pure omissions. In many civil law systems there are specific statutory duties[28] (often in criminal law)[29] that would oblige you to help someone in extreme danger, if it is possible to do so without endangering yourself. Violation of such a duty would be wrongful, being a breach of a statutory duty.

Common law tends to be more restrictive. Omissions may only lead to liability if there is a duty of care: this is presumed in the first element of negligence, that there must be a duty of care. But if there was no prior involvement, a pure omission is usually not a violation of a duty of care as the mere possibility to intervene does not create a duty of care at common law. 'It is common ground that under our law two persons can stand aside and watch a third jump to his death: there is no legal duty to rescue.'[30] Only if you do attempt to rescue him, you assume responsibility and can be liable for negligence.[31] If on the contrary you didn't lift a finger to help, an action for negligence will fail. The law thereby seems to punish persons who try to help.

However, even in common law systems this outcome is considered to be unjust. Therefore several common law jurisdictions have adopted statutes that impose an obligation to provide aid in certain cases.[32] As it also seems unfair to expose rescuers to the threat of liability for any harm caused during the rescue operation (as the rescuers were obligated to rescue and did not choose to undertake that risk), several US states have also adopted 'Good Samaritan' statutes that exclude liability if you attempted a rescue in good faith.[33] The UK has recently adopted the Social Action, Responsibility and Heroism Act 2015, which applies when 'a court, in considering a claim that a person was negligent or in breach of statutory duty, is determining the steps that the person was required to take to meet a standard of care' (s. 1). The courts should then take into account whether the person was acting for the benefit of society or any of its members, demonstrated a predominantly responsible approach towards protecting the safety or other interests of others, or whether the act occurred when the person was acting heroically

---

[27] A rare explicit provision to that effect is found in § 2900 of the Czech Zákon občanský zákoník (Civil code 2014). Another example is the Serbian Law on Contracts and Torts, art. 182

[28] A civil law tort is found in Croatia: art. 1082 Civil Obligations Act (2005).

[29] For example § 323c of the German Strafgesetzbuch (Criminal code).

[30] *Vellino v Chief Constable of Greater Manchester* [2001]EWCA Civ 1249, at 13. This position was confirmed in *Poole Borough Council v GN* [2019] UKSC 25, at 65. Further Winfield and Jolowicz 2020, 5-030.

[31] Winfield and Jolowicz 2020, 5-040 through 5-047.

[32] For example § 361.062 of the Florida Statutes (Duty to give information and render aid): 'The driver of any vehicle involved in a crash resulting in injury to or death of any person … shall render to any person injured in the crash reasonable assistance, including the carrying, or the making of arrangements for the carrying, of such person to a physician, surgeon, or hospital for medical or surgical treatment if it is apparent that treatment is necessary, or if such carrying is requested by the injured person.' A similar exception to liability is found in Germany (§ 680 BGB).

[33] For example, § 41.711a of the Ambulance and Inhalator Service and Hospital Support Act of 1960 in Michigan.

by intervening in an emergency to assist an individual in danger (ss. 2–4). Thereby the harshness of the general common law attitude towards voluntary assumption of a duty of care in rescue cases is mitigated.

The notion of pure omissions can be construed as one way in which balance is achieved: pure omissions involve cases where the harm is particularly serious, and only in such cases is there a reason to limit the freedom of individuals and force them to help another in need. For less serious cases it may be a friendly gesture to voluntarily offer aid, but there certainly is no legal requirement to do so.

6.4   STATUTORY DUTIES

As mentioned in § 6.2, one particular way in which rules outside tort law can influence whether an act is wrongful is through *breach of statutory duty* as a ground of liability. This applies where there is a statutory duty that is not in itself a tort, and that duty has been breached: the question is whether this breach should lead to civil liability. Cases where a statute creates a tort and explicates that certain conduct leads to liability (and/or remedies), such as the Protection from Harassment Act 1997, do not involve the breach of a statutory duty, rather they constitute independent torts. In such case the ground for liability is that specific act, and *not* the tort of breach of statutory duty.

Breach of statutory duty is only invoked if there is a statutory duty that does not in itself prescribe civil law remedies (in English law such civil law remedies are referred to as a 'private right of action'): these are typically rules of criminal law or administrative law. An example: violation of traffic rules in a specific act may be considered wrongful and lead to liability as constituting breach of a statutory duty.[34] Liability on the basis of breach of statutory duty has the advantage that there is clear support by relying on the authority of the legislator for finding an appropriate balance between the interests of tortfeasor and victim. However, it may be necessary to look into the legislative intent to determine whether the legislator not only wanted the defendant to refrain from certain behaviour, but also wanted to have provide a victim with remedies towards the defendant.

An explicit codification of this ground of liability can be found in art. 823 II BGB (see § 4.4). Some countries do not have a separate tort of breach of a statutory duty. French law for instance only has one general rule for fault liability, but legal scholars recognize that courts in practice apply a category of violation of a legal duty (*devoir légal*) within the general norm. US tort law also does not have a tort of breach of a statutory duty. Instead, there is the doctrine of *negligence per se*, which means that in case of violation of a statutory duty the courts may have to find that the conduct was negligent.[35] Hence you might say that the US tort of negligence has simply engulfed the breach of a statutory duty.

---

[34]   For example, the Manitoba Highway Traffic Act (of the Canadian province of Manitoba) provides rules and fines for traffic, but does not provide a private law remedy.

[35]   Goldberg and Zipursky 2010, pp. 154–9.

The tort of breach of a statutory duty is often limited to the harm that falls within the 'scope of the rule' (§ 9.1). This is an explicit element of both the English tort and the German § 823 II BGB. Note that French law does not recognize this restriction (§ 9.1), whereby the breach of a statutory duty is a more important basis for liability in French law than in other jurisdictions.

Closely related is the breach of another official rule that is not a statutory duty, for example a local city ordinance. It depends on the legal system whether the breach of such localized rules also falls under breach of statutory duty. In France, for example, such a local rule may be considered a 'devoir légal' (legal imperative), the breach of which constitutes a fault in the meaning of art. 1240 Cc. Breach of a local ordinance may also be breach of a statutory duty if there is a statute that criminalizes such a breach.

Acting without mandatory government licence may also constitute a breach of a statutory duty. However, the converse does not hold: having a licence does not exempt from liability. This is easy to see if we consider that a licensed driver may still be liable when he causes an accident.

6.5   RIGHTS AND FUNDAMENTAL RIGHTS

Finally, another way to find wrongfulness is with the notion of infringement of a right. This is fairly often recognized as a distinct category of wrongfulness.[36] In French doctrine the infringement of right is recognized as a subcategory within violation of a legal duty (breach of statutory duty), while in German law the protected interests of § 823 I BGB are also perceived as rights. Witness the phrase 'another right' in that provision.

It can be argued that rights represent a well-established manner in which society tries to keep freedom to act from interfering with relevant interests. The idea is that rights on the one hand confer an individual with the freedom and power to use or act within that right, and on the other hand delimited a certain interest that should not be infringed. That is evident in the case of property: you may use the property as you see fit (without harming others), and the interest in the property may not be infringed upon. However, further analysis quickly makes clear that rights on their own cannot completely decide the issue. If rights have any meaningful content, the exercise of one right will occasionally clash with the interests protected by another right. The doctrines of abuse of right and defences are two ways in which further nuances are added to the concept of rights as a basis for determining wrongfulness.[37] Still, rights do represent interests that in principle deserve protection. As we will see in the following chapter, many specific torts can be conceived as ways to protect against infringement of certain rights, or the interests covered in such rights.

A subset of rights are so-called *fundamental rights*.[38] Fundamental rights are rights that protect certain important or fundamental interests of individuals against infringement by the

---

[36]   For instance, art. 483(1) of the Portuguese Código Civil. Similarly, in art. 6:162(2) Dutch Civil Code (Burgerlijk Wetboek), infringement of a right is one of three categories (besides breach of statutory duty and negligence).

[37]   See also the complicated discussion in § 4.2.

[38]   See further Ferreira 2011, Emaus 2013, Wright 2017, Gilleri 2021.

state. Fundamental rights are explicated in in national constitutions and international treaties. A well-known example of constitutional protection of fundamental rights is the US constitution. In France and Germany there are similar constitutional protections.[39]

An example of a treaty protecting fundamental rights is the European Convention on Human Rights (ECnHR, also called the Rome Treaty). The ECnHR lists several fundamental rights that aim at the protection of individual interests from infringement by the state. Examples are the right to family life (art. 8 ECnHR) and the right to life (art. 2 ECnHR). These rights primarily protect against infringements by the state. They therefore primarily give rise to state liability.

However, the European Court of Human Rights (ECtHR) that interprets the ECnHR has in standing case law upheld the principle that the State also has *positive obligations* to protect individuals against infringement of such rights by third parties. The state would, for example, be held to protect a citizen against a possible attempt of murder of a fellow citizen. The extent of such obligations is not settled, but it is clear that this makes the state liable for certain torts committed by third parties (jointly, besides the tortfeasor).

Furthermore, the ECtHR also holds the state responsible for court decisions in conflicts between private parties. In this way the ECtHR can in effect oblige national courts to find wrongful conduct in a specific case where the infringement of a protected right is at stake. A case in point is the decision in *Von Hannover v Germany*,[40] where the ECtHR held that the German courts applied an incorrect rule for deciding whether the press was allowed to print pictures taken from princess Caroline of Monaco in private situations. In effect this decision overrides the various national rules on this issue. Thereby the ECnHR influences national tort law.

There are other international fundamental rights instruments,[41] in particular the Universal Declaration of Human Rights and the International Covenant on Civil and Political Rights. However, these usually do not have the binding force of the ECnHR and lack effective enforcement mechanisms (in particular a supranational court). The African Charter on Human and Peoples' Rights and the American Convention on Human Rights[42] do have courts for their enforcement.

The effectiveness of these instruments may vary; individuals may be able to invoke the protection of national courts or fundamental rights courts (such as the ECtHR), but otherwise may be at the mercy of voluntary compliance by the state. As fundamental rights are usually formulated as involving certain interests that are to be respected by the state, such as family life, freedom of expression, property, there is a natural connection to tort law, which also arguably protects these interests. But precisely because of this overlap in aim, it seems super-

---

[39]   In France there are the *Constitution* and the *Déclaration des Droits de l'Homme et du Citoyen*, in Germany the *Grundgesetz* (basic law or constitution). These are principally interpreted and enforced by constitutional courts.

[40]   ECtHR 24 June 2004, case 59320/00 (*Von Hannover v Germany*). See later ECtHR 7 February 2012, cases 40660/08 and 60641/08 (*Von Hannover 2*) and ECHR 19 September 2013, case 8772/10 (*Von Hannover 3*).

[41]   Gilleri 2021 provides an analysis of various instruments.

[42]   Which is ratified by most countries in South America and Middle America, but not by the USA or Canada.

fluous to look at the fundamental rights dimension. The violation of a fundamental right will generally be considered wrongful simply because the right serves to protect an interest that is already protected by tort law.

Before discussing the influence of international instruments such as the ECnHR on national tort law, it should be pointed out that these are not the only instruments that protect fundamental rights in associated states: in Germany and France, particularly, the constitution also offers similar protection of fundamental rights. In England, principles such as *habeas corpus* serve a similar function in the absence of a written constitution, as does the Human Rights Act 1998 (discussed later in this section).

For German law, a direct violation of a fundamental right can be considered an injury of a protected interest in § 823 I BGB. Intentional violation of fundamental rights is considered wrongful on the basis of § 826 BGB, as being by definition a violation of public policy.[43]

In French law fundamental rights are principally approached through the French Constitution, which can be interpreted to offer at least the same protection as the ECnHR. Infringement of a fundamental right can thereby simply be classified as violation of a legal duty (*dévoir legal*), a species of the 'breach of statutory rule'. An exception applies to liability for violation of the right to privacy, which has obtained an independent basis with the introduction of art. 9 Cc (see § 7.5).

In English law, courts assess breach of fundamental rights by the state primarily on the basis of the Human Rights Act 1998.[44] § 8 HRA provides a ground for an award of damages, but this is limited to infringement by the state. The HRA does not provide a direct claim from one individual onto another, it is not a 'tort statute'.[45] There is not a specific or general tort of breach of fundamental rights or breach of the convention on human rights. Nonetheless courts do need to take into account whether a victim has obtained just satisfaction when there has been a breach of a right protected by the ECnHR. They may do so, if necessary, by lifting limitations to compensation for particular torts.[46]

In common law there is no specifically applicable tort. A fundamental right is not in itself a statute and hence there is no breach of a statutory duty, except if the right has been codified in some statute. Neither is there a tort of violation of fundamental right. However, several torts do cover interests that are protected by fundamental rights. We can point to trespass to the person which protects against infringement of the right to personal integrity.

Hence, we can usually rely on the system of tort law without having to explicitly acknowledge the fundamental rights aspect of the case. There are however reasons to devote a few more words to fundamental rights.

First of all, some fundamental rights are fairly new and their protection in tort law is therefore more explicitly linked to the fundamental right. This applies particularly to privacy (§ 7.5).

---

[43]   Deutsch and Ahrens 2014, para 324.

[44]   Wright 2017.

[45]   *R v Secretary of State of the Home Department* [2005] 1 UKHL 14.

[46]   See for example the discussion in Horsey and Rackley 2019, pp. 573–7.

Similarly, a fundamental right can bolster a claim in tort law if it is unclear whether the general tort law rules support a claim but there is clearly a violation of a fundamental right.

Secondly, violation of a fundamental right may help a court to obtain jurisdiction. A tort is as a rule litigated in the country where the tortious actions and the harm occurred, but in the case of violation of a fundamental right a court might be more likely to assume jurisdiction for torts that occurred abroad.[47] This is one reason why fundamental rights are often invoked when trying to litigate against multinational companies for infringements by subsidiaries. However, once the court has jurisdiction and the claim has to be decided under its national tort law, the claim will need to be qualified again as a delict or tort under the specific system. The fact that a fundamental right is at stake may influence the application of the tort, but is not always a tort in itself.

Thirdly, fundamental rights are important when the issue is state liability, also called liability of public authorities. The system of most conventions on fundamental rights is that the state is bound to observe these rights and is obliged to provide a remedy, which may consist of compensation paid by the state. In England the Human Rights Act 1998 contains specific rules for liability of public authorities when human rights have been violated (s. 8). This topic flows over into the general issue of state liability which is not discussed in this introduction (see briefly § 7.6). The finer details of compensation and satisfaction under the European Convention on Human Rights are outside the scope of the present text.

---

[47]   The reasons for this are found in Private International Law.

7
Categorizing fault (II): torts and protected interests

7.1   INTRODUCTION

In this chapter we will look at an alternative way to approach liability, by concentrating on specific areas within tort law. Many English torts do in essence carve up the entire field of tort law into specific domains that cover particular areas of social life or specific kinds of interests. Doctrinal literature in other countries uses a similar approach, as witnessed by books on business liability or personal torts.

The present chapter takes a middle road between the English specific torts and the protected interests of German law. The categories discussed here typically make connections between the kind of actions that are wrongful and the kind of protected interests. The resultant ordering has intuitive appeal. By going over the way in which three jurisdictions approach these groups of cases you will hopefully obtain a better understanding of the way in which lawyers in these jurisdictions actually analyse and structure tort cases. I will discuss how the three jurisdictions regulate issues in different ways, which explains why certain peculiarities of, for example, the English property-related torts do not directly apply in French and German law.

This chapter overlaps with materials discussed in other chapters: it explicates connections between the several elements of fault liability. The description may at first appear quite complicated because of those connections. You should approach this chapter primarily as a way to enhance your understanding from the previous chapters: it explains a bit of the background of torts we have already encountered.

7.2   PERSONAL INJURY

An important area of tort law is the torts that deal with personal injury. Personal injury here refers principally to bodily harm (including mental harm). Certain personal torts can protect immaterial interests, but these are primarily dealt with elsewhere, as being the subject of fundamental rights or involving wrongful statements, as in the tort of defamation.

7.2.1　The place of personal injury in the system of torts or delicts

English law covers personal injury as one kind of harm that may result from several specific torts. The primary category of personal torts in English law is the group of torts that comprise *trespass to the person*, in case the injury was caused intentionally. These are the torts of battery, assault, and false imprisonment. An important characteristic is that these torts do not require the presence of damage: they are actionable per se (§ 5.4.1). The claimant can start an action even where there is no discernible damage and may still obtain at least nominal damages. If there is damage, there is no foreseeability requirement.

In the context of the system introduced in Chapter 2 and the discussion on damage and damages in Chapters 10–11, this can be rephrased as follows: the definition of these torts implies the presence of harm in the sense of infringement of certain interests. Even if there is no identifiable loss, it can be argued that there is immaterial damage (as it is called in civil law systems) because of the mere infringement, which provides the basis for an award of immaterial damages. The end result is similar to what is achieved with nominal damages in common law. Civil law systems also tend to apply the condition of legal causality in a generous manner: even fairly remote damage is compensated in case of personal injury.

Personal injury can also be the result of negligence or the intentional infliction of injury. Negligence can of course be applied as well in case of intentional injury and indeed it often is, where it is uncertain whether the claimant will be able to prove the presence of intention.

In a system like French law, personal injury cases can be resolved, as always, under the general rule of art. 1240 Cc. The specific sub-categories of art. 1240 Cc can be applied fairly easily as well: first consider whether there is a statutory rule, as that would provide a clear presumption of wrongfulness, and alternatively examine whether the defendant's conduct can be considered negligent.

In German law you would primarily look at § 823 I BGB as the basis for a claim, since life, body and health are among the interests protected by that provision. Additionally, there is the category of *Verkehrspflichten* which also protects against personal injury.

Ultimately the combination of several grounds in the respective systems is usually sufficient for determining whether there is liability for personal injury. These grounds have been discussed previously and need not be investigated again. In each case, there is a strong interest to protect against personal injury, without, however, requiring the avoidance of all risks. The importance of personal injury torts as a separate category lies rather in the specifics regarding causality and damages, which differ from the operation of tort law in other areas. We will briefly look at a few of those details.

7.2.2　Personal injury consisting of mental harm

A specific category that does require consideration is the possibility of a claim for personal injury consisting of mental harm.[1] The Palsgraf case discussed in § 2.1 provides an early

---

[1]　Van Dam 2013, para 705.

example. The reason for treating mental harm as a particular category of personal injury is that mental harm is not as clear-cut as physical injury. While it is undesirable that every slight inconvenience could give rise to liability, it is also unfair if serious mental harm could not be compensated. The law in the three systems under consideration attempts to draw the line between the one and the other.

In English law the traditional heading was 'nervous shock', but nowadays lawyers prefer to speak of psychiatric injury or mental injury.[2] An action for negligence leading to mental injury requires proof that the claimant suffers a recognized psychiatric illness.[3] Mere mental distress is insufficient. A related problem is that there is intuitively a difference between the direct victim developing a mental illness, and others who are related to the primary victim or witnessed the accident developing an illness. It seems to make sense not to compensate the latter group, or to have a higher threshold for compensation. The law in this area is complicated.[4]

In French law mental harm is simply another kind of harm that may be occasioned by a fault. There is no threshold for compensation like a mental injury or a traumatic injury, compensation is simply found under the heading of immaterial damage (*préjudice extrapatrimoniaux*), in particular the subcategories of temporary functional disability (*deficit fonctionnel*) and moral suffering (*souffrances morales*).[5]

§ 823 I BGB lists health as one of the protected interests, and this includes mental health. Hence even in the absence of actual physical harm, mental harm can suffice as a ground for damages. Nonetheless, it is recognized that it may be difficult in practice to assess whether there is actual harm to mental health.[6] The BGH has in a consistent line of case law upheld that there must be a 'traumatic' injury, that consists of serious psychopathologic failure over a certain period, to count as infringement of health in the sense of § 823 I BGB.[7]

7.2.3   Problems of causality with personal injury

In cases of personal injury it is often hard to establish causality because of the uncertainty regarding the prior medical condition of the victim, and the medical outlook for recovery. Generally speaking, the fact that the victim is particularly prone to illness or serious consequences of relatively minor harm will not lead to a reduction of damages. As the English maxim holds, 'the tortfeasor must take the victim as he finds him'. This may seem unfair to the tortfeasor who may face significant higher damages than they would with an average victim,

---

[2]   Winfield and Jolowicz 2020, para 5-069.

[3]   Winfield and Jolowicz 2020, para 5-070.

[4]   See for instance the discussion in Winfield and Jolowicz 2020, paras 5-071 through 5-086.

[5]   See, for instance, the case Cass., 2, 23 March 2017, no 16-13350.

[6]   Deutsch and Ahrens 2014, para 243.

[7]   Wagner 2021, para 5.44, refering to BGH 11 May 1971, BGHZ 56, 163 and BGH 22 May 2007, BGHZ 172, 263 where the state of the law was paraphrased as: 'Durch ein Unfallgeschehen ausgelöste, traumatisch bedingte psychische Störungen von Krankheitswert können eine Verletzung des geschützten Rechtsguts Gesundheit im Sinne des § 823 Abs. 1 BGB darstellen'.

but from the viewpoint of the victim who did not choose to suffer an accident this principle is justified.

As a general note, courts appear to apply legal causality fairly liberally in cases of personal injury: even rather remote heads of damage may still be compensated.

7.2.4   Damage and damages for personal injury

As to the kinds of damage, these are typically medical costs, loss of income and costs for care and equipment to cope with disability. A peculiarity of many personal injury cases is that they involve recurring damage over a long period of time: a disability may lead to a loss of income over the span of several decades. To deal with this, courts can apply the doctrine of future damages (§ 11.1.4).

A victim may also claim damages for immaterial damage (non-pecuniary loss in English law). This is a complicated field, characterized by various intricate rules and categories particularly relevant to personal injury. A quick overview may suffice (see also § 11.1).

English law allows an award of damages for three categories of non-pecuniary loss:[8]

- Pain and suffering. Simply put, this means physical pain or discomfort, and the mental or emotional distress.
- Loss of amenity. This means the loss of enjoyment of life experienced after the injury. Typical examples are not being able to play sports or enjoy a prior hobby, due to the injuries.
- The injury itself.

The amounts that are paid out may differ greatly, one may see awards in the order of £1,000–10,000, but far lower sums are not uncommon.

In French law, similar categories apply for immaterial damage (*préjudice extrapatrimoniaux*):[9]

- Endured suffering (*souffrances endurées*)
- Temporary loss of quality of life and usual pleasures of life (*perte de qualité de vie et à celle des joies usuelles de la vie courante*)
- Temporary and/or permanent disfigurement (*prejudice esthétique*)
- Temporary and/or permanent functional disability (*deficit fonctionnel*)
- Permanent loss of amenity (*Le préjudice d'agrément*): being limited or unable to practice certain sports or hobbies[10]
- And other specific heads such as loss of ability to have sex, loss of opportunity to lead a normal family life or start a family.

---

[8]   Winfield and Jolowicz 2020, para 23-071 points out that the first two categories are usually lumped together, under the acronym PSLA.

[9]   Since 2005 the courts use a list of categories, the so-called *nomenclature Dintilhac*. Viney, Jourdain and Carval 2017, pp. 295–332, Le Tourneau 2020, paras 2125.101–2125.192.

[10]   Cass., 2, 28 May 2009, Bull.civ. II no. 131, Cass. civ 2, 29 March 2018, no 17-14499, Cass., 2, 10 October 2019, no 18-11791.

These categories could in other legal systems simply be recognized as specific instances of immaterial damage.

In German law, the court can award damages for pain and suffering (*Schmerzengeld*) on the basis of § 253 II BGB.[11] German law does not clearly distinguish each of the separate kinds of immaterial damage recognized in French and English law, presumably the courts simply take into account all circumstances to arrive at an amount that seems just, and thereby implicitly recognize the particular kinds of immaterial damage that were suffered.

7.2.5   Secondary victims

In case of personal injury there can also be third-party damage caused by the injury (also referred to as the issue of secondary victims, *victims par ricochet*, or ricochet damage). This may occur because a third party compensated the damage from the actual victim and would like to retrieve that compensation from the tortfeasor, because family members of the victim also suffer damage because of the disability or death of the victim, or because family members directly suffer immaterial damage because of the accident.

Many jurisdictions allow family members of victims who have been killed a claim on the tortfeasor, not only for loss of consortium (loss of the income that would have been generated by the spouse, partner or parent) but also for the immaterial damage (grief) caused by losing a beloved family member. This will be discussed under the heading of third party damages (§ 11.4).

Sometimes a caretaker such as a parent may also claim loss if the parent personally cares for an injured child and thereby loses income greater than the cost of hiring a professional caretaker.[12]

7.3   PROPERTY-RELATED TORTS

The category of torts related to property is important in practice.

7.3.1   Kinds of property

First of all we need to clarify the concept of property. Property relates primarily to tangible objects, goods such as land, houses, cars, apples, animals, clothing, furniture, computers. Such objects may serve human needs, may indeed be indispensable (in the case of food). Owning a good provides you with the right to *use* the object as you deem fit: to consume it, to keep it in a collection. You may enjoy the freedom of sitting on your own lawn, to sleep in your own bed. Property furthermore has value: it can be sold or leased, it can also be stored for future consumption or sale. The law protects the interests of the owner, and part of that protection is found in tort law. More abstractly, property rights can be conceived as a balance that the

---

[11]   See Geigel 2020, chapter 6 for a detailed overview of case law.

[12]   For instance Cass., 2, 14 April 2016, no 15-16697.

legislator achieved between the interests of individual citizens: the freedom to do what you want, versus the security of the owner that certain of their needs will be met in the future (and being secure in enjoyment).

The protection that tort law provides primarily deals with infringement of property rights, including damage to the property. Damage is not essential: the thief of your bicycle infringes your property right in your bicycle but does not damage it (indeed has an interest in not damaging it needlessly). Damage to property, such as breaking a smartphone, can, however, be conceived as infringement to property.

Property is in common law divided into real property and personal property. Real property means primarily land (including objects more or less permanently affixed to the land, such as houses, fences, trees). Personal property includes tangible objects that are not real property (such as cars, books, computers, jewellery: physical objects that you can touch), and also certain intangible objects (such as the copyright in a novel, software, bank accounts, licenses). Alternative terms are chattels versus choses in action: this division corresponds broadly to that between tangible and intangible property.[13]

In civil law systems lawyers speak of goods: you may own a good, the good is your property. The main division is between incorporeal and corporeal goods. Incorporeal goods correspond to intangible property in common law. Corporeal goods are divided into movables and immovables. Immovables correspond by and large to what common law calls real property. Movables are like tangible personal property.

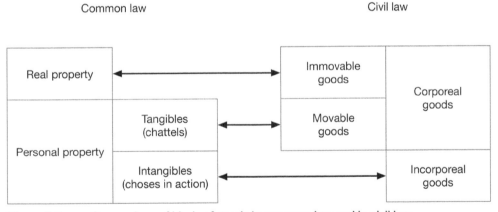

Figure 7.1   Comparison of kinds of goods in common law and in civil law

Here we can leave out discussion of intangible property. Infringement of intangible property is typically the province of distinct areas of law, in particular intellectual property law. Some

---

[13]   The terms chattels and choses in action are used in a slightly different context and may have additional elements; in the present introduction we can ignore these details. It is useful to know these terms as you may encounter them in case law and literature.

forms of intangibles can be protected by tort law, in particular by economic torts. An example is interference with a subsisting contract: the contract might – depending on the precise classification – be considered an incorporeal good or intangible. In this section we will focus, however, on corporeal goods: tangible personal property and real property.

7.3.2   Infringement of the good or the possession of the good

The first group of torts to investigate involve injury to property, property damage. The principal English torts in this group are trespass to land and trespass to goods. Trespass implies intentional, direct infringement of land or goods. Unintentional direct infringement to property must be litigated on the basis of negligence. Furthermore, there is the tort of conversion for cases of depriving someone from the possession of the property, without damaging the property itself.

Although trespass as a category of torts does have a certain unifying force, civil law systems typically see no reason to make a principled distinction between infringement of movables and immovables, or between intentional or negligent action. The primary basis in civil law is infringement of a right, which is considered wrongful. A property right is a right that can be infringed. In German law § 823 I BGB explicitly protects property (*Eigentum*) regardless whether the infringement is intentional or negligent. There is therefore liability in the case of having your cattle eat someone else's grass, letting someone's parrot escape, park your car on another's parking area.[14] The French art. 1240 Cc is considered to encompass infringement to a statutory right (including property right) as a specific category of fault, besides negligent conduct. Cases of conversion would in civil law be considered an infringement with property right, which gives right to compensation in the form of damages, provided that actual damage can be proven. If another remedy would be required, civil law systems would typically look outside of tort law.[15]

7.3.3   Nuisance

The other main category is infringement of property where no property damage has resulted. As the law aims to protect the interests of the owner, the law also needs to act against infringement of the enjoyment of property.[16] This differs from trespass and conversion in that the possession as such is not infringed. For instance, when sitting in your garden reading a book, your neighbour is having a party with loud music. Cases like this are covered by the tort of nuisance. As the example already suggests, not every nuisance is actionable: you are supposed to bear a certain amount of discomfort in life. The threshold may differ between jurisdictions and may depend on local circumstances. Frequently there are also administrative or environmental

---

[14]   Wagner 2021, para 5.51.

[15]   See § 7.3.4.

[16]   Incidentally, cases where someone walks over your land are formally trespass to land but also do not constitute damage.

rules that determine what is allowed. A lawyer might therefore, if applicable, prefer to litigate on the basis of breach of a statutory duty (or also public nuisance in England).

The actions that common law regards as private nuisance are in civil law systems either considered a form of wrongful conduct (fault), or covered under a different area of law called the neighbour law (*droit de voisinage, Nachbarrecht*) which is part of property law. Neighbour law may contain rules such as the right to an unhindered view. Some parts of neighbour law overlap with trespass to land in common law: rules on overhanging branches for example. This part of the law contains fairly detailed provisions that delimit the respective rights and duties between neighbours. Those rules go back to Roman law but have been modified to keep up with modern circumstances. A general norm is for instance found in German law:

---

§ 906 BGB
(1) Der Eigentümer eines Grundstücks kann die Zuführung von Gasen, Dämpfen, Gerüchen, Rauch, Ruß, Wärme, Geräusch, Erschütterungen und ähnliche von einem anderen Grundstück ausgehende Einwirkungen insoweit nicht verbieten, als die Einwirkung die Benutzung seines Grundstücks nicht oder nur unwesentlich beeinträchtigt. ...

§ 906 BGB
(1) The owner of a plot of land may not prohibit the entry of gas, fumes, smells, smoke, soot, warmth, noise, vibrations and similar influences emanating from another plot of land insofar as this influence does not or only insignificantly interfere with the use of his land. ...

If the interference of the enjoyment is significant, the owner can prohibit the interference on the basis of § 1004 BGB. The same provision provides a ground for damages if the interference happened in the past.

Public nuisance would in civil law typically be discussed under the equivalent of breach of statutory duty.

Finally, some forms of private nuisance might be discussed under the doctrine of *abuse of right*. If you cause nuisance without good reason, this is often considered wrongful in itself. Otherwise the nuisance must be proportionate to the aim: loud noises because of building activity have to be borne as this is unavoidable, but loud noises merely because you like to play music at high volume are not. In French law the erection of an ugly building just to annoy your neighbour could be wrongful as being an abuse of your property right.[17] In English law this would need to be considered under private nuisance, and incidentally would probably not be actionable as there is no right to a view, not even if blocking the view was malicious.[18]

---

[17]   As in the classic precedent of Colmar, 2 May 1855, DP 1856.2.9. See further Le Tourneau 2020, para 2213.42.

[18]   Winfield and Jolowicz 2020, paras 15-012 and 15-013.

7.3.4   Remedies

In civil law jurisdictions some of the issues of property-related torts are governed by property law. The reason for this difference is in the available remedies. In case of infringement of property you may need remedies other than damages. In case of trespass to land you may want the person to desist from further infringement, in case of infringement by building on your land (or less permanent, by leaving a broken car on your land) you may want the infringing object removed. If the infringement consists of stealing or otherwise disallowing you access to and control of your property (conversion in English law), you may wish to have an action to have your property returned to you.

Such remedies are in civil law considered part of property law, since they are different from the general remedies in tort law. In English law there is no systematic body of property law as a whole,[19] and cases like the aforementioned are actionable in tort law. Since the infringement may not involve actual damage, it is said that (some of) these torts are actionable per se, meaning that they can lead to an action even in the absence of damage.

Incidentally, if there is damage, there is ground for an award of damages. In English law this follows directly from the fact that it is a tort, in civil law the violation of a property right is generally considered wrongful. The difference is therefore not in whether the conduct is wrongful, but as to whether a specific action (remedy) is part of tort law or not.

In civil law systems the focus of tort liability regarding property is on damage caused to property or loss of enjoyment of the property. If the property is unharmed but is inaccessible, the primary ground of action is a property law action: revindication (retrieval, repossession) if the good is outside the control of the owner, removal of an object that is infringing on the land (such as a tree fallen on land or a shed built illegally on the land). Tort law may play a supplemental role in case the other party refuses to comply by the duty to remove a tree from land or return a stolen good: the owner may for example then remove the tree himself and claim the costs as damages based on infringement of his property right. From a common law viewpoint this approach may seem needlessly fragmented. An advantage, however, in placing certain remedies outside tort law is that civil law can do without the notion of 'actionable per se': the owner has a right to put a stop to an infringement in the absence of actual damage or harm, as property law actions do not require harm. Thereby it remains true that a delictual action in civil law always requires harm.

There are also self-help remedies for property-related torts.[20] For instance, for cases of nuisance there is the remedy of abatement in common law, whereby the person suffering nuisance by encroaching roots of a tree is allowed to cut off the roots on their own.[21] In civil

---

[19]   Textbooks focus mainly on land law or real property.

[20]   For English law see Clerk and Lindsell 2020, paras 29-06 through 29-33.

[21]   For example, Section 3502 of the California Civil Code: A person injured by a private nuisance may abate it by removing, or, if necessary, destroying the thing which constitutes the nuisance, without committing a breach of the peace, or doing unnecessary injury. Section 3503 makes clear that abatement may even allow the person to access his neighbour's land.

law this remedy is part of property law, in particular the duties of neighbours. See for instance in France:[22]

> *Art. 673 Cc*
> *Celui sur la propriété duquel avancent les branches des arbres, arbustes et arbrisseaux du voisin peut contraindre celui-ci à les couper. …*
> *Si ce sont les racines, ronces ou brindilles qui avancent sur son héritage, il a le droit de les couper lui-même à la limite de la ligne séparative. …*
>
> Art. 673 Cc
> He on whose property encroach branches of trees, bushes or shrubs of the neighbour can force his neighbour to cut those. …
> If there are roots, brambles or twigs that invade his land, he has the right to cut those himself up to the line separating the lands. …

7.4   WRONGFUL ECONOMIC CONDUCT

Economic torts are an important category in practice, as many court procedures are fought out between corporations that have the means and the incentive to litigate. In a market economy it is expected that businesses compete, which implies that they deliberately try to outdo each other. In doing so, they may harm the economic interests of others. It is not wrongful to operate your business efficiently and offering low prices to customers, even if this leads to a less efficient and therefore more expensive competitor losing customers and ultimately having to file for bankruptcy. Hence the economic interests of companies are not protected as a matter of course. A liberal economy could not function otherwise. This reasoning lies partly behind the German exclusion of pure economic loss from the scope of protection of § 823 I BGB.[23]

However, it is also recognized that there are limitations. Not all behaviour in the marketplace should be condoned, some restrictions are necessary to prohibit conduct contrary to good market practices and morality. The problem is how to set the limits. This, in a nutshell, is the problem of economic torts. We can reformulate the problem as one of finding a balance between the interest of businesses to pursue profit maximization, and the interest of fair play in the marketplace.

We have seen how English courts work with a collection of irregular torts. Civil law systems do not seem to offer a clearer system. The tendency in economic torts is to look at the means that are employed, as the effects of permissible competition and wrongful economic conduct are indistinguishable: causing bankruptcy or other kinds of loss. Furthermore, because of the

---

[22]   Similarly § 910 BGB. There is also a general right to perform an obligation yourself at the expense of the debtor, in art. 1222 Code civil.

[23]   Wagner 2021, para 5.6.

value of freedom in a market economy we tend to set a high threshold before considering behaviour to be unacceptable.

One solution is that we outsource the decision on what conduct is allowed on competitive markets: this is the area of competition law. In tort law we could simply refer to the rules of competition law. These tend to be laid down in specific statutes, and can have effect in tort law through the breach of a statutory duty. An example is German law: witness the prohibition on unfair commercial acts in § 3 UWG (*Gesetz gegen den Unlauteren Wettbewerb* (UWG), Unfair Competition Act)[24] and the prohibition of anti-competitive behaviour in § 33 III 1 GWB (*Gesetz gegen Wettbewerbsbeschränkungen*). However, competition law may not cover all kinds of unacceptable commercial behaviour. Furthermore, competition law is a relatively new field, and in the past tort law was used to achieve the aims of competition law, whereby there still is an interest in tort law as a supplementary mechanism to competition law.

7.4.1   Economic torts in comparative overview

The primary economic torts in English law are: interference with trade by unlawful means, interference with a subsisting contract, intimidation and conspiracy. We will not again go over these torts in detail, as they have been described at some length in § 5.7. Suffice to say that there is no general rule for economic torts. The House of Lords rejected the idea of a 'unified theory' of economic torts in *OBG v Allan*.[25] One commonality is that these are all intentional torts.

The civil law approach to wrongful commercial behaviour is not much clearer. In German law, several different grounds cover this area. § 823 I BGB protects the right to an established and operative enterprise as one of the 'other rights'. Violation of that right entitles the victim to recovery of pure economic loss, even though § 823 I BGB as a rule does not cover pure economic loss. Examples of such infringement are the case of a sports trainer who was excluded by the army from training soldiers (because the trainer used to be member of the East-German Stasi), sending out spam e-mails.[26] This ground requires a *direct* infringement to the enterprise itself, hence indirect infringements such as caused by lack of electricity are outside the scope of this provision.[27] This ground furthermore requires balancing the interests involved to see whether the court should really assume wrongfulness.[28]

More important is § 826 BGB, which covers many intentional actions that infringe economic interests of businesses. Among the kind of cases that have been litigated are cases of deceit (*Täuschung*), conspiracy (*Kollusion zum Nachteil Dritter*), falsely giving the appearance of creditworthiness (*Gläubigergefährdung*), disproportionate statements (*Unangemessene Äusserung*), deloyal behaviour (*Treuwidrigkeit*), enticing breach of contract (*Verleitung zum Vertragsbruch*), boycott (*Ungerechtfrertiger Ausschluss*), abuse of monopoly (*Missbrach einer*

---

[24]   Wagner 2021, para 5.10.

[25]   [2007] UKHL 21.

[26]   Wagner 2021, paras 7.58–7.62, referring to BGH 15 May 2012, VI ZR 117/11, BGHZ 193, 227, BGH 20 May 2009, I ZR 218/07.

[27]   Deutsch and Ahrens 2014, para 260, referring to the well-known cable case BGH 20 March 1967, BGHZ 29, 65.

[28]   Wagner 2021, para 7.60.

Monopolstellung).[29] As you can see, these cases overlap to a significant extent with the economic torts in English law.[30] Although there is formally a single ground in § 826 BGB, the variety under this provision is just as bewildering and diverse as the English economic torts. Note that this provision also requires intention on the part of the tortfeasor.

French treatises on tort law usually give only scant attention to economic delicts. This can be explained by the fact that this is considered to be the province of commercial law, for which there is a separate code (the *Code de commerce*) and concomitant doctrinal literature. Behaviour considered objectionable under English economic torts can be classified as unfair competition, which may be disallowed under abuse of a dominant economic position (art. 82(1) EU Treaty) and may amount to violation of a legal obligation[31] and therefore is a *faute*. But art. 1240 Cc can also on its own provide a ground for holding businesses liable. In the extensive treatment of Le Tourneau, wrongful commercial conduct is discussed mainly under the general category of abuse of right, in particular the category of 'concurrence déloyale' (unfair competition).[32] Examples are:[33] obtaining trade secrets (nowadays covered in intellectual property law), providing facilities to employees of a competitor on strike, to use unfair means to induce the personnel of a competitor to leave, to knowingly participate in violation of an exclusivity clause binding a contractual party to a third party. These actions bear a certain similarity to the English economic torts, even though there may be differences in detail and extent. Furthermore, these cases also seem to imply the presence of intention (as shown for instance by 'knowingly'). Abuse of right typically requires intention as well.

In summary, the field of economic torts in the three jurisdictions covered here is not very clear. In English law you would have to consider whether a specific case satisfies the conditions of one of the economic torts. In German and French law, you could formally find refuge in § 823 I or 826 BGB or art. 1240 Cc, but would then be left with the task to research doctrine and case law to determine whether your case is sufficiently close to a recognized category of wrongful conduct under one of those provisions. A common thread is the requirement of intention in most cases.

7.4.2   Torts against consumers

Besides behaviour that is wrongful to competitors, there is also commercial conduct that harms consumers. Such torts are not covered under economic torts in common law. In the EU there is principally the Unfair Commercial Practices Directive 2005/29/EC.

---

[29]   Deutsch and Ahrens 2014, paras 310–325b.

[30]   Markesinis, Bell and Janssen 2019, pp. 82–6 compares the German case law with the English economic torts.

[31]   In particular art. L 420-1 Code de commerce and further.

[32]   Le Tourneau 2020, chapter 2214. At para 2214.24 the doctrine of *concurrence déloyale* is based (with reservations) on the doctrine of abuse of right.

[33]   Le Tourneau 2020, para 2214.61.

> art. 5: Unfair Commercial Practices Directive 2005/29/EC
> 1.   Unfair commercial practices shall be prohibited.
> 2.   A commercial practice shall be unfair if:
> (a) it is contrary to the requirements of professional diligence, and
> (b) it materially distorts or is likely to materially distort the economic behaviour
> with regard to the product of the average consumer whom it reaches or to whom it is
> addressed, or of the average member of the group when a commercial practice is directed
> to a particular group of consumers.
> …
>
> 4.   In particular, commercial practices shall be unfair which:
> (a) are misleading as set out in Articles 6 and 7, or
> (b) are aggressive as set out in Articles 8 and 9.

This Directive has been implemented in specific acts: in Germany in § 3 UWG (Gesetz gegen den Unlauteren Wettbewerb (UWG), Unfair Competition Act),[34] in France in the Code de la Consommation,[35] in England in the Consumer Protection from Unfair Trading Regulations 2008.

Outside the European Union there is a large variety of approaches to protect consumers. Quite often there are specific regulations for competition law and consumer protection, but these rules may also partly be found in a general civil code, or developed in case law. Finally, the protection of consumers may be in the hands of specific agencies such as the Federal Trade Commission in the US.

7.4.3   Other wrongful conduct among businesses

To close our overview, we can point out that there may be more specialized rules in statutes that also provide remedies for rather specific wrongful actions. An example is the *actio pauliana*, what in common law is also known as fraudulent conveyance: deliberately assigning assets from a debtor to another party, whereby they are outside of reach to the creditors of the debtor.[36] Fascinating as this topic is, the area of economic torts is a specialized field and you would be wise to consult an expert or conduct a thorough investigation if you wish to ensure that you covered every conceivable ground for action in a specific case.

What you can take away from this discussion is that the economic torts are a mixed bag. In civil law countries this is for a large part covered by competition law, but may also be covered

---

[34]   Wagner 2021, para 5.10.

[35]   Art. L121-1 (*pratiques commerciales déloyales*).

[36]   In the UK this was already prohibited by the 1571 Fraudulent Conveyances Act. Nowadays the Insolvency Act 1986, part XVI (arts. 423–5) prohibits defrauding creditors.

under more general grounds of liability. The above overview gives a flavour of the kind of commercial conduct that is not condoned.

7.5   INFORMATION-RELATED TORTS

The torts that base wrongfulness on the dissemination of information do not form a systematic whole. Due to the complicated picture that arises, it is impossible to give a complete overview that holds for every legal system. Instead, we will discuss the approach in several jurisdictions, pointing out some relevant considerations and concepts, and a few generally recognized torts. That should help you to find your way in the variety of systems you may encounter.

First of all, we may consider what information involves. Here we can simply say that information may be any form of expression or communication that is meaningful to others (the public). The technical term 'data' may also be used when it refers to information sent and received by computers. On the Internet the term 'content' is used to refer to information on platforms and websites.

Theoretically it is possible that incorrect information causes physical injury or property damage. An example is a radiation robot that is supplied with incorrect information about the level of radiation for the treatment of a patient suffering from cancer. Such cases do occur but are relatively rare. Liability is attributed primarily to the person who operated such a device and should have checked the information. Such cases are often brought under professional liability, which in civil law is primarily an issue of breach of contract, not tort law.

Information typically only causes pure economic loss or infringement of intangible interests such as privacy. Many tort law systems are hesitant in offering protection against such harms. This approach is further justified because prohibitions on spreading information may well lead to a restriction of fundamental rights, in particular the right of freedom of expression.[37] This right encompasses the right to disseminate (and receive) opinions and information, which is considered fundamental to the functioning of a well-ordered democracy and to the growth of scientific knowledge. Furthermore, in the distant past it may have been more difficult to spread information due to the absence of mass-media. Consequentially information-related torts are fairly new, with the exception of defamation.

To further delimit the current topic, we can leave out IP rights such as copyright and trademarks. IP rights are a form of intangible property: the infringement of such rights leads to liability. As IP law is a specialized subject, regulated in particular statutes and treaties, it is outside the scope of the present introduction.

This leaves us with two distinct groups: privacy, and defamation and similar torts. In addition a brief note on the liability of ISPs is in order. And to start off, the 'personality right' of German law must be discussed separately, as it is a distinct approach to this area which is sufficiently important to discuss in an integrated manner.

The discussion of privacy and defamation is intended only to give an impression of how the main information-related torts are regulated in France and Germany. It is impossible to

---

[37]   As protected by art. 10 ECnHR and the First Amendment to the US Constitution.

give a complete overview of information-related torts across the world in a few pages. As an example, we may consider the tort of 'false light' which is accepted in some US states but not in others and is considered a kind of infringement of privacy by maliciously putting someone in a false light that would be highly offensive (as for instance by a fictional account).[38] This tort bears some similarity to the German notion of a personality right under § 823 I BGB,[39] although that does not require malice.

7.5.1   The German general personality right

One of the 'other rights' of § 823 I BGB is the general personality right (*allgemeine Persönlichtkeitsrecht*).[40] Introduced with the *Schacht*-judgment,[41] this right has found wide application in a large variety of cases. These include distortion of public image (similar to 'false light'), infringement of privacy, what is called the right to informational self-determination[42] (controlling the use of your personal data, nowadays also under the European General Data Protection Regulation), appropriation of commercial personality attributes (using someone's likeness or name for commercials). Some categories are also protected by other provisions, such as defamation or the exclusive right to your portrait. Hence this serves as catch-all category for cases that elsewhere tend to be distributed over separate grounds.

7.5.2   Violation of privacy

Violation of privacy is generally considered violation of a fundamental right which leads to different forms of protection than with normal interests; I will only discuss this very briefly as it is a specialized topic. English law does not recognize a tort of violation of privacy, but there is the related action for misuse of private information, while other torts also protect against some of the conduct that violates privacy (§ 5.8). In German law, violation of privacy can lead to liability in tort law.[43] In French law, art. 9 Code civil states that everyone has the right to have his private life respected. That provision furthermore lists several remedies that courts can award to protect this right. This article provides a solid basis for liability for infringement of privacy.[44] In the European Union the right to privacy is further regulated by the General Data Protection Regulation 2016/679.

---

[38]   Le Morvan 2018. Goldberg and Zipursky 2010, pp. 331–41, provide an overview of privacy torts in US law.

[39]   Wagner 2021, para 7.29.

[40]   Markesinis, Bell and Janssen 2019, pp. 43–9, Geigel 2020, Chapter 23, Wagner 2021, paras 7.5–7.52.

[41]   BGH 15 May 1954, BGHZ 13, 334, about the lawyer of a former Nazi who in his capacity as lawyer complained to a journal of a publication about his client. The journal printed the letter in modified form whereby it appeared as if the lawyer had written the letter as a personal opinion, suggesting sympathy with the Nazi cause. This conduct was found wrongful on the part of the journal for violation of the personality right of the lawyer.

[42]   Bundesverfassungsgericht 15 December 1983, Case 1 BvR 209/83 et al. (Volkszählungsurteil).

[43]   It does lead to an action in tort, see Wagner 2021, paras 7.31–7.32. It can also be considered a violation of the personality right (§ 823 I BGB), see Deutsch and Ahrens 2014, para 269.

[44]   See further Le Tourneau 2020, nr. 2125.250–374.

7.5.3 Defamation and related torts

We may now consider the way in which various jurisdictions treat the liability for wrongful information that injures commercial or personal interests.

In common law, more particular in English law, the economic torts cover various ways in which information may harm commercial interests. The torts of passing off and malicious falsehood in particular protect against wrongful information. Passing off involves a trader passing off (misrepresenting) his goods or services as those of associated with another trader, thereby profiting from the other's goodwill. Malicious falsehood involves publication of a false statement with 'malice', causing damage to claimant.

Besides these torts there is the tort of defamation, which applies to businesses as well as to persons. Defamation means publication of a statement that has caused or is likely to cause serious harm to the reputation of the claimant.[45] While originally a common law tort, it is frequently modified extensively by statute. In England there is the Defamation Act 2013, in many other common law jurisdictions there similarly are specific Defamation Acts. The details of these acts may differ significantly in the kind of exceptions allowed, the remedies and so on. In English law, defamation primarily applies to false factual statements, as the truth of a statement is a defence (s. 2 Defamation Act 2013). Opinions can be actionable, but s. 3 Defamation Act 2013 allows the defence of honest opinion, which would stand in the way of most actions (including actions against insulting opinions).

In France, wrongful behaviour involving information causing harm can lead to liability on the basis of general fault-based liability or on the basis of contractual liability for professional services. In particular three categories of infringement are recognized:

Denigrating expressions (*Le dénigrement*), which are actionable as a fault on the basis of art. 1240 Cc. This can be defined as publicly discrediting the products, enterprise or personality of a competitor for gain.[46] More briefly it may be defined as divulging information which discredits a competitor.[47] It is viewed as a form of unfair competition.

Injurious expressions (*L'injure*) are prohibited in art. 29(2) of the Law of 29 July 1881 on freedom of the press.[48] This amounts to strong abusive words.

Defamation (*La diffamation*). This is prohibited in art. 29(1) of the Law of 29 July 1881 on freedom of the press. One relevant defence is the truth of the allegation (art. 35 Law 29 July 1881).

---

[45]   See s. 1(1) Defamation Act 2013.

[46]   '[J]eter publiquement le discrédit sur les produits, l'entreprise ou la personnalité d'un concurrent pour en tirer un profit.'

[47]   Cass. (com.), 24 September 2013, no 12-19.790: 'la divulgation d'une information de nature à jeter le discrédit sur un concurrent constitue un dénigrement'.

[48]   Arts. 30 and 31 of this law regulate specific forms of defamation, against state organs and the President. Art. 32 regulates discriminatory expressions. Art. 34 sanctions defamation against the memory of the deceased.

> *Art. 29 loi du 29 juillet 1881 sur la liberté de la presse*
> *Toute allégation ou imputation d'un fait qui porte atteinte à l'honneur ou à la considéra-*
> *tion de la personne ou du corps auquel le fait est imputé est une diffamation. La publication*
> *directe ou par voie de reproduction de cette allégation ou de cette imputation est punissable,*
> *même si elle est faite sous forme dubitative ou si elle vise une personne ou un corps non*
> *expressément nommés, mais dont l'identification est rendue possible par les termes des*
> *discours, cris, menaces, écrits ou imprimés, placards ou affiches incriminés.*
> *Toute expression outrageante, termes de mépris ou invective qui ne renferme l'imputation*
> *d'aucun fait est une injure.*
>
> Art. 29 of the Law of 29 July 1881 on the freedom of the press
> Allegations or imputations of a fact that violate the honour or the esteem of a person or
> a corporate body to which the fact is imputed constitute defamation. The direct publica-
> tion or the reproduction of such an allegation or imputation is punishable, even if it is
> expressed in a way that leaves room for doubt or if it refers to a person or corporate body
> not expressly named, but of which the identification is possible by the terms of the lecture,
> cries, menaces, writings or prints, placards or incriminating posters.
> All outrageous expressions, contemptuous terms or invective hat do not contain the
> imputation of any fact are injurious.

The latter two injuries can be litigated on the basis of the Law of 1881, but it appears also possible to base a claim on art. 1240 Cc.[49] You should take note of this approach, as a similar approach may be found in other jurisdictions: the limitations of freedom of expression (and therefore liability for defamation or other information) may be found in specific statutes relating to freedom of the press. You may therefore need to research that area of the law to obtain a complete overview.

In Germany, information that infringes business or personal interests is typically treated under several headings.

There is only a single codified tort, § 824 BGB, about endangering credit. Further protection is given under the umbrella of the kind of interest that is harmed.

For businesses, the publication of information that harms the business may be an economic tort, which can be protected under § 826 BGB (which protects against pure economic loss of conduct violating public policy, which is applied in particular to unacceptable commercial conduct). In some instances, true statements may lead to liability on this basis.[50] Furthermore, the right to an established and operative enterprise is protected as 'another right' in § 823

---

[49]   Cass. (civ.), 1, 2 July 2014, no 13-16730 suggest the Law of 1881 is exclusive, but later case law shows that a claim on the basis of art. 1240 Cc is still allowed (Le Tourneau 2020, para 2212.21).

[50]   Deutsch and Ahrens 2014, para 315 mention cases where a true fact is published without sufficient reason, because the general reaction is expected to be disproportionate. An example is as a butcher informing the press that the son of a competitor suffers from hoof-and-mouth disease. See also Wagner 2021, paras 7.71–7.81 on wrongful criticism.

I BGB. Thereby a business can for example find protection against true statements taken out of context.[51] Also a business may invoke the general personality right (see above for persons).[52] Finally, and possibly most importantly, statutory protection may lead to tort liability (§ 823 II BGB). The relevant provisions can be found in the German Criminal Code (*Strafgesetzbuch*). § 185 StGB prohibits insult (*Beleidigung*) on punishment of a fine or incarceration. § 186 StGB prohibits malicious gossip (*üble Nachrede*), defined as stating or disseminating a fact about another that is suitable for making that person despicable or lower his public esteem.[53] That implies that the fact is true. § 187 StGB punishes defamation.

German Criminal Code (*Strafgesetzbuch*)

§ 187 Verleumdung
Wer wider besseres Wissen in Beziehung auf einen anderen eine unwahre Tatsache behauptet oder verbreitet, welche denselben verächtlich zu machen oder in der öffentlichen Meinung herabzuwürdigen oder dessen Kredit zu gefährden geeignet ist, wird mit Freiheitsstrafe bis zu zwei Jahren oder mit Geldstrafe und, wenn die Tat öffentlich, in einer Versammlung oder durch Verbreiten von Schriften (§ 11 Abs. 3) begangen ist, mit Freiheitsstrafe bis zu fünf Jahren oder mit Geldstrafe bestraft.

§ 187 Defamation
Whoever against better judgement states or disseminates an untrue fact about another person which is suitable for making that person despicable or lowering his public esteem or endangering his creditworthiness, will be punished with imprisonment for up to two years or a fine, and, if the act was committed publicly, in a meeting or by disseminating of publications (§ 11 (3)), with of imprisonment up to five years or a fine.

As you can see, defamation is hereby also recognized as a ground of liability. § 187 Strafgesetzbuch shows that the truth of the statement is a defence.

For individual persons, the publication of wrongful information is protected both under the personality right as another right in § 823 I BGB,[54] and again through breach of a statutory duty (§ 823 II BGB in conjunction with the aforementioned provisions of the German Criminal Code). It should be mentioned that on occasion the publication of a true statement may also be wrongful as infringing the personality right, for instance when it concerns a crime committed years ago for which the person had served a prison sentence.[55]

Defamation is also generally recognized in civil law jurisdictions in a broadly similar way, but the actual way in which it is categorized differs substantially, as we have seen for France

---

[51]   Deutsch and Ahrens 2014, para 261, referring to BGHZ 8, 142.

[52]   Standing case law, confirmed in BGH 4 April 2017, VI ZR 123/16.

[53]   'Wer in Beziehung auf einen anderen eine Tatsache behauptet oder verbreitet, welche denselben verächtlich zu machen oder in der öffentlichen Meinung herabzuwürdigen geeignet ist …'.

[54]   On which Deutsch and Ahrens 2014, para 264, Wagner 2021, paras 7.5–7.56.

[55]   Bundesverfassungsgericht 5 June 1973, BverfGE 35, 202, discussed in Wagner 2021, para 7.23.

(specific statute) and Germany (through the protection of the relevant interests and by specific statutes). English law is more restrictive in that opinions, even insulting opinions, are only rarely actionable, while under French and German law strong insults may lead to liability. Some civil law jurisdictions do have a specific rule against defamation in the provisions on torts.[56]

A particular problem with defamation, and also with violation of privacy, is that it may be difficult to assess damages. The damage may be immaterial in kind, although damage to commercial reputation may be material and significant. Defamation is noteworthy as it may lead to specific remedies, in particular the remedy of retraction[57] and an injunction against publication.

7.5.4   ISP liability

Finally, at this place we can point out the relevance of the doctrine of the liability of internet service providers (ISP-liability). Internet Service Providers (including platforms such as YouTube, TikTok and Facebook) would be quickly liable on the basis of general tort law for hosting infringing content. This was found undesirable, and as a consequence it was decided to establish rules that would remove liability of ISPs if they did not know (or need not know) about the infringing content, as long as the ISP removes the information once it has been informed about it (notice and take down). In the EU these rules are based on the E-commerce Directive 2000/31.[58] Elsewhere there are specific rules.[59] Thereby the liability for information is restricted for a specific category of parties that aid in the dissemination of information.

7.6   MISCELLANEOUS TORTS AND DELICTS

Finally, there are a number of torts that do not fit into one of the earlier categories. I will briefly go over these and explain how they are treated in French and German law.

7.6.1   Malicious prosecution

First of all, malicious prosecution. This tort involves instigating or causing a court case (or a criminal prosecution) intentionally, knowing that the case is entirely unfounded. Using other instruments of civil procedure knowing that there is no foundation for doing so may also be brought under this tort.

In Germany liability for abuse of legal proceedings is not based on § 823 I BGB (as there is no definite protected interest involved), rather on § 826 BGB as requiring an intentional

---

[56]   See for instance Ecuador (Art. 2231 Codigó Civil).

[57]   Also called 'rectification', see for instance art. 6:167(1) Burgerlijk Wetboek (Dutch Civil Code).

[58]   For England see also art. 5 Defamation Act 2013.

[59]   Such as in China, art. 36 Tort Liability Law (2010), in India, s. 79 Information Technology Act, 2000. In the USA there are in particular the Digital Millennium Copyright Act, Title II, and the Common Decency Act, s. 230.

wrongful action. While litigation and enforcement of judicial decisions in itself is not wrongful (following from the fundamental right of access to court, art. 6 ECnHR), there may be liability in specific circumstances.[60]

In French law the related doctrine is *abus des droits processuels*.[61] This is a sub-category of *abus de droit* (abuse of right) which is a category of fault in the meaning of art. 1240 Cc.

7.6.2   State liability

The description of German and French law regarding abuse of procedure does miss one important element: the possibility that the state is liable, in particular where criminal prosecution is concerned. In English law such forms of state liability are as a matter of course treated under tort law. In Germany and France, state liability is a separate topic that is partly outside private law.[62] For that reason we will not discuss this any further.

The tort of misfeasance in public office is also partly covered by state liability in civil law systems. The civil servant who is guilty of abuse may also be personally liable, see for German law § 839 BGB. However, in most instances liability would actually be covered by the German State on the basis of art. 34 Grundgesetz (German Constitution).[63]

7.7   CONCLUSION

Our overview has shown many additional details to the outlines of Chapters 3–5. The landscape of torts is varied and not easily captured by general principles if we wish to remain cognizant of the actual details. By the description in this and the previous chapter you have hopefully obtained a better understanding of this area of the law. It should also have become clear that the differences between civil law and common law are not as extreme as sometimes presented. If you examine the entire field in sufficient detail, all systems operate with a mix of statute law and case law, and thereby try to cover the whole of the area with distinct categories and subcategories. To reconstruct the state of the law you will need to research case law and doctrine extensively to flesh out the bare outlines provided by the provisions of statute law.

As regards the balance sought between the different interests involved, you may have noticed that this is not at the foreground of the discussion. This can be explained by the concentration on rights, which assumedly tip the balance towards protection of the right against infringement. The balance is mainly found in the frequent recourse to the idea of abuse of right (or the English concepts of malice and intention), whereby disproportionate harm from the use of a right is prohibited. This is especially noticeable in the case of economic torts where there is usually no clear infringement of a right. At the other side there is the discussion of

---

[60]   See the extensive discussion of case law in Bamberger Kommentar 2019 § 826 (Förster), paras 189–219. Also Wagner 2021, para 7.67.

[61]   Le Tourneau 2020, paras 2213.150–2213.170.

[62]   The outlines are discussed in Van Dam 2013, chapter 18.

[63]   Deutsch and Ahrens 2014, paras 477–98, mentioning exceptions at 495.

information-related torts, where there are two fundamental rights at stake that have to be balanced: freedom of expression, and the right to family life (including privacy).

8
Subjective fault: accountability and intentionality

8.1   INTRODUCTION

The discussion of tort law up to now presumed a tortfeasor who acted deliberately with the knowledge of a mature, responsible person: the standard of the reasonable person. In real life, individuals have varying mental capabilities. These varieties occasionally warrant differentiated legal treatment. This is captured by the notion of subjective fault. Did the tortfeasor actually want to risk injuring the victim?

This question has two aspects. Firstly, in some cases there is reason to doubt whether the tortfeasor should really be held responsible for the conduct, even though the conduct objectively was wrongful. This is the issue of accountability (§§ 8.2 and 8.3). Secondly, for the assessment of liability it is in some instances relevant whether the tortfeasor really wanted the injury to occur, or merely happened to be careless towards the interests of the victim. This is the issue of the degree of intentionality (§ 8.4).

8.2   ACCOUNTABILITY AND TEMPORARY INCAPACITY

When assessing individual conduct, we presume that the conduct was conscious, even if it was negligent and the harmful consequences were not intended. A clumsy person who drops a mirror is still held accountable for his carelessness. This is the consequence of applying the objective standard of the reasonable person. Nonetheless there are situations where one may doubt the fairness of holding someone accountable for certain actions.

The question is not whether the person was capable of sound judgement at the time, rather it is whether he is accountable for his actions. For instance, if someone commits a tort when seriously inebriated, he is held accountable even though a drunk person may not be able to fully oversee the consequences of his actions. The justification for doing so is that presumably it was the tortfeasor's own choice to get drunk. This presumption is explicated in many codes.[1]

---

[1]   For instance, in § 827 BGB (making an exception if he did not cause that state, for instance when being drugged by someone else), also in art. 2318 Chilean Código civil and other codes in South and Central America.

For persons whose judgement has become impaired due to temporary mental disability, tort law generally tends to cling to an objective standard. In France, as is clear from the treatment of children (§ 8.3), the law without exception applies an objective standard. In English law the torts of defamation and battery are defined without reference to the insight of the defendant in the consequences of his actions. For the tort of negligence, similarly, the reasonable person standard is applied without restriction. An example is the case *Dunnage v Randall*[2] where a schizophrenic not only set himself on fire but also his nephew, when he tried to stop his uncle. The nephew suffered severe burn wounds and sued the estate of his uncle (who had died). The insurance company of his uncle and aunt was found liable, as the actions of the uncle were voluntary even if under the influence of a disturbed mind. In Germany, in contrast, temporary disability may remove liability for the tortfeasor (§ 827 BGB).

But what about a person who becomes almost completely mentally incapacitated, and in that state causes an accident? The English case *Roberts v Ramsbottom*[3] involved a case where the driver suffered a minor stroke before entering his car, which caused him to drive extremely negligently and causing several accidents. The court held that if the driver had completely lost control, he would not have been liable, but as he still had some control over his actions, he was fully liable to the standard of the reasonable person.[4] In Germany, being unconscious leads to a lack of accountability if that state occurred without any fault of the tortfeasor. See § 827 BGB, quoted in § 4.7.

8.3   ACCOUNTABILITY AND CAPACITY IN GENERAL

Certain persons are treated as a special category because their accountability is generally in question, not merely temporarily. These are typically minors and mentally disabled adults. For those groups the law frequently has special rules, whereby the requirement of subjective fault becomes explicit.

In English law there is no dispensation for persons of unsound mind. In § 8.2 we saw that the law holds on to an objective standard. For children, however, an exception is made. Although age is not an absolute defence, the age of a child is taken into account in the assessment of negligence: the standard of behaviour is that of an ordinarily prudent and reasonable child of the relevant age.[5]

In Germany there is a rather complicated rule in § 828 BGB that restricts the liability of children by distinguishing between 0–6, 7–9 and 10–18 years (§ 4.8). For persons of unsound mind § 827 BGB may apply. Incidentally, § 829 BGB allows the court to hold a minor or person of unsound mind liable despite §§ 827 and 828 BGB, if this is fair and just in the circumstances

---

[2]   [2015] EWCA Civ 673.

[3]   [1980] 1 All ER 7.

[4]   See further Clerk and Lindsell 2020, paras 5-63 through 5-64, 7-168, Winfield and Jolowicz 2020, para 6-011.

[5]   *Mullin v Richards* [1998] 1 All ER 920 about two girls, aged 15, fencing with plastic rulers, where one ruler shattered and a splinter injured the eye of one of the girls. See further Winfield and Jolowicz 2020, para 6-009.

of the case (the *Subsidiäre Billigkeitshaftung*).[6] This applies only in cases where there is no contributory negligence on the part of the victim.[7]

In French law the courts have over time moved to an objective requirement of fault of the child, which appears to be influenced by a desire to give wide application to the strict liability of the parent. However, we need to distinguish here between the liability of the child and that of the parents. In case of liability of the child, the rule is as described in § 3.5: an objective standard is applied for wrongfulness. In case of liability of the parents, there is an even broader rule: it is not necessary that the child acted wrongfully according to an objective standard. It suffices that there is a 'fait du mineur' (act of the minor), a 'faute' of the minor is not necessary (§ 14.4). Persons of unsound mind are held liable regardless of their mental disability, based on art. 414-3 Cc (§ 3.5).

Note that the restrictions on liability of minors and persons of unsound mind are usually compensated by simultaneously holding the parents, wardens or other supervisors strictly liable (§ 14.4).

A related question is whether the specific rules regarding negligence by children and persons of unsound mind are also applied when it comes to *contributory negligence*. That is indeed the case for the three systems discussed here. English law extends the approach of negligence to contributory negligence: the standard of the reasonable child.[8] An example is a 13-year-old child crossing a road from behind a school bus on a rural road, and being hit by a car going 50 miles per hour.[9] German law applies §§ 827 and 828 BGB also to contributory negligence,[10] hence persons of unsound mind and children that meet the conditions of those provisions may be excused from contributory negligence. French law applies an objective standard to the contributory negligence of children (§ 3.5), which has been criticized.[11] Courts do attempt to restrict the harsh consequences by factually finding that the contribution of the child was limited, and in the proposed reform of French tort law this rule is to be abolished.[12]

8.4 DEGREES OF CULPABILITY: NEGLIGENCE, INTENTION, MALICE

There is another aspect of subjective fault besides accountability. The mental attitude of the tortfeasor towards the wrongful act, the motive, may be relevant for certain torts as an additional requirement for liability. In moral terms this is culpability, a term that is still in use

---

[6]   Deutsch and Ahrens 2014 paras 175–9.

[7]   Wagner 2021, para 6.64.

[8]   Clerk and Lindsell 2020, para 7-170, Winfield and Jolowicz 2020, para 23-048.

[9]   *Jackson v Murray* [2015] UKSC 5. The Court of Appeal had set the child's contributory negligence at 90 per cent, this was reduced by the Supreme Court to 50 per cent.

[10]   BGH 28 May 1957, BGHZ 24, 325, Wagner 2021, para 6.57.

[11]   It is as yet unknown whether an objective standard also applies to persons of unsound mind, although that seems likely given art. 414-3 Cc and the case law regarding children.

[12]   Fabre-Magnan 2021, p. 110.

in civil law systems. In common law the general notion is usually called intention,[13] which is somewhat confusing as intention also is used to denote a specific kind of intentionality. Lawyers typically distinguish between three attitudes that the tortfeasor may have had towards his conduct.

The tortfeasor may have been *negligent*. In essence this means that he did not want the harm to occur, indeed if he had known that his action would result in injury, he probably would have refrained from it or would have attempted to be more careful. For example, the driver of a car is briefly distracted by the sound of an incoming app message, takes his eyes off the road, and causes an accident when he swerves into the opposing lane. The act of driving was conscious and deliberate, and he did consciously look away from the road, but he would have paid more attention if he would have realized the consequences. His mental state was therefore simply one of 'negligence'. Note that we are here talking about negligence as a qualifier of behaviour, not 'negligence' as the tort.

The next degree of culpability is that the tortfeasor was guilty of an intentionally wrongful act.[14] You have to be careful: this is not the same as saying that his action was intentional. A negligent act is usually intentional, but the harm was unintended. If you playfully throw a ball at a friend but accidentally hit his head and cause a broken nose, you may be negligent but presumably did not intend any negative consequence. That is different if you throw the ball to someone you hate in order to cause injury. 'A person intends to bring about a given consequence if it is his goal to cause it.'[15] It is not necessary that the tortfeasor intended the exact result that materialized, it suffices if he intended a similar consequence, even if less severe. An example is the case of *Wilkinson v Downton*[16] where the court held that the prankster intentionally caused injury: the intention was inferred from the facts of the case which clearly showed intent to cause at least some distress even if it was not to the extent that actually emerged. This case also shows that courts can infer the state of mind of the tortfeasor simply from his conduct, foregoing an actual psychological examination.

Intention also encompasses cases of *recklessness*.[17] Civil law systems usually refer to recklessness under the name of *gross negligence* which is negligence short of actual intention, and is treated the same as actual intention. An example would be setting off fireworks in the midst of a crowded area: even in the absence of actual intention to harm bystanders, we can surely agree that such an act shows a clear disregard of safety which is grossly negligent (or in common law terms, reckless). Recklessness or gross negligence allow us to treat cases like intention even where it is doubtful whether the consequence was actually intended. For instance, if a bystander suffers a heart attack during and because of a bank robbery, one can hardly maintain that the robber intended this consequence, but one could argue that robbery does lead to fear and stress that contributes to a risk of a heart attack.

---

[13]   In criminal law the Latin phrase *mens rea* is also used.

[14]   See further Liew 2015.

[15]   Winfield and Jolowicz 2020, para 3-005.

[16]   [1897] 2 Q.B. 57, discussed in § 5.4.2.

[17]   Winfield and Jolowicz 2020, para 3-009.

An even stronger degree of intent is that the tortfeasor acted with *malice*. Malice generally means intention combined with an improper motive aimed at the victim. The prime example is that the defendant had the purpose of injuring the victim. Imagine that the owner of a company threatens another company to cancel a contract unless they fire an employee against whom the owner bears a grudge. The threat may lead to an intentional harm suffered by the company that loses a valuable employee, but it is malicious towards the employee.[18] If, in the case of *Wilkinson v Downton*, the tortfeasor would actually have aimed at the severe shock of Ms. Wilkinson, he would have acted maliciously. However, it is not always sufficient that the tortfeasor desired to harm the victim. If the claimant wants the defendant to suffer from loss of a court procedure, that is not sufficient for malice, if the claimant litigated fairly. The motive becomes improper if an instrument (such as starting litigation) is used outside of its proper purpose. This can be compared to the way 'abuse of right' operates in civil law countries.

You must be careful when considering malice in common law. In common law there is no unified concept of malice. For malicious falsehood it appears that the aim to injure the victim is not required, although for other torts (malicious prosecution, misfeasance in public office, conspiracy by lawful means) it is argued that malice does have the meaning we just discussed.[19] Arguably malicious falsehood can better be understood as involving intentional falsehood.

The threefold distinction between negligence, intention and malice is fundamental to English tort law. Several torts refer to these concepts. In French and German law these categories are also recognized, but are at first sight of lesser importance. The main rule is that negligent behaviour suffices for liability. As art. 1241 Cc and § 823 I BGB state, the tortfeasor is liable for negligent as well as intentional acts. Malice is usually not discussed in civil law as a separate category, as it can simply by considered as a form of intention. However, on closer examination degrees of intention do matter.

Although the Code civil seemed to do away with distinctions in gravity of the fault, French law occasionally attaches consequences to the 'gravity of the fault' (*la gravité de la faute civile*).[20] French doctrine distinguishes between non-intentional fault, serious fault (*faute lourde*), inexcusable fault and intentional/malicious (*dolosive*) fault.[21] In rare cases a higher degree of fault is required for liability. For instance, the employee is not liable towards his employer for damage caused by his labour, except in case of serious fault equivalent to malice.[22] The liability of a carrier extends also to unforeseeable damage in case of inexcusable fault.[23] In case of intentional or malicious fault, similarly, contractual limitations to damages may be ineffective.

---

[18] The example resembles the facts of *Rookes v Barnard* [1964] AC 1129 HL about intimidation.

[19] About which: Murphy 2019.

[20] Fabre-Magnan 2021, p. 118, Viney, Jourdain and Carval 2013, p. 706ff.

[21] Viney, Jourdain and Carval 2013, pp. 720–76.

[22] Viney, Jourdain and Carval 2013, p. 713, 'faute lourde équipollente au dol'.

[23] Art. 133-8 Code de commerce: 'Seule est équipollente au dol la faute inexcusable du voiturier ou du commissionnaire de transport. Est inexcusable la faute délibérée qui implique la conscience de la probabilité du dommage et son acceptation téméraire sans raison valable. …'. Thereby the limitation of compensation to direct and certain damage is bypassed.

In German law, the main distinction is between negligence (*Fahrlässigkeit*) and intention (*Vorsatz*). Usually negligence suffices, but sometimes intention is required, among others for § 826 BGB. However, German law also recognizes several other stages, in particular gross negligence (*grobe Fahrlässigkeit*), which is required by a few specific provisions outside the general tort provisions.[24]

Furthermore, the degree of intention is relevant in civil law systems when assessing causality and damages. The general tendency is that in the case of intentional and malicious acts the courts may compensate more remote heads of damage, compared to cases of negligence. For assessing immaterial damage, courts may also take into account whether the behaviour was intentional or malicious. However, the precise concepts used here are slightly different from solely intention and malice.

Finally, we can observe a similarity in the role of intention for economic torts. In English law the main intentional torts are economic torts. In German law, the main provision dealing with economic torts, § 826 BGB, also requires intention. Similarly, in French law, liability for wrongful economic behaviour is covered to a large degree by 'abuse of right', which also requires the presence of intention (§ 7.4). Hence intention does serve in a similar way as a threshold for economic torts.

---

[24] Deutsch and Ahrens 2014, paras 153–8.

9
Causality

First of all, a quick recapitulation of the role of causality may be in order. As explained in § 2.7, the element of causal connection consists of two cumulative requirements:

- *factual causation*, and
- *legal causation*.

Factual causation, in civil law also called *condicio sine qua non (c.s.q.n.)*, simply means that the harm is an actual consequence of the wrongful act. The concept of factual causation is intuitive, but runs into difficulties when it comes to proving causation (§ 9.2), particularly when there are multiple causes of the harm (§ 9.3). The solution in some cases of multiple causes is simply to hold someone liable even though there is no certainty whether their action really caused the harm. Effectively we thereby move from a strict factual causation to legally attributing the harm to the action. Hence even factual causation is not purely factual but may be corrected for reasons of equity.

There are other techniques related to causation to correct or supplement the general causality rules. One example follows from the analysis of multiple causes, that is the notion of an intervening cause, whereby an action that stands in factual causal connection to the harm is deemed not to be a legally relevant cause anymore due to another cause intervening in the causal chain (§ 9.4).[1] Another is the rules of how to treat cases where only probabilities can be established and the normal rules of factual causality lead to unfair results (§ 9.5).

Legal causation as a concept is intended to restrict the extent of liability. Considered on its own this may seem simple enough. However, the general idea of restricting the extent of liability is developed in several ways that are not always directly connected to causality. In § 9.1 we shall first discuss legal causation, and the related doctrine of 'scope of the rule'.

9.1   LEGAL CAUSATION AND SCOPE OF THE RULE

Legal causation as a concept is intended to restrict the extent of liability. Considered on its own this may seem simple enough. However, the general idea of restricting the extent of liability is developed in several ways that are not always directly connected to causality. I will first discuss the various interpretations of legal causality, and then will describe the related doctrine

---

[1]   In Winfield and Jolowicz 2020, paras 7-046 through 7-058, intervening causes are discussed under legal causality, but separately from remoteness.

of 'scope of the rule'. To confuse matters, German law combines these doctrines, while other jurisdictions may keep them separate. This will hopefully become clear.

Legal causality limits liability to consequences that are insufficiently related to the wrongful act. This occurs in two ways: when the *harm* is insufficiently related to the wrongful act, or when the *heads of damage* that are claimed are insufficiently related. The distinction between the causal link to the harm and to the heads of damage is discussed in § 10.2. The difficulty of legal causality lies in what is meant by 'insufficiently related'. We have seen two different approaches: the idea of remoteness, and the notion of adequacy.

Remoteness is principally used in English and French law. This approach appears to look at the length of the causal chain between conduct and harm or damage. Although apparently simple, there is no clear way to determine when the causal chain is too long. Although experienced lawyers can usually make a good prediction as to the outcome of court cases, the criterion seems opaque for others. This is aggravated by apparent inconsistency in application: why can personal injury damage be compensated even if the heads of damage are decades in the future, while in commercial settings judges may show a tendency to a more restrictive attitude?[2] The alternative notion of foreseeability seems to provide more guidance, but in practice does not fare much better. Was the fire in the case of the *Wagon Mound*[3] really unforeseeable as a consequence of spilling oil? Furthermore, foreseeability does not solely imply that the causal chain was not too long, it also seems to require that the kind of harm or damage that was caused was a fairly obvious risk from the wrongful act. Thereby foreseeability may actually work like the adequacy criterion. The same can be said of remoteness, insofar as the application of remoteness depends on the kind of tort or harm.

The adequacy criterion, as used in German law, indeed explicates the idea that it is not so much the length of the causal chain, as well as the kind of harm and conduct that matter. Arguably, spilling oil does seem to be adequate to the risk of causing fire: the conduct matches the harm. As explained in § 4.9, German law nowadays tends to interpret the adequacy criterion by applying the doctrine of scope of rule, which works by focusing on the rule that is violated by the act, instead of looking at the act on its own. This deserves further inspection.

The doctrine of 'scope of the rule' can be found in German law and English law, where it limits the protection provided by a specific tort or ground of liability.[4] If liability is restricted by the scope of the rule, that means that the legal rule only aims at the protection of

- a certain group of persons (protected class), and/or
- certain interests.

For instance, the rule that prohibits speeding on public roads appears to aim at protection of safety of other persons on the road, but is not clearly intended to protect someone living

---

[2]   Incidentally, the concept of pure economic loss may also be used to restrict the extent of liability (§ 10.4): in some situations this concept may fulfil a role that in other jurisdictions is accomplished by means of legal causality.

[3]   *Wagon Mound (No. 1)* [1961] UKPC 2, [1961] AC 388, discussed in § 5.10.

[4]   The German term is *Schutzbereich*. You may also encounter *Schutzzweck* (protective purpose) which has a similar meaning, see Wagner 2021, paras 5.90–5.94.

next to a road against noise or pollution. It seems fairly logical to restrict compensation for violation of a rule to only those interests and persons that fall within the scope of the rule. You might also argue against that position by pointing out that the tortfeasor did act wrongful and that there is factual causality with some harm, so why should victims have to bear their own damage if they did not do anything wrong? If the tortfeasor would have behaved as he should have, the harm would not have occurred. German doctrine, like English law, finds the justification for such restrictions in the idea that everyone should bear the ordinary risks of life themselves (in German: *allgemeines Lebensrisiko*).[5]

In German law a clear limitation of protected interests is found in § 823 I BGB to the interests listed there, and (implicitly) to personal injury and property damage. Furthermore, in doctrine the element of legal causality tends nowadays to be interpreted by means of the 'scope of the rule' instead of the older doctrine of adequate causality (§ 4.9).[6]

In English tort law we find a restriction similar to the 'scope of the rule' with the tort of breach of a statutory duty, where the private right of action may be restricted to a particular class of individuals.

For the sake of completeness we can also point to a similar restriction to liability which is also referred to as 'scope of the duty' (duty, not rule) and was formulated in the SAAMCO case:[7]

A mountaineer about to undertake a difficult climb is concerned about the fitness of his knee. He goes to a doctor who negligently makes a superficial examination and pronounces the knee fit. The climber goes on the expedition, which he would not have undertaken if the doctor had told him the true state of his knee. He suffers an injury which is an entirely foreseeable consequence of mountaineering but has nothing to do with his knee.

It seems obvious that the injury is not within the scope of the duty that was violated, therefore should not be compensated. The 'scope of the duty' principle serves as a further restriction to liability for harm or damage, and can be considered an additional part of the requirement of remoteness. The SAAMCO case concerned liability for negligent valuation of property, and the 'scope of duty' was used to limit the damages to only compensate the direct damage due to the difference between valuation and actual value, and leave out compensation for losses due to a drop in the property market.[8] It appears that this principle is restricted to cases of professional liability, and thus outside the scope of this introduction. We included it here as illustration of a further similarity between legal systems, and because it may help you to understand how restrictions as to scope are applied.

---

[5] Wagner 2021, para 5.92.

[6] Deutsch and Ahrens 2014, para 56, Geigel 2020, paras 16–22.

[7] *South Australia Asset Management Corporation v York Montague Ltd* [1996] UKHL 10, [1997] AC 191, at 19.

[8] A similar application was given in a case of professional negligence: *Gabriel v Little (BPE Solicitors v Hughes-Holland)* [2017] UKSC 21. In *Khan v Meadows* [2021] UKSC 21 (concerning medical professional liability) and *Manchester Building Society v Grant Thornton UK LLP* [2021] UKSC 20 the application of the 'scope of the duty' restriction has been further clarified.

In French law the 'scope of the rule' requirement is generally rejected. Nonetheless scholars argue that courts do in practice apply a similar limitation through the application of the causality requirement.[9] An example is the case of a gambler who lost his bet because a soccer player violated the soccer rules.[10] The *Cour de cassation* rejected the claim, a decision that appears to be motivated at least partly by considerations similar to the idea of scope of the rule.

The consequence of a 'scope of the rule' restriction is that there is a connection between the ground of wrongfulness and the harm: you cannot assess these elements independently, but have to analyse them in conjunction. When investigating a specific tort or delict it is therefore necessary also to check what kinds of harm it covers for the jurisdiction you are researching.

In practice it is not always clear what is the scope of a rule, as rules themselves usually only explicate what is prohibited, not why this is so. To determine the scope, an investigation of the intention of the legislator may be necessary. In some cases, however, the legislator has explicated that certain interests are protected, or that certain persons have an action when the rule is violated.

To conclude: there are several ways in which liability may be restricted for certain consequences. The primary way to do so is by legal causality, which can be interpreted as relating to the length of the causal chain (remoteness) or whether the defendant should have anticipated the consequence (foreseeability), or by assessing whether the consequence is 'adequate', sufficiently related to the fault. Alternatively, there is a doctrine called 'scope of the rule' (and related doctrines such as 'scope of the duty' in the SAAMCO case) that achieve a similar restriction like the 'adequacy' approach to legal causality. In English law these approaches are kept separated, while in German law adequacy is principally interpreted as by means of the 'scope of the rule', essentially combining the two. French law formally rejects the doctrine of scope of the rule, although French courts may on occasion use argumentation similar to that doctrine.

9.2   PROOF OF CAUSALITY

Factual causation has to be proven.[11] While all criteria for liability have to be proven as far as the factual component of those criteria is concerned, the proof of causality turns out to be particularly complicated. The reason for this is that factual causation involves a comparison between what actually happened, and what would have happened in a hypothetical situation

---

[9]   Viney, Jourdain and Carval 2013, pp. 259–65, Fabre-Magnan 2021, pp. 246–8.

[10]   Cass., 1, 14 June 2018, no 17-20046 (facts abbreviated). The Court considered inter alia 'solely an act having as aim to deliberately harm the inherent probability of a sports bet is of a kind to lead to liability of the player or as the case may be, the club, against the gambler' (*seul un fait ayant pour objet de porter sciemment atteinte à l'aléa inhérent au pari sportif est de nature à engager la responsabilité d'un joueur et, le cas échéant, de son club, à l'égard d'un parieur*).

[11]   Legal causation is not proven in the strict sense of the word. Legal causation involves a legal assessment as to whether given all facts, it is fair to consider the harm as a consequence of the wrongful act. While the relevant facts themselves can be proven, the court has to determine on the basis of the facts whether there is indeed legal causation.

where the cause would not have occurred.[12] As a hypothetical situation is by definition not reality, it cannot be proven directly but has to be inferred from other evidentiary materials.

To begin with, the threshold of proof for factual causality differs between jurisdictions. Courts generally decide on the basis of a conviction that there really is factual causality. Such a conviction seems to require a high degree of probability: while the English approach seems to be satisfied if claimant's scenario is more than 50 per cent likely ('balance of probabilities'),[13] in Germany the courts actually want near certainty, while allowing a modicum of doubt.[14] In France there is no clear rule, but we can assume it is something between the English and German approaches.[15] Bear in mind, however, that these theoretical differences may in practice not lead to very different outcomes.

While in principle the victim bears the burden of proof of all elements of a tort, the proof of causal connection may be especially difficult to accomplish, as causation is inherently not feasible for conclusive proof. Courts everywhere have therefore looked at ways to enable the victim to establish causation. A few examples may suffice:[16]

–   Prima facie evidence: from the facts it seems self-evident that there is a causal connection. Therefore, causality is presumed, while the defendant is allowed to disprove causality. In England the Latin expression *res ipsa loquitur*[17] is used for this way of reasoning.[18] The German notion of *Anscheinsbeweis* works in the same way.
–   Reversal of the burden of proof: for some kinds of wrongful conduct, such as violating a safety rule, it seems fair to assume a causal connection with the harm, particularly if the rule aims to prevent the kind of harm that has occurred. An example is speeding in traffic: we may presume, in the absence of disculpating evidence, that this was a cause of the subsequent accident. The effect is quite similar to prima facie evidence.[19]

---

[12]   The 'but-for' test.

[13]   Sorabji 2019. In the US the phrase 'preponderance of the evidence' is used.

[14]   Althammer and Tolani 2019, citing the Anastasia case BGH 17 February 1970, III ZR 139/67, BGHZ 53, 245ff., 'The court may and must however satisfy itself in actual doubtful cases with a degree of certainty useful for practical life, that silences doubt without completely excluding it' (*Der Richter darf und muss sich aber in tatsächlichen zweifelhaften Fällen mit einem für das praktische Leben brauchbaren Grad von Gewissheit begnügen, der den Zweifeln Schweigen gebietet, ohne sie völlig auszuschliessen*).

[15]   Jeuland 2019, Fabre-Magnan 2021, pp. 252–3.

[16]   See extensively Van Dam 2013, nr. 1107, also Fabre-Magnan 2021, pp. 252–61.

[17]   The facts speak for themselves.

[18]   *Res ipsa loquitur* may be used for other elements of a tort as well, for example to prove negligent behaviour.

[19]   The difference can be explained in that reversal of the burden of proof is typically required on the basis of a legal rule when certain conditions apply (such as violation of a protective rule and occurence of a matching accident), while prima facie evidence is usually based on the particular facts of the case (hence not on a general rule). Furthermore, prima facie evidence is easier to remove by presenting evidence that raises doubt, while a reversal of the burden of proof requires actually proving the opposite (absence of causal connection), for instance by proving that there was a different cause.

— Proof by exclusion: defendant may propose alternative causes, but if all of those alternatives have been shown not to apply (have been excluded), causality with the remaining cause is proven. This argumentation can be found in French law.[20]

These instruments range from applications of common sense (such as prima facie evidence) to rather technical argumentations. As these instruments do not apply to all jurisdictions, you will have to check which tools for proving causality are available in the legal system that you are investigating.

9.3 MULTIPLE CAUSES

A topic that has given rise to considerable debate amongst legal scholars is what to do when there is more than one possible cause of the harm. The 'but for'-test does not work well for such cases.

This can be illustrated by means of a simple example. Two criminals shoot a man at the same time, and their victim dies from two bullets through the heart. Either bullet would have been fatal on its own. If we apply the 'but for' test to one criminal, the result is that the shooting of one bullet was not causal for the death of the man, as he would have died anyway from the other bullet. The same reasoning can then be applied to the other criminal. The result would be that neither shot is in causal connection to the victim's death. Clearly this is an unacceptable, even absurd outcome.

A related problem occurs if in the above example it would be discovered that only a single bullet hit the victim, presuming that there is no means to determine who fired that bullet. These are in essence the facts of the Californian case *Summers v Tice*.[21] During a hunting trip, two hunters were shooting quail, and both happened to hit a third hunter who was climbing further away up a hill. One shot hit the victim's right eye, another his upper lip. The injury of the eye caused the most damage. It could not be proven which of the hunters had hit his eye and which hit his lip. Ordinarily the victim would have to prove who hit which body part in order to claim the corresponding damages for that specific injury. The California Supreme Court held that it was fair that the burden of proof of (lack of) causality should be shifted from the victim to the defendants, as they acted wrongfully and brought themselves in the position of having to disprove causality. Furthermore, the defendants would be better placed to provide evidence. The result was that the tortfeasors were both held liable, with the exception that either would be absolved if he could prove that his actions did not stand in causal connection to the harm.

This approach is generally taken in cases where there are multiple tortfeasors. Those tortfeasors are held *jointly and severally liable*.[22] This means that the tortfeasors are both

---

[20]   Viney, Jourdain and Carval 2013, p. 311.

[21]   *Summers v Tice*, Supreme Court of California, 33 Cal.2d 80, 199 P.2d 1 (1948).

[22]   In French law (and countries that derive their law from French law) this is referred to as 'solidary' obligations. There are minute distinctions between various forms of solidary obligations and the notion of joint and several liabil-

liable (together, jointly) for the entire damage,[23] but that the victim does not have to sue both tortfeasors together: the victim may choose to sue only one of the tortfeasors, who then has to compensate all the damage suffered by the victim.[24] That tortfeasor may subsequently recover part of the damages from the other tortfeasors (usually proportionate to each contribution to the harm), but that doesn't concern the victim. The victim can also sue all tortfeasors together if the victim wants to do so.

A rule of joint and several liability for multiple tortfeasors amount to an exception to the requirement of factual causation as regards the individual tortfeasors: it is possible that an individual tortfeasor is held liable even though their act did not actually cause the damage. The tortfeasor usually has the opportunity to prove that there is no actual c.s.q.n.-connection between their act and the harm.

To deal with such and other cases of multiple tortfeasors, most jurisdictions have developed special rules which usually lead to joint and several liability. For many legal systems the development of this part of the law is left to the courts, in case law. Other countries have codified provisions to deal with such cases.[25] In German law §§ 830 and 840 regulate these cases in general, for France see arts. 1313 and 137 Cc. In England the Civil Liability (Contribution) Act 1978 explicates that the victim may sue tortfeasors independently, and that the tortfeasors can recover from each other a contribution to any damages paid.

The general principle of joint and several liability does not apply in a few cases that involve multiple causes. The general line of reasoning is recognized in most jurisdictions, but they may not always allow the same outcome, or may arrive at a similar outcome by different means.

- If there is another cause that is simply a natural cause not attributable to anyone, and if the tortfeasor's contribution to the harm is negligible compared to the other cause, it is possible that the other cause is considered *force majeure*, whereby the tortfeasor is not liable.[26] Force majeure may also be considered a defence (§ 12.3).
- If the other cause can be attributed to another tortfeasor, but the contribution of the other is so large that the first tortfeasor's contribution is negligible, the effect may be that the first tortfeasor is found not to be liable. A case like this could also be treated like an intervening cause (§ 9.4).
- If there are multiple causes of the harm or (amount of) damage, some of which are attributable to the victim, this may lead to a reduction of the amount of damages on the basis of contributory negligence (§ 12.2).

---

ity. Although you need not learn these at this stage, you should be aware that in practice you may have to understand these differences when you have to advise on a concrete case.

[23]   In English law 'joint' actually means that there is a common design of the tortfeasors, which is stricter than simply the result of being liable together. There is also the concept of 'pure several liability', where each tortfeasor is only liable for the proportion of the damage that they are actually responsible for.

[24]   An individual tortfeasor can get out of liability by proving that they did not act wrongfully or that their fault did not actually have a causal connection to the harm.

[25]   A very extensive set of rules is found in China, art. 8–14 Tort Liability Law.

[26]   As in French law: Viney, Jourdain and Carval 2013, pp. 332–58.

A related issue to multiple causality is the possibility of multiple actors cooperating to intentionally cause harm. Such cases may give rise to group liability, whereby all persons in the group are liable regardless of their actual contribution to the harm. An example of this approach can be found in § 830 BGB for accomplices and participants (*Mittäter und Beteiligte*).[27] While interesting, this topic is too complicated to deal with extensively in an introductory text.

9.4   INTERVENING CAUSES

A wrongful act may set a chain of events in motion that ultimately results in harm. This chain may include other acts. It is possible that one of those acts is of such a nature that it eclipses the original act and thereby breaks the chain of legal causation (notwithstanding that there is factual causality) from the original act to the harm. That act is considered an *intervening cause*.

Consider an example: someone negligently causes a friend to trip and fall down, leading to a visit to the doctor for a sprained ankle. The doctor makes a mistake in treatment, whereby the victim's ankle doesn't heal well and leads to permanent disability. Are those consequences also attributable to the original negligence, or is the medical negligence an intervening cause?[28]

The notion of intervening cause again shows that causation is not merely factual but also *legal*: the intervening cause is determined to be the sole legally relevant cause. The intervening cause is so important or decisive that it is to be considered the real cause, instead of the act that originally gave rise to the entire chain of events. Incidentally, this must be distinguished from cases where another cause increases the damage. If a victim of a collision is transported to the hospital in an ambulance, which subsequently collides with another vehicle, the second collision will probably not be considered an intervening cause but rather a further contributing cause to the entire harm.

If the intervening cause is attributable to a third party, the effect can only be that there is no causal connection between the act of the defendant and the damage, hence the defendant is not liable. It is possible, depending on whether the third party acted wrongfully, that the third party is liable instead. If the intervening cause is a natural event, that may also be considered force majeure (§ 12.3).

If the intervening cause is attributable to the victim, the effect may be that there is no causal connection to the damage, hence a necessary element of an action in tort is absent. Alternatively, one might argue that this is a case of contributory negligence where the contribution of the victim is 100 per cent (§ 12.2). Either approach can be found.

It is hard to assess when another cause actually intervenes instead of simply being another contributing cause.[29] Case law appears to be influenced by many factors, such as the foreseeability of the intervening cause, whether the intervening cause was tortious and/or intentional.

---

[27]   Including instigators and assistants (*Anstifter und Gehilfen*). For French law see Fabre-Magnan 2021, pp. 112–13.

[28]   Clerk and Lindsell 2020, paras 2-124 through 2-126 discusses divided case law on this issue.

[29]   See for instance the cases discussed in Clerk and Lindsell 2020, paras 2-110 through 2-143, Winfield and Jolowicz 2020, paras 7-047 through 7-058.

The results of the doctrine of intervening causes can often also be accomplished by application of the criterion of remoteness or scope of the rule. For instance, the case of traffic on the pavement, discussed in § 4.9, could, from the perspective of the person who caused the original accident, be viewed as caused by the intervening cause of the cars that drove on the pavement. Similarly, the defence of force majeure (§ 12.3) can also be perceived as a way to refuse liability when there is an intervening natural cause.

Incidentally, there are other complications with causality that resemble the topic of intervening causes. An example is what are called supervening causes or successive tortfeasors. Imagine the victim of a collision has become 30 per cent disabled, and then suffers a second collision leading to full disability. The question is how the consequences are to be distributed over the two tortfeasors of both collisions. This topic is too specific for an introduction, it is only mentioned here to introduce you to the terminology.

9.5 CAUSALITY AND PROBABILITY

As causality often cannot be proven with absolute certainty, it is usually assumed that the claimant has to prove that it was sufficient likely that the act is indeed the cause of the harm (§ 9.2). This leads to complications when there is a fundamental uncertainty in the outcome.

The classic example is professional negligence: the lawyer who forgets to file an appeal in time. It is uncertain whether the appellate court would have found for the lawyer's client: chances might well be estimated at 40–60, which is below the threshold of proof of 50 per cent in English law. In cases like this it appears unfair to decline the award of damages merely because causality with a positive outcome is insufficiently probable. For such cases some jurisdictions (in particular France) accept that the damage may consist of *loss of a chance*.[30] That means that the victim is awarded damages, but only to the proportion that he lost a chance. If the appeal could have resulted in an outcome of €100,000, and there was a 40 per cent chance of winning the appeal, he would be awarded damages for € 40,000.[31] See also § 11.1.4. In France the case law is unclear as to whether any serious chance, even slight, suffices, or whether there must have been a reasonable chance.[32] Recognition of loss of a chance is usually developed only in case law.[33]

There are other instruments for awarding damages in cases where causality is not certain. An example is damage that was caused by a medicine which was produced by several companies, while it cannot be proven which company produced the medicine that the victim took. In such cases legal scholars have argued that damages could be awarded against any of these companies (joint and several liability), who could subsequently distribute the damage on market share.

---

[30]   In English law the position is unclear; the case *Gregg v Scott* [2005] UKHL 2 is interpreted by some as allowing loss of a chance in certain cases.

[31]   =40% × €100,000.

[32]   Cass., 1, 12 October 2016, 15-23230 and 15-26147, versus Cass, 1, 30 April 2014, nos 13-16380 and 12-22567, about which also Le Tourneau 2021, para 2123.92. Possibly both formulations can be reconciled.

[33]   A codified rule can be found in Article 1385 of the Djibouti Code civil (2018).

Or alternatively the victim would have to sue each company for obtaining damages based on the actual damage, to the proportion of market share of the company. If a company had 33 per cent market share, you could at most obtain compensation 33 per cent of your damage.

Finally, there is a doctrine called *proportional liability* for cases where it is hard to prove factual causality between the wrongful act and the harm. The classic example is lung cancer that could have been caused by exposure to asbestos (which is wrongful) but might as well have been caused by the smoking habit of the victim. In such cases the Dutch courts have awarded damages to the proportion of the chance that the harm had been caused by the exposure, even though it was not clearly proven that the asbestos actually caused the lung cancer.[34] In England the House of Lords accepted proportionate liability in *Barker v Corus*,[35] but the legislator intervened to abolish this for asbestos cases.[36]

---

[34]   Hoge Raad 31 March 2006, *NJ* 2011/250 (Nefalit). See also articles in ERPL 2008, pp. 1009–117. French courts appear to apply the doctrine of loss of a chance to these kinds of cases.

[35]   [2006] UKHL 20. The case was preceded by *Fairchild v Glenhaven Funeral Services Ltd* [2002] UKHL 22 where the House of Lords allowed joint and several liability where several tortfeasors had materially increased the risk of causing mesothelioma (alleviating the threshold of proof for causality in cases of multiple tortfeasors).

[36]   S. 3 Compensation Act 2006. Proportionate liability is still available for cases that do not fall under this provision, such as cases from Guernsey and non-asbestos cases (Winfield and Jolowicz 2020, para 7-041).

10
Harm and damage

In the discussion of various torts in the previous chapters, we could not avoid several conceptual distinctions related to harm and damage which were not fully explained in Chapter 2. In this chapter we will finally get around to explaining what was left implicit earlier.

First of all, the concepts of harm, damage and damages need to be distinguished clearly (§ 10.1). Subsequently the relation between damage and causality is explained (§ 10.2). Finally, we will discuss two different classifications of damage (§§ 10.3–10.4).

10.1   DISTINGUISHING HARM, DAMAGE AND DAMAGES

If we consider a typical tort case like negligent conduct that resulted in a car crash, we can distinguish between the accident (*harm*), the negative consequences (*heads of damage*), and the monetary sum that the tortfeasor has to pay to compensate for those consequences (*award of damages*). The accident can be distinguished from later consequences such as medical treatment. Those consequences can be assessed at monetary value but are not identical to that value. We can therefore distinguish between:

– the original harm: an infringement or injury (*Verletzen, dommage*)[1]
– the resulting damage: losses or disadvantages suffered by the victim (*Schaden, préjudice*), and
– the award of damages by the court (*Schadensersatz, dommage-intérêts*),[2] the monetary compensation for damage.

In schematic form, the three elements are related as follows (improving on the simplified figure 2.1).

Damage results from the harm, and is usually required for an award of damages. The English concept of damage often refers to losses and other disadvantages, but may also be used

---

[1]   In French law *dommage* is also used to refer to the 'disadvantage' or prejudice, the *préjudice* (for example *dommage moral*).

[2]   See the country reports in Magnus and Busnelli 2001, also Von Bar 2011 and Heinze 2017. On English law see McGregor 2018, on German law Lange and Schiemann 2021, for French law see Viney, Jourdain and Carval 2017. The current French reform of the law of liability runs along lines similar to those sketched here, see also Sirena 2019.

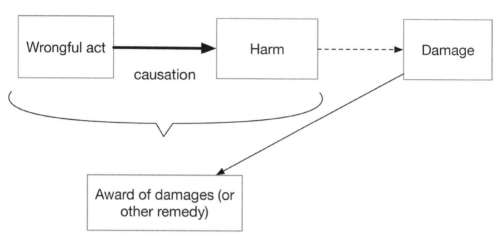

Figure 10.1   The elements of fault liability and the resulting remedy (advanced)

in the meaning of harm or infringement (similar to the French *dommage*).[3] Here I will use damage in the first sense.

Harm was in § 2.6 already defined as an injury to an interest. In the French Code civil this is not explained any further.[4] Other legal systems, in particularly German law, clearly specify the interests that are protected by several grounds. Many English torts can be analysed as protecting specific interests.

The distinction between harm and damage (losses) is not always clear-cut and may not be wholly accepted in every jurisdiction. An example where harm and damage cannot be easily separated is in case of defamation. A defamatory statement causes harm (injury to the reputation of a person), but this harm seems to be identical to the damage (which consists of this injury to reputation).

Nonetheless, it serves an analytical purpose to distinguish between harm and damage where this is feasible.[5] In case of a car crash, for instance, it makes sense to differentiate between the accident itself and the losses that result from the accident. In German law such a distinction is an integral part of the system of tort law, where the analysis proceeds in two phases. First you need to assess whether there is a *haftungsbegrundender Tatbestand* (set of facts establishing liability), in order to establish whether there is liability, which requires among others the presence of harm. Secondly, there must be a *haftungsausfüllender Tatbestand* (set of facts determining the extent of liability). In that phase you determine what damage has been caused by the wrongful act.

---

[3]   Nolan 2017 argues that English law should maintain a strict distinction between *damage* as infringement and *loss* as disadvantage.

[4]   Doctrine does discuss in more detail the interests that are protected under the general notion of harm. Incidentally, as of 1 October 2016 arts. 1246–1252 Cc contain rules for protection of environmental harm (*préjudice ecologique*), which allow the State and special interest groups to litigate for the protection of the environment.

[5]   Such as the difference in causality between infringement and harm, and between infringement and loss.

Finally, keeping harm distinct from damage is useful to pinpoint that harm is a necessary condition for liability (and remedies in general), while damage is not. In particular for injunctions and other forms of reparation in kind, damage is not required. Damage is only required for obtaining an award of (compensatory) damages. In English law there are non-compensatory damages that do not require the presence of damage (§ 11.1.3). These can be awarded for torts (such as defamation and trespass) that are actionable per se. But as an award of (compensatory) damages is in the vast majority of cases the primary goal of an action in tort, it is tempting to simply say that damage is always required for liability, even though that is not entirely correct.

10.2   DAMAGE AND CAUSALITY

At this point you may be confused by the different ways in which causality seems to come into play. Up to now we appeared to focus mainly on the causal connection between the wrongful act and the harm, the injury that gives rise to liability. But what about damage: is causality required between act and damage? Furthermore the 'scope of the rule' requirement appears to make a connection between the rule that was violated and the protected interests, and thereby also to the kind of damage that would be protected. There is reason to explicate the relation between these concepts.

Using the terminology as explicated in § 10.1, we can first of all establish that causality (legal and factual) is required between act and harm in order to grant a remedy. But if the claimant wishes to obtain an award of damages, this usually requires also the presence of damage, more particular, concrete heads of damage.[6]

Heads of damage are specific kinds of loss that the victim suffered. The costs of repair of a bicycle, the loss of value of an office building damaged by a crane falling on its roof, the mental distress and anguish caused by a knife attack, the decline in profits due to false rumours concerning a restaurant's hygiene: these are all examples of heads of damage. A major element of the lawyer's job is to determine the various heads of damage that are involved in the client's case. These heads are typically divided by type and by factual basis. For example, if a car and a bicycle were damaged, this can be construed as two separate heads of damage, which are both of the same kind (repair costs). It is also possible that a single event may give rise to several different heads of damage. For instance, a wrongful dismissal following a smear campaign by the directors of the company may lead to a claim for loss of income as well as a claim for mental distress.

Only those heads of damage can be compensated that stand in a causal connection to the wrongful act, the fault. There has to be factual causality (c.s.q.n. connection),[7] while the damage also needs to be sufficiently related to the fault to be recoverable (legal causality). Both forms of causality are required, not only between the act and the *harm*, but also between the

---

[6]   An exception are non-compensatory damages (§ 11.1.3).

[7]   In practice it suffices to establish that the damage stands in factual causal connection with the harm, as the harm is already a factual consequence of the act.

act and the *head of damage* for which the victim wants compensation. This is what German law explicates in two different phases of assessing tort liability (§ 10.1).

As regards factual causality: this is generally established by comparing the actual situation with the hypothetical situation that the victim would be in but for the wrongful act. In German law this is called the *Differenzhypothese*, the 'difference theory'. At first sight this might seem no more than a repetition of the analysis for factual causality between act and harm. On closer examination there is a difference. When assessing damage, you need to look at the specific damage that is at the basis of the claim. It is possible that a certain kind of damage has already been remedied or disappeared, even though there clearly has been a harm. For example: a publisher prints 1,000 books but finds out that the author plagiarized another book. The publisher immediately destroys all the books. While there has indubitably occurred an infringement of copyright which in itself is a harm, an injury, the fact that the books were subsequently destroyed means that in the comparison with the final situation there is no damage, as there are in actuality no infringing books anymore, just like there would be no infringing books in the hypothetical situation that no infringement had ever taken place. The fact that for a brief time there were infringing books does not seem to constitute damage.

If there are many heads of damage, it is possible that some are compensated while others are not recoverable. A court may find that only some of the heads of damage do not have sufficient connection to the wrongful act. Such an assessment may be based on the mere remoteness in the sense that the damage is too far removed, too many causal steps away from the act. It is also possible that the kind of damage or victim does not match up with, is not 'adequate' to, the rule that was violated. Legal causality allows for finetuning of the compensation.

Although theoretically the court would have to examine all causal connections between fault, harm and heads of damage, this is not necessary in practice. Often the causal connections are undisputed as they are self-evident, and the defendant concentrates their energies on the one causal link that seems the weakest. That link may be common to several heads of damage, and the court can then assess the causal connection for several heads simultaneously.

10.3   KINDS OF DAMAGE: MATERIAL AND IMMATERIAL DAMAGE

The principal categories of damage in civil law systems are as follows:

1. material damage:[8] detriment to material interests, such as property, money. English law speaks of *pecuniary loss*.
   a. losses: a direct diminishing of value, or loss of money.[9]

---

[8]   *Préjudice patrimoniaux* in French law, patrimonial losses. Note that this is not restricted to tangible goods, rather the concept refers to material value, assets.

[9]   The Latin phrase 'damnum emergens' is also found in literature.

b. Loss of profit:[10] profits that would have been gained in the hypothetical situation that no fault would have occurred, but did not materialize in reality because of the fault.

2. immaterial damage:[11] harm to immaterial interests such as reputation, mental health. Some jurisdictions call this *moral damage* (damage consisting of immaterial harm, such as suffering nervous shock or violation of privacy). In English law the term is *non-pecuniary loss*.

Losses tend to be relatively easy to assess, as they can be proven by bills, valuations, changes in bank account.

Loss of profit is not as easy to prove, as it involves an estimate of how much profit would have occurred in a hypothetical situation. A particular form, loss of income, may be easier to assess if the income would have been obtained from a permanent employment contract.

The factual basis of immaterial damage can be proven by the facts that gave rise to it, but it is not straightforward to attach a value to an immaterial harm. In § 7.2 we discussed several kinds of immaterial harm. In § 11.1.2 we discuss how to assess immaterial damage.

It should be noted that a group of facts may form the basis for several kinds of damage. For instance, harm to reputation may lead to loss of income as well as immaterial damage.

10.4 PERSONAL INJURY, PROPERTY DAMAGE, PURE ECONOMIC LOSS

Another important classification of damage is the following:

-   personal injury,
-   property damage, and
-   pure economic loss.

First of all, we have to distinguish between three kinds of harm: bodily harm, harm to property and other kinds of harm (typically non-tangible). These kinds of harm may correspond to certain kinds of loss, or may result in loss. For instance, damage to a painting constitutes immediate damage in the form of loss of value. However, it can also cause further losses, such as the costs for restoring the painting in proper condition, the loss of profit due to being unable to loan the painting for an exhibition.

Now we also speak of economic loss as the kind of damage that does not correspond to a tangible harm, even if it may be caused by or serve to compensate that harm. The restoration costs in the earlier example are economic costs, as is the loss of profit. They are economic, in the sense that they have economic value.

For the purposes of legal analysis lawyers operate with a threefold distinction in damage.

Personal injury consists of all damage consisting an injury to a person's body or health, and consequential damage (which usually consists of economic loss) .[12]

---

[10] The Latin phrase is 'lucrum cessans'.

[11] French law also calls this *préjudice extra-patrimoniale*. In German law the term is *Immaterialschaden*.

[12] Including the further economic losses following from this damage, such as loss of income.

Property damage is the damage of physical property and the damage as a consequence of the damage to the property (which again may consist primarily economic loss).

Pure economic loss is all damage that is not the consequence of personal injury or property damage.[13]

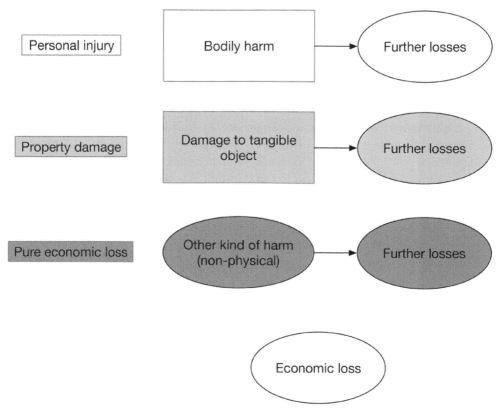

Figure 10.2   Personal injury, property damage and pure economic loss

The decisive element therefore is the harm that is at the root of the losses: that harm decides what kind of damage we are discussing. Economic loss can be a consequence of physical injury and of property damage, but if neither of those harms were at the origin of the economic loss, all the losses that have occurred are called *pure* economic loss. It is *pure*, as there is no harm other than economic loss. Hence this categorization does not depend on the kind of loss on its own (such as loss of income, which is a form of economic loss) but on whether this loss is a consequence of a physical harm (personal injury or property damage). Loss of income would

---

[13]   This definition is found also in Swedish law, Ch.1, § 2 *Skadeståndslagen* (Tort Liability Act) 1972. Cf. also the case *Spartan Steel & Alloys Ltd. v Martin & Co Ltd.* [1973] QB 27.

be compensated as personal injury, but might not be compensable if it is part of pure economic loss.

The type of damage is relative to the victim. For example: Mary is driving her colleague John to work in her car, and her car is hit in a traffic accident, whereby both do not make it to their work and do not get paid for that day.[14] Assume that they did not suffer injuries. John has suffered pure economic loss, but it can be argued that Mary's loss of income is a consequence of the harm to her property (the car) and is therefore contained in her property damage.

The principal importance of this distinction is that pure economic loss is not always recoverable, particularly not in negligence.[15] In particular common law systems are hesitant to allow recovery of pure economic loss,[16] except in specific cases.[17] Civil law systems take varying positions. For example, in German law pure economic loss is not covered under *Verkehrspflichten*, but can be compensated on the basis of § 826 BGB.[18] In French law, there is no strict limitation to compensation of pure economic loss: the courts may apply the requirement of legal causation to refuse an award for pure economic loss where they find such an award inappropriate.

---

[14] Whether you are paid in such a situation depends on the local labour laws and the kind of contract you have.

[15] There is much comparative literature about this. See with further references Palmer 2021.

[16] This is often recognized, such as in *OBG Ltd v Allan* [2007] UKHL 21, Lord Hoffmann at 99: 'it is a commonplace that the law has always been very wary of imposing any kind of liability for purely economic loss'.

[17] For example, professional negligence. However, this does not apply to all common law jurisdictions. Even among US states there are variations.

[18] Wagner 2021, para 5.131 discusses the reasons why the German legislator was hesitant in allowing compensation for pure economic loss.

11
Damages and other remedies

In this chapter we will discuss damages and other remedies. The ultimate goal of most liability cases is to obtain compensation in the form of an award of damages. A claim needs to be supported by several heads of damage. The final step in the assessment of damages is to set a value at each head of damage.[1] This is easy if the damage consists of a repair bill: the corresponding damages are the amount payable on the bill.[2] However, there are additional details to cover, and for other types of damage the assessment process may not be as straightforward.

Lawyers distinguish several kinds of damages, and the classification in common law is quite different from the civil law system. We will discuss both approaches (§ 11.1). This is followed by a brief description of the way in which damages are typically assessed by courts (§ 11.2). We continue with other remedies (§ 11.3). To conclude our overview, we also discuss third party damages (§ 11.4) and the role of insurance and compensation funds (§ 11.5).

11.1 KINDS OF DAMAGES AND THEIR ASSESSMENT

11.1.1 Introduction

Legal systems recognize various kinds of damages. The problem, from a comparative point of view, is that there is little uniformity in the categorizations. When discussing kinds of damages in an English text, it may seem logical to use the terminology of English common law. However, these terms are rather idiosyncratic and are not always easily translated to kinds of damages in civil law countries. We will approach the topic of damages by using a general terminology, while also pointing out the corresponding terms and concepts in specific jurisdictions.

It should be noted that many modern codifications contain extensive rules on assessment of damages. Often these are part of the general rules on obligations (which would also cover contractual damage). An example is the German BGB (§ 4.10).

---

[1]   This means that each head is 'assessed': assessment of damages (with an 's') is therefore achieved by assessing heads of damage.

[2]   There can also be additional costs, such as monetary interest.

11.1.2   Compensatory damages

Damages aim at full compensation. This means that 'everything must be returned to the previous situation, or, if this is not feasible, its estimated value must be compensated ...'.[3]

Compensation is, however, not the only aim of damages, as we shall shortly see. The just quoted Austrian provision also mentions the need for making estimates when it is not possible to give a precise assessment, which indeed is an important tool to achieve a decision on damages.

In common law one of the major categories of damages is compensatory damages, damages to compensate loss. As indicated above, the position in civil law systems is that damage is solely intended for compensation, hence civil law systems simply speak of 'damages'. For the purpose of this comparative text, we first discuss 'compensatory damages', bearing in mind that in civil law these comprise the entirety of damages. Within that category, the assessment differs according to the kind of damage that is to be assessed.

Note that French and German law usually do not speak of specific kinds of damages, rather speak of compensation of specific kinds of damage. Although there are concepts that denote certain kinds of damages (such as in German *Immaterialschadenersatz* or *Schmerzengeld*, which are damages for non-pecuniary loss), these are the exception.

In § 10.3 we introduced a general classification of damage that may serve to organize our discussion.

1. material damage
    1. losses
    2. loss of profit
2. immaterial damage/moral damage

Damages for *material damage* tend to be mainly compensatory, as the award of damages is in principle set at the exact value of the losses caused by the fault. These may involve expenditure and other costs that have been incurred because of the harm. Such cases are easily assessed. However, it is also possible that no precise value can be given. Courts usually also have discretionary power to estimate the damage at the value that seems appropriate. In some instances there are further rules.

Property damage is usually assessed at the loss of value of the property. There are two principal approaches: valuation at the repair costs, or an estimate of loss of market value. These approaches generally lead to a similar result, but that is not always the case. For instance, the repair costs of a four-year-old laptop where the screen has been scratched may far exceed the actual loss of value caused by that scratch. In such cases corrections are necessary to obtain fair results (for instance, when the property has sentimental value). More complicated is the question whether compensation is due for the loss of use of property. While the costs for renting

---

[3]   To quote s. 1323 of the Austrian *Allgemeines bürgerliches Gesetzbuch* (ABGB).

a substitute car may be compensable, courts are hesitant to compensate the lack of availability of the object.[4]

Loss of profit. This is often specifically mentioned (for example in § 252 BGB). It is hard to prove how much profit has been lost (for example if a restaurant was burnt to the ground). This is often assessed on the basis of expert valuations.

A specific form of loss of profit is loss of income. This can be easier to assess, if there is an employment contract with a fixed salary. If an employee has been injured and thereby is unable to work, it is possible that they still receives salary.[5] In such a case the employer may have a claim on the tortfeasor for third party damages (§ 11.4).

Two specific forms of material damages need to be mentioned here.

First of all, damages for compensating the loss suffered because the victim was for a period of time deprived of money: this is called *monetary interest*. The victim may for instance have had to borrow money to pay his rent, and wants to be compensated for the corresponding interest that the victim had to pay over the loan. The monetary interest may be fixed by the legislator at a certain percentage that can vary over time, thereby abstracting from the actual financial loss suffered by the victim.

Another category is *procedural costs*: the lawyer's fees and other costs related to the court procedure (such as expert reports, fees for the summons, court fees). There are differing opinions as to the right for compensation of procedural costs. On the one hand it seems fair that the victim is fully compensated for all expenditure, which would support full payment of procedural costs by the winner. On the other hand, full compensation may have a chilling effect. If the victim happens to lose a good case because a crucial witness dies, it seems unfair to make him even worse off by having to pay the costs of the other party. It is also possible that the losing party could in good faith argue against the claim, or it is not clear who is winner and who is the loser (if the main claim is rejected and only a tiny award is given). Access to justice might be impaired if the procedural costs would be too high. Countries take various approaches: some have a system where the loser pays the actual procedural costs, others have a system where costs are compensated by a fixed system, and sometimes the costs are divided between winner and loser on a discretionary basis by the court.

Damages for *immaterial damage* compensate for immaterial harm (§ 7.2). In Germany this is regulated in § 253 BGB (*Schmerzengeld*, payment for pain and suffering). These are similar to what common law calls damages for non-pecuniary loss. Such damages put a value at something that does not have a clear monetary value. The assessment of immaterial damages is far from easy. In practice courts tend to rely on earlier precedents or overviews that list figures that are found to be fair compensation for certain injuries. Immaterial damage may be compensated on top of actual material damage, such as in the case of loss of a limb where there is immaterial loss (having to miss a body part) besides the loss of income.

---

[4]　　BGH 23 January 2018,VI ZR 57/17 allows compensation for the loss of use of a motor cycle, although not essential for its owner, under restrictive conditions.

[5]　　This depends on the applicable labour laws, which may require the employer to continue paying salary for a period of time during the employee's sick leave.

A final note on assessment of damages: in practice it is often necessary to also take into account the effect of taxes. An award of damages may result in a higher income for that year, and any consequential additional taxes also need to be compensated. Calculation of these effects is the work of specialists.

11.1.3   Non-compensatory damages

If we turn to non-compensatory forms of damages, we need to apply the common law categories, since in civil law systems all damages are purportedly compensatory in nature.

First of all, there are *punitive damages*, also called *exemplary damages*. The aim of punitive damages is, as the name says, punishment of the tortfeasor. They may be awarded in cases where the conduct of the defendant is sufficiently outrageous to merit punishment. This is primarily a common law category. Civil law jurisdictions are generally averse to punitive damages.[6] However, the gain-based damages discussed below may also have a punitive effect.

A species of punitive damages is the sub-category of *aggravated damages*.[7] These are intended for compensation of certain intangible injuries. 'Aggravated' refers to the injuries, not to the damages. Cases involve mental distress or injury to feelings; relevant is the motive (such as intention to injure the victim). This category is specific to common law. However, in civil law countries so-called immaterial damages or moral damages may also be awarded in cases of mental distress. Hence immaterial damages in civil law may partly overlap with aggravated damages in common law.

The second category is *gain-based damages*: this is a remedy that requires the tortfeasor to hand over the profit he gained from the tort. Other names are *restitutionary damages* or *disgorgement damages*. An example is producing illegal copies of a copyrighted product. The profit from sales of these copies may be higher than the loss of profit to the copyright holder. It seems unfair that the infringer may keep the surplus profit, in particular as this does not discourage infringement. It is not always clear whether this remedy is actually a form of damages or rather a remedy outside of damages. It is also to be distinguished from punitive damages: while the damage may feel like punishment, the aim is not really meting out punishment but rather turning over profit.

Gain-based damages are recognized in civil law systems, but may be categorized in various ways.[8] In Germany there is no general clause, but there do exist various grounds for specific situations.[9] Courts may also effectuate payment of money related to the gains of the other party by using specific constructions, such as implied agency/mandate (see § 667 BGB), *negotiorum gestio* (§ 684 BGB), unjustified enrichment (specifically §§ 816 and 818 BGB).[10] Restitution for

---

[6]   A comparative overview is Koziol and Wilcox 2009. A rare example of punitive damages in a civil code can be found in article 2229 Philippine Civil Code (1950).

[7]   Tilbury 2018.

[8]   Hondius and Janssen 2015.

[9]   See for the case of IP infringement BGH 16.2.1973, BGHZ 60, 206.

[10]   Dannemann 2009, Helms 2015.

IP infringement may also be based on specific provisions in IP codes.[11] Similarly, in France, there are only specific provisions for disgorgement.[12]

Finally, common law recognizes the category of *nominal damages*. This refers to what elsewhere may be called symbolic damages: an award of damages that is of no real value and is awarded solely to provide a response to the tort, while the court finds insufficient reason to award a significant amount of money. Similar is the category of *contemptuous damages*, a negligible amount awarded to show that a wrong has been committed. In civil law, immaterial damages may be used to award damages for satisfaction where there is no clear value for the harm that has been incurred. From a civil law perspective such damages may have a partly punitive, partly satisfactory purpose to show a legal response to a harm. An example is the breach of privacy: quite often it is hard to put a real value on such a breach, while clearly such breaches are undesirable. It would add insult to injury if the court would not award any damages at all. Hence civil law courts would argue that the immaterial interest of privacy has been harmed, giving rise to compensation for immaterial damage.

11.1.4　Specific ways to calculate damages

Two kinds of 'damages' need special mention, as they involve a particular technique for calculating damages.

First of all, there are *future damages*. While damages are intended to compensate for the past, it is found to be unfair if certain damage can already be predicted with reasonable certainty that the victim would still need to wait until the damage materialized. A particular example is loss of income. Hence the law may allow a victim to claim an award to compensate for future losses, which are estimated by the court. The payment of personal injury damages often occurs in the form of a *lump sum*: a sum of money that is paid at once, instead of yearly paying out damages for the damage suffered in that year. The idea is that the lump sum generates sufficient yearly revenue or interest to compensate the victim for the yearly loss of income.

Another instrument is *loss of a chance* (§ 9.5). This is used to calculate damage for an event that did not clearly cause a fixed loss but rather caused the loss of the chance of profit (or conversely opened up a risk of loss). Common examples are an incorrect medical diagnosis whereby a disease was not treated in time (but where it was not sure that a timely diagnosis would have led to better prospects), a lawyer who forgets to appeal a decision in time leading to the loss of a chance of a better outcome in appeal. Damages are usually calculated by multiplying the respective outcomes with the probability of that outcome being realized, and adding those sums together. For instance, one estimates that there was a 30 per cent chance of a better outcome in appeal (worth €100,000) against a 70 per cent chance of losing the appeal (leaving the outcome the same, but adding own costs and procedural costs of the other party of €10,000). The result would be 30 per cent × €100,000 + 70 per cent × −€10,000 = 30,000 − 7,000 = €23,000. Most jurisdictions allow compensation on the basis of loss of a chance, but there may be specific restrictions as to its scope of application.

---

[11]　Such as § 2 *Urheberrechtsgesetz* (Copyright act).

[12]　Sejean 2015, referring to provisions in IP law, criminal law and commercial law, besides other constructs.

11.1.5 The entire system of damages

The kinds of damages we have been discussed may be represented graphically as follows, to show the connections between the common law concepts and the civil law terminology.

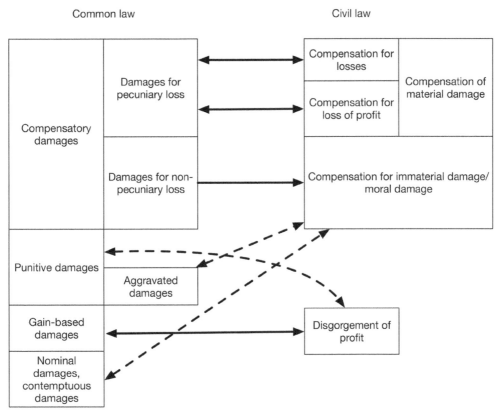

Figure 11.1   Kinds of damages in common law and civil law

The upper part of this overview is for practical purposes the important part, as most damages relate to compensatory damages in one form or another.

11.2   THE PROCESS OF ASSESSMENT OF DAMAGES

If we abstract from the specific rules, the process of assessment of damages generally involves the following stages (which need not be followed in this order).

a.   Identify all heads of damage.
b.   Check whether there is a causal connection between each of the heads of damage and the wrongful act: only heads of damage that are in legal causal connection can be compensated.
c.   Assess each head of damage to a certain amount of money.

d. Apply corrections if necessary (contributory negligence, deducting collateral benefits).

a. In order to identify the various heads of damage, you need to apply the categories that were introduced in the previous section. There are often typical kinds of damage that occur. For example, in a traffic accident the typical heads of damage are personal injury, property damage (to the car), and possibly medical expenses, loss of income.

b. See § 10.2. Here the general notions of factual and legal causality are applied. In practice courts usually do not check each head of damage separately. It usually suffices to determine which head of damage is too remote; all damage following thereafter is also too remote. Incidentally, in certain systems the court may use the notion of legal causality in a way that resembles the 'scope of the rule' requirement (§ 9.1).

In the example, the costs of the holiday might be too remote, or it could be argued that there is contributory negligence specifically for these costs.

c. Assessment of individual heads of damage involves matters of proof, for example the proof that the property damage amounts to a certain value, that repair costs were incurred to a certain amount. There are many specific rules that govern the way in which various kinds of damage have to be assessed. Some civil codes contain intricate rules for the assessment of damages, while usually there are additional rules to be found in case law. In certain cases there may be statutory limitations to the amount of damage that may be awarded. Some aspects will be discussed in the next section.

d. Furthermore, some corrections may be necessary. First of all, contributory negligence may lead to a reduction of the award of damages (§ 12.2).

Secondly, sometimes the victim may have received material benefits (profit or gain) from the wrongful act. For example, because your car is a total loss after the accident, you get a reduction on your road taxes. These *collateral benefits* may be deducted from the award of damages. Some systems have an explicit rule to this effect. For example, the Dutch art. 6:100 BW contains a rule for 'attribution of advantages' (*Voordeelstoerekening*).[13] In other systems this deduction is simply part of the assessment of damages: the reasoning is that such a benefit reduces the net amount of damage.

However, not all benefits are deducted from the award of damages. It may be unjust to allow the tortfeasor to profit from an independent source of benefits which he doesn't have to do with. For example, a thief steals your bicycle and afterwards throws it in the canal. Your friends buy you a new bicycle. It seems clear that the thief, if apprehended, cannot successfully defend himself by pointing out that you have not suffered any damage since you have already obtained a new bicycle.[14] For this reason art. 6:100 BW also contains an exception where deduction of collateral benefits is not allowed if this would be unjust. Other legal systems have similar restrictions in place.

---

[13]   § 3-1 of the Norwegian Skadeserstatningsloven contains a detailed rule for which benefits are to be deducted, similarly art. 6.290 Lithuanian civil code.

[14]   A particular important issue is how to deal with compensation that the victim obtains from insurance. One possible approach is to allow the insurance company to take recourse to the tortfeasor.

In the third place, a few systems allow *mitigation of damages* for reasons of equity.[15] The typical example is if the victim is extremely rich and the tortfeasor poor, and the award of damages would ruin the tortfeasor.

11.3   OTHER REMEDIES

The main alternative to an award of damages is a court order or injunction. In this way the defendant can be forced to achieve certain effects other than payment of money. Also, some kinds of infringement may be prevented, as in the case of a restraining order. Such orders have been discussed above (§§ 3.8, 4.10, 5.11).

In civil law systems there is also the concept of reparation or compensation in kind or reparation 'in natura'. This is simply a way to conceive of the aim of full compensation in a different manner than by an award of damages. An example is that the thief must return the good that he stole, which is a more appropriate form of compensation than having to pay the replacement value, particularly in cases of unique goods. Such forms of compensation are usually awarded in the form of an injunction or court order. Sometimes a declaration of rights may also suffice, for instance to establish that the claimant is indeed the holder of the copyright in a certain work.

As we have seen in the section on property torts, there are various remedies for the loss of or infringement of property (§ 7.3).

There is also the possibility of a declaration of rights. This means that the court simply declares as its decision that the defendant acted wrongfully and is liable, without attaching any further consequences to that declaration. One might argue that this is not really a remedy as the declaration does not force the defendant to do anything. However, from a more abstract point of view the declaration of rights may serve the goal of satisfaction or recognition (§ 2.3). It may be a useful outcome for cases of defamation, whereby the victim can point to the decision to show that the allegation was baseless. Furthermore, a declaration of rights may be a first step to obtain damages: parties can be incentivized to negotiate about the damages to be paid and might reach agreement without requiring a further costly assessment by the court.

Finally, for cases of defamation there is the specific remedy of rectification or retraction (§ 7.5).

11.4   THIRD-PARTY DAMAGES

A related topic is what are called third-party damages. There are cases where the primary victim may or may not have a claim, while there are third parties who do have a justified claim on the tortfeasor even though they are not the direct victim. This is particularly important when the victim has died: the dead can't claim in court as they do not suffer loss. However,

---

[15]   See for example art. 52 Turkish Code of Obligations (*Türk Borçlar Kanunu*), art. 6:109 Dutch civil code (*Burgerlijk Wetboek*).

their family members may end up destitute if the victim provided the sole income for the family. Another example, mentioned above, is the employer who may temporarily lose the benefit of the labour of an injured employee, but still has to pay the employee's salary. In such cases there is reason to provide third parties with a claim for their damage.

Often these claims are fairly easy to assess: the employer's damage can be assessed at the lost value of the labour, the costs of hiring a replacement, or the costs for the employee that now have become useless (salary plus possibly taxes). Sometimes a claim can be construed on the basis of taking recourse. For instance, if a family member provides a victim with money to pay for medical bills, the family member may have a direct claim on the tortfeasor, either because the victim transferred ('assigned' is the legal phrase) their own claim to the family member, or because the law provides for these kinds of cases (such as 'subrogation', § 11.5).

For three cases there need to be specific rules. In English law, such claims are based on the Fatal Accidents Act 1976, which provides dependents with an action in case of the death of aa partner, parent, child or other close family member (see s. 2 Fatal Accidents Act 1976). In German law, § 844 BGB provides the basis for compensating these kinds of damage. Claimants are in principle restricted to partners and children. In France the developments are mainly based on case law.

First of all, relatives will usually bear the funeral expenses and it is fair to also provide them compensation for those costs. There are usually specific provisions to that effect (§ 844 I BGB, in England art. 3(5) Fatal Accidents Act 1976).[16]

Secondly, there is the loss of consortium, also called loss of maintenance. This happens when the bread-winner of a family dies. The family members have a claim for the loss of the income that would have been brought into the household. Complications arise as to the kinds of relationships where compensation is due: only for married couples and families, or also for non-married couples, same-sex marriage, couples who do not live together, divorced couples? In England such a claim can be based on art. 1A Fatal Accidents Act 1976. In Germany there is § 844 II BGB. § 845 BGB also provides a ground for compensation for loss of service, meaning not the financial support provided by the deceased but other kinds of services provided, such as providing care, taking care of the household. In France, loss of revenue has been recognized in case law and is compensated rather liberally, as there is no restriction to partners or children: anyone who can prove the loss of monetary support by the deceased can claim compensation.[17]

Thirdly, family members and other relatives may have a claim for their own emotional damage when they have lost a family member. In England, s. 1A Fatal Accidents Act 1976 provides for an award of 'damages for bereavement' in case of loss of a partner or parent. The damages are fixed by law (in 2021 GBP 15.120). Damages for bereavement cover what other jurisdictions compensate as affectional distress. In France the courts do allow the indirect victim an award for the *préjudice d'affection*, the affectional distress due to a close relative dying or suffering serious physical injury.[18] In Germany § 844 III BGB (introduced in 2017)

---

[16]   For France the rules have been formed in case law (Viney, Jourdain and Carval 2017, p. 344).

[17]   Viney, Jourdain and Carval 2017, pp. 333–45.

[18]   Viney, Jourdain and Carval 2017, pp. 346–8. The case law shows awards between €3,000–30,000.

provides compensation for emotional distress for persons in a particularly close relationship to the deceased.[19]

Before § 844 III BGB was enacted, courts occasionally awarded damages for nervous shock suffered by hearing of the death.[20] That route presumes that the victim is a direct victim, the legal question there is whether nervous shock following the witnessing of such an event is compensable. That was discussed in § 7.2. English courts have largely rejected claims for nervous shock or other psychiatric harm on hearing of or witnessing death.[21] French law does allow such a claim and does not require a medical condition for awarding damages (§ 7.2). As there is also a claim in French law for being an indirect victim, this raised the question how those two actions are related. The Cour de cassation decided in 2017 that a victim can obtain damages simultaneously as direct and as indirect victim,[22] leading to the critique that the victim is thereby compensated twice for the same harm.

11.5   INSURANCE AND ALTERNATIVE COMPENSATION SCHEMES

Quite often damages are not actually paid by the tortfeasor. Rather the award of damages is paid by an insurance company,[23] or in some instances, by specific funds.[24] These companies or funds may in turn attempt to *recover* the damages they have paid from the tortfeasor: they ask the actual tortfeasor (or someone who is responsible for him) to pay the amount paid to the insurance company or fund. The law of insurance is a specialist topic that we cannot discuss in detail in an introductory text. As insurance companies and funds are nonetheless a fixture in the whole landscape of tort law, it is befitting to devote a few remarks to this topic.

An insurance company is, simply put, a corporation that allows private individuals (and companies) to spread the risk of suffering damage or being held liable. Individuals and companies contract with the insurance company, by which they are obliged to (periodically) pay an insurance fee. In return the insurer is obliged to pay out an insurance claim if the event that is insured materializes. For example, the insurance policy stipulates that the company will pay out if the policy holder dies or suffers an injury, suffers property damages in a fire or because of bad weather or natural disasters. The insurance policy specifies in detail for what kind of events the insurer will pay out, which limitations apply (for example not all natural disasters, no payment in case of suicide), up to which amount (usually there is an upper limit). The insurer calculates the risk of having to pay out and sets the insurance fee to such an amount that the sum of all fees received exceeds the amount it has to pay out, and in this way may turn

---

[19]   Geigel 2020, chapter 7, Wagner 2021, paras 10.67–10.71.

[20]   Kötz and Wagner 2016, paras 738–9.

[21]   Such claims are generally rejected due to the lack of proximity for assuming a duty of care, see in particular *Alcock v Chief Constable of South Yorkshire Police* [1991] UKHL 5, [1992] 1 AC 310.

[22]   C.Cass. civ. 2, 23 March 2017, no 16-13350.

[23]   Ebert 2021.

[24]   Jutras 2021.

a profit. Calculations are further complicated by taking into account expected profits from investment of the insurance fees, while the insurance company may spread its risk further by asking others to partake in the risk (co-insurers).

If the insured event is caused by someone else who is liable for the damage, the victim has in principle two sources for obtaining compensation: they can sue the tortfeasor, or they can ask their own insurance company to pay out (this is called *first party insurance*, it is the insurance of the first party, the victim). Often the victim takes the second cause of action. But it would seem highly unfair if the tortfeasor would thereby not have to bear the consequences of his actions. The insurance company may want to recover its payment from the tortfeasor. The insurance company can do so on the basis of a legal doctrine called *subrogation*, whereby the party that has compensated the victim takes the place of the victim in a claim on the tortfeasor. The tortfeasor in turn can in this procedure invoke all defences they had towards the victim. The intervention of insurers in the process of tort litigation has many advantages: the insurance company may be able to assess the claim more objectively and spare the victim the trouble of actual litigation, the company has the benefit of more expertise and may be able to view trends and stimulate preventive actions, the company has no trouble undertaking costly litigation if necessary.

Another possibility is that the tortfeasor has an insurance policy whereby the insurance company will bear the damages for which the tortfeasor is liable. This is called *third party insurance*. The victim may in such a case be allowed to sue the insurance company of the tortfeasor (the third party) instead of the tortfeasor themself, or the tortfeasor may ask the insurance company to step in and take over the burden of the litigation. The precise legal details may differ between jurisdictions and may also depend on the actual content of the policy. Such insurance policies are particularly beneficial when unavoidable risks of normal activities are concerned. An example is car accidents: drivers may make small mistakes when driving which may cause substantial damage. It seems preferable to spread the risk over all drivers, who individually pay only relatively small fees, and thereby avoid the risk that they would become bankrupt following a slight error in driving. A disadvantage is that reckless drivers are hereby not incentivized to drive more carefully (although insurance companies may penalize drivers who cause many claims). Third-party insurance does remove part of the preventive effect of liability. Nonetheless, there is also an advantage for the victim: if the tortfeasor is poor and unable to pay their debts (is insolvent, as is the legal phrase), they would be unable to pay damages and the victim would be left partly uncompensated. The intervention of an insurance company provides the victim with an additional source of indemnification.

The effectiveness of insurance has led to the introduction of compulsory insurance schemes. An example is, again, compulsory insurance for owners of motorized vehicles.

A different institution for arranging compensation is the compensation fund. Such a fund exists to offer victims of certain events compensation under specific conditions. It functions somewhat like third party insurance. However, funds are not based on an insurance policy of the tortfeasor. The legal basis is instead usually found in statutory law. An example is the EU rules for travel agents.[25] Travel agents have to take measures against insolvency, to ensure that customers who bought packages travel arrangements are compensated if their travel agent goes bankrupt. An appropriate measure is that travel agents collectively establish a compensation fund, filled with contributions by all agents based on the arrangements that they sold. A compensation fund has several advantages: it is not bound by the sometimes very intricate legal rules on damages and may instead have a simple, fast pay-out schedule. Furthermore, a fund can pay out without burdening the courts, which is particularly useful in the case of mass claims.

A fund can also be established voluntarily by companies in a specific economic sector. A fund may promote confidence to customers or to citizens who would thereby be less inclined to oppose an activity that might cause injuries to many people. For this reason some legal scholars are proposing the establishment a compensation fund for damage caused by AI or robots.

A well-known example is the New Zealand Accident Compensation Act 2001.[26] This act provides a basis for compensating personal injury caused by certain kinds of accidents: work-related accidents, motor vehicle accidents, and injury following medical treatment. Funding is obtained through a combination of levies (principally from employers, self-employed, employees and motor vehicle licence holders, and medical professionals and hospitals and the like), and government funding. The operation somewhat resembles a mandatory insurance scheme. An important difference is that the scheme does not require fault: the victim only has to prove injury, he does not need to establish that someone else did something wrong. As a consequence of this scheme, most tort law claims become superfluous as the victim can obtain compensation far easier through the administrative body in charge of paying out under this scheme. It can be argued, though, that such a scheme is really a form of social security that overlaps with, but has no real bearing on, tort law. Nonetheless the practical effect is that tort law has become mostly irrelevant for several major areas of liability in New Zealand.

Economically speaking insurance companies and funds fulfil the role of spreading risks over the persons who benefit from certain risky activities. They raise the costs of the activity (though the insurance fees) and thereby internalize the negative externalities.

[25] Currently the Package Travel Directive 2015/2302.
[26] As is the latest name of this statute. See Brown 1985, Jutras 2021.

12
Defences and limitations

12.1   INTRODUCTION

Even if all the criteria for liability have been fulfilled, the tortfeasor may not be obliged to reparation. The tortfeasor may mount several defences against an action based on tort (§ 1.5). In this section we focus not on defence as a rebuttal in litigation, but on defences in the sense of 'arguments that lead to the conclusion that there is no liability', even though at first sight the conditions for liability appear to be fulfilled.

You can either argue that a defence removes the wrongfulness of the act (i.e. provides a *justification* for the act), or that the act is in itself wrongful, but should not lead to liability given the presence of a valid defence.[1] For most defences either approach could be applied. Contributory negligence alone is solely a defence, not a justification: it usually does not remove wrongfulness but may only lead to a reduction of damages.

One problem in finding applicable defences is that you may need to look elsewhere in the code. For example, the German tort provisions are §§ 823–853 BGB but defences can be found among others in § 227 (self-defence), § 904 (necessity). Some defences may not even be found in the code at all, being established in case law.[2]

You can generally presume that the defences listed in this chapter are recognized, and if a particular defence seems to apply to the case under consideration you should make an effort to research whether this specific defence has a legal basis (in statute or in case law) in the jurisdiction you are investigating. It is possible that a certain defence mentioned here is in a specific system classified under another defence: the categorization employed here is only indicative.

12.2   CONTRIBUTORY NEGLIGENCE

Contributory negligence is in common law regularly considered a defence, while in civil law systems it is typically viewed as a separate doctrine, or is discussed under multiple causality whereby one of the causes is attributable to the victim (like in France). The general concept and the way in which it works is however fairly similar.

---

[1]   A theoretical and practical examination of English law is Goudkamp 2013.

[2]   In French law the defences are mostly derived from criminal law and are recognized in doctrine and case law, Viney, Jourdain and Carval 2013, pp. 644–82 (*Les faits justificatifs*).

Contributory negligence exists where the harm or the damage was at least caused partly by the victim. This may also involve causes that are to be attributed to the victim. An example is that the damage was partly caused by an employee of the plaintiff.[3] The consequence of contributory negligence is a reduction of the amount of damages that is awarded.[4] If the contribution of the victim is the most important cause, the result may even be that the judge finds that the defendant did not act unlawfully or that there is no causal connection between his act and the harm.[5] This doctrine is also applicable in contract law.

As mentioned, French law discusses contributory negligence as a kind of multiple causality (§ 3.6). This makes sense as multiple causality is viewed as involving all cases where there is another cause of the harm besides the behaviour of the tortfeasor. If the other cause is attributable to the victim, it is a case of contributory negligence, otherwise it is a case of multiple tortfeasors (or possibly force majeure). If there is contributory negligence (i.e. a cause attributed to the victim), this may lead to a reduction of the award of damages.

In German law contributory negligence (*Mitverschulden*) is regulated in § 254 BGB. This includes contribution to the occurrence of harm and contribution to the extent of damage flowing from the harm. In English law contributory negligence is regulated by a specific act,[6] as earlier precedent law in this area was found to be too strict, hence the legislator intervened.

Contributory negligence principally relates to factors that were causal to the occurrence of the harm. It is also possible that the victim did not partly cause the harm but failed to take steps to mitigate the damage. The victim will then be barred from recovering the damage that they could reasonably have prevented from occurring. In English law this is called the doctrine of *mitigation of damage*. In civil law systems this is typically covered also under contributory negligence, where the cause has contributed to the extent of damage. However, French law does not recognize an obligation on the victim to mitigate damage.[7] An example of mitigation is the victim of a car accident, who doesn't follow the doctor's orders and consequentially doesn't improve as quickly and as well as would normally happen. In both cases the consequence may be a reduction of damages. The presence of a particular medical weakness before the accident is usually not a cause for contributory negligence. As the maxim goes, 'the tortfeasor takes the victim as he finds him'. For instance, if the victim has brittle bones and thereby suffers severe injuries from a relatively minor accident, the defendant still has to compensate the damage, even though the damage is unusually large.

---

[3]   Contributory negligence may also cover some cases that could be brought under consent or assumption of risk; this depends on the jurisdiction.

[4]   The assessment of the percentage of reduction is usually left to the discretion of the courts, who tend to look at the (estimated) proportionate causal contribution, as well as the seriousness of the wrongfulness of the act (in particularly the presence of intent/malice).

[5]   In Madagascar these two possibilities are separately explicated in art. 230 and 235 of La théorie générale des obligations, Loi n° 66-003 du 2 juillet 1966.

[6]   The Law Reform (Contributory Negligence) Act 1945.

[7]   Recently affirmed in Cass., 1, 2 July 2014, no 13-17599.

The reduction of damages is usually determined by looking at either the causal proportion to the harm, or the seriousness of the faults of each party (intention, negligence).

12.3   OTHER DEFENCES

There are several other defences that by and large cover the same cases, but there is no consistent terminology. Here we will briefly go over several of the most important defences found.

French law recognizes several kinds of defences, or as it is called in French law justificatory facts (*faits justificatifs*), influenced by criminal law and mostly recognized in case law.[8] In German law some defences are found in the BGB, while others have a different legal basis.[9] English tort law recognizes a number of defences, but the available defences vary according to the tort.[10]

Permission (consent).[11] An action is not unlawful if the person who suffers the consequences consented to the action (*volenti non fit injuria*). A good example is medical treatment: cutting a patient would be wrongful, but if the patient consented to being operated upon, the surgery is of course allowed.[12]

A closely related concept is *assumption of risk* (in English law: voluntary assumption of risk). An example is horse-riding: although it is known that there is the danger of incurring serious harm if the horse throws you off, a rider does not expect or hope to be harmed. Strictly speaking the rider does not consent to harm, only assumes the risk of getting harmed, and thereby may be barred from holding the keeper of the horse liable. Participating in boxing may involve consent (to being hit), but could conceivably also be categorized as assumption of risk.

Force majeure. This means an overpowering external cause,[13] which is not to be attributed to either the victim or the defendant. French law also speaks of a 'chance event' (*cas fortuit*) that was unforeseeable and irresistible for the defendant.[14] The latter is a concept often found in jurisdictions influenced by French law.[15] The two are usually considered to be synonymous.

The defence of force majeure is primarily relevant for strict liability.[16] We will see an example in the liability for motorized vehicles (§ 14.2). Another example is the liability of

---

[8]   Viney, Jourdain and Carval 2013, pp. 332–58, 644–82, Le Tourneau 2020, paras 2141.11–40.

[9]   Deutsch and Ahrens 2014, para 91-110, Wagner 2021, paras 5.18, 5.95–5.99.

[10]   Goudkamp 2013.

[11]   In German: *Einwilligung*. See Wagner 2021, para 5.97–5.99.

[12]   A codification of this principle can be found in art. 52 of the Turkish Code of Obligations (*Türk Borçlar Kanunu*).

[13]   A definition of force majeure can be found in art. 129 of the Senegalese Code des Obligations Civiles et Commerciales (COCC): 'an external, insurmountable event that was impossible to foresee' (translation author).

[14]   Viney, Jourdain and Carval 2013, p. 336, Fabre-Magnan 2021, pp. 262–9, referring to numerous cases.

[15]   Other examples are art. 1388(2)(c) Civil code of Seychelles (2021), art. 393 Civil code of Brazil (see Celli 2021, at 548–9).

[16]   In German law *höhere Gewalt* (greater force) is an exception to the liability for motorized vehicles (§ 7.2 Straßenverkehrsgesetz, Road Traffic Act, see § 15.2 below and Wagner 2021, para 8.35 and 8.53).

a train company, based on the French liability for objects (§ 14.4): if an unknown person pushes a victim waiting on the platform before the train, that constitutes *force majeure* for the train company.[17] In French law, force majeure is also applied to fault liability, although not very often. For instance, the train company is liable for a collision of a train with a car that broke down on the tracks, as this is not unforeseeable.[18] A hurricane, armed robbery, and similar events may constitute force majeure dependent on the specific circumstances of the case.[19] The consequence of force majeure may simply be that the causal connection is broken, or that the behaviour of the defendant does not constitute fault. Force majeure is applied particularly in cases of strict liability.

In English law, force majeure (or as it used to be called in the past, Act of God) is recognized as a defence only for the rule of *Rylands v Fletcher* (§ 15.4).[20]

Necessity.[21] This defence involves actions undertaken to protect the defendant's interests or the good of other people, in particular in urgent cases of imminent peril. Of course, it does not apply when the defendant caused the necessity in the first place. The defence requires that the actions were reasonable. An example is tearing down houses to prevent fire from spreading. Another example (from English law) is erecting barricades on your own land against an incursion of water, with the result that the water floods your neighbour's land.[22] Another example is injuring a dog that attacks you, in order to avoid being bitten.[23] In French law, this defence is rarely used, as it overlaps with force majeure. It requires that the defendant was threatened with a danger which they could only evade by causing a less serious harm to another's interests. French lawyers treat the act of saving someone else in peril as a form of necessity.[24] While necessity may remove the wrongfulness of an act, most legal systems[25] still require the person who acted in necessity to compensate for the damage he caused.

Self-defence.[26] This involves defence against an attack, typically restricted to physical attack (like the torts of assault or battery). This differs from necessity in that necessity may arise

---

[17] Cass., 2, 8 February 2018, no 16-26198 and 17-10516. It should be noted that the relatives of the victim (who were the claimants) had already received compensation from the Compensation Fund for the Victims of Terrorist Attacks and Other Crimes (*Fonds de Garantie des Victimes des actes de Terrorisme et d'autres Infractions*).

[18] Cass., 2, 10 nov. 2009, no 08-20971. The liability of the train company was based on strict liability for the train as an object.

[19] Viney, Jourdain and Carval 2013, p. 344.

[20] Clerk and Lindsell 2020, para 19-93.

[21] French: *L'état de nécessité*. German law recognizes *defensiver Notstand* (§ 228 BGB) and *aggressiver Notstand* (§ 904 BGB), defensive and aggressive necessity when harming another's good to save a more important interest (Deutsch and Ahrens 2014, paras 97 and 99, see also para 108).

[22] *Home Brewery v William Davis and Co (Leicester) Ltd.* [1987] Q.B. 339.

[23] This is not self-defence, as self-defence is against an attack of a human being.

[24] Viney, Jourdain and Carval 2013, p. 666. Here we discuss this under pure omissions (§ 6.3).

[25] See § 228 BGB, similarly for French law.

[26] In English law: private defence, in German: *Notwehr* (§ 227 BGB), in French: *La légitime défense* (see arts. 122-5 through 122-7 Code Pénal (Criminal code)).

from a natural danger, while self-defence is against a danger posed by the person you defend yourself against (and who you thereby injure). In French law, 'legitimate defence' as it is called may also encompass aggression against another person, or against goods, including economic interests. Other systems might view those as cases of necessity.

Illegality. If the harm was caused during or because of an illegal activity in which the victim knowingly participated, the victim cannot obtain compensation. Most legal systems restrict protection to legitimate interests.[27] This is often expressed in the Latin maxim *ex turpi causa non oritur actio*, no action can arise from a dishonourable act. An example from English law is *Gray v Thames Trains*[28] about a man who suffered Post-Traumatic Stress Disorder after a train crash, then killed a man in an argument and was subsequently convicted of manslaughter and detained under the Mental Health Act 1983. His claim for loss of income due to the detainment was rejected as the detainment was caused by the criminal act of manslaughter.

Statutory duty. If you are obliged by law to do something, this cannot be considered wrongful.

In English law there is the defence of statutory authority, which applies for instance to the tort of private nuisance: if you are obligated by statute to use your land in a certain way, you cannot be held liable for the inevitable nuisance caused by that use.[29]

Order by legitimate authority.[30] If a police officer commands you to drive on the wrong side of the road in order to circumvent an obstacle, you are not acting wrongfully by doing so. This defence can be considered a species of statutory duty.

12.4   PRESCRIPTION AND STATUTE OF LIMITATIONS

In addition to defences and grounds of justification, there is another important bar to liability: *prescription*. This means that if the claimant waits too long before filing a claim,[31] they will no longer obtain a remedy in court. The claim has 'prescribed', it is 'time-barred'. In common law systems this is usually referred to as the *statute of limitations*, since there is an actual statute that contains these limitations.[32] Rules for prescription are often found in an entirely different part of a civil code, and not in the part about tort law. However, some countries do have prescription rules in the tort law section.[33]

---

[27]   For French law see Viney, Jourdain and Carval 2013, pp. 111–18.

[28]   *Gray v Thames Trains* [2009] UKHL 33. Since then, the Supreme Court gave a general approach to illegality in *Patel v Mirza* [2016] UKSC 42, which also applies in tort law (see *Henderson v Dorset Healthcare University NHS Foundation Trust* [2020] UKSC 43).

[29]   *Manchester Corporation v Farnworth* [1930] AC 171.

[30]   An example of this defence can be found in Thailand, s. 449 Civil and Commercial Code (2008).

[31]   The claim usually has to be filed in court, but it is possible that you can also restart the prescription period by sending a notice to the tortfeasor.

[32]   For example, the Limitation Act 1980 in England and Wales, the Limitation Act, 1963 in India.

[33]   For instance, Chile in art. 2332 Código Civil (1855).

Prescription law is an extremely complicated area due to the presence in every system of numerous detailed exceptions. In the following overview only the main outlines and concepts are discussed, with a few examples that are by no means exhaustive. You should carefully examine the requirements and effects of prescription if you are confronted with prescription in practice.

In German law the prescription (*Verjährung*) of tort claims starts from the moment the victim is cognizant of the circumstances that ground liability and the person of the tortfeasor (§ 199 BGB). The general prescription period (*Frist*) is three years (§ 195 BGB). In French law, *la prescription de l'action* is five years for general actions (art. 2270-1 Cc), ten for physical injury (art. 2226 Cc) and 20 years for particularly grievous acts like torture or sexual abuse of minors (art. 2226 Cc).[34] Crimes against humanity do not prescribe at all.[35] For English law, tort actions must generally be brought to court within six years after the cause of action 'accrues',[36] according to s. 2 Limitation Act 1980. After that, the action is 'time-barred'. For many actions for personal injury the limit is three years (ss. 11–14 Limitation Act 1980), and other limits apply to specific torts.

English law does not yet have a general 'long-stop period', a rule that absolutely bars claims after a very long period even if the claimant lacked knowledge to start a claim.[37] There is only a long-stop period of 15 years for negligence (s. 14B Limitation Act 1980). In French law there is a long-stop period (*délai-butoir*) of 20 years (art. 2232 Cc). § 199(2) BGB contains for German law a long-stop period of 30 years from the moment of the wrongful conduct or injury or another harmful event.

The prescription usually starts when the victim is able to sue in court, or as they say in English law, when a cause of action 'accrues'. This is the moment when all the necessary elements for a claim have been fulfilled and are known to the claimant (§ 199(1) BGB). One element is usually the presence of actual damage, and in French law that is the main criterion: the moment at which the damage materializes.[38] As damage may take some time to materialize, the actual start of prescription may be some time after the harm. In English law the cause of action accrues when the claimant can establish the facts necessary to prove all the elements of the cause of action, similar to German law. But as some torts do not require the presence of damage, the limitation period may start immediately with the occurrence of harm.

The limitation period can be temporarily halted or suspended ('tolled' is the English term) by various means, principally by filing a suit (starting a procedure in court). In German law, suspension (*Hemmung*) is achieved by a court procedure, negotiations and other actions (§ 204 BGB), as well as in a few specific cases as between spouses during marriage (§ 207 BGB and

---

[34]   Fabre-Magnan 2021, pp. 547–8.

[35]   Art 213-5 Code Pénale, Fabre-Magnan 2021, p. 549. The operation of the criminal code for civil liability is too complicated to discuss here.

[36]   This concept is explained later in this section.

[37]   Several other common law jurisdictions do have a long-stop period, such as the ten-year period in New South Wales for damage arising out of defective building work (s. 6.20 Environmental Planning and Assessment Act 1979).

[38]   Such as in art. 2226 Code civil: 'from the date of consolidation of the initial or aggravated damage'.

others). After the suspending event is removed (such as after divorce), the term continuous from when it was suspended (§ 209 BGB), but in some cases the term starts anew (*Neubeginn*, § 212 BGB), such as after an award of damages by the court.[39] French law similarly makes a distinction between suspension and interruption (starting anew), see arts. 2230 and 2231 Code civil. Suspension may occur for instance by force majeure (art. 2234 Cc, listing other cases as well) or during marriage (art. 2236 Cc) or mediation (art. 2238 Cc). Starting a court procedure interrupts the prescription (art. 2241 Cc) until the procedure has ended (art. 2242 Cc). The English Limitation Act 1980 provides that the limitation period may be extended in several cases, such as mediation in cross-border disputes (s. 33A Limitation Act 1980). A fresh accrual of action (starting the period anew) occurs upon acknowledgement of the claim or partial payment (s. 29 Limitation Act 1980).

Different limitation periods apply for different jurisdictions (countries) and kinds of tort. At the lower end are three years for many English torts and German law, at the higher end five to ten years for French law. Specific actions and grounds may have different periods, such as the three-year period for product liability on the basis of art. 10 Product Liability Directive 85/374/EEC. For particularly grievous torts (such as sexual abuse) or torts that are harder to detect (particularly environmental harm), a longer limitation period may apply.

12.5 OTHER LIMITATIONS ON LIABILITY

Finally, for the sake of completeness, there are a few other limitations on liability that can be mentioned.

Firstly, in some cases the liability of the defendant may be limited by a prior contractual agreement. This usually occurs in cases that are primarily contractual in nature. If the jurisdiction allows a tort action in a contractual case,[40] it is possible that a limitation clause in the contract may restrict the liability of the defendant. An example is a lawyer who uses terms and conditions that limit professional liability to €1,000,000. If the client sues the lawyer, the limitation will usually hold up in court. A limitation clause, incidentally, may also limit liability to the *kind* of damage that the defendant needs to compensate. A very common clause is to restrict liability to only personal injury and property damage, excluding compensation for pure economic loss.

Secondly, for particular types of cases there are statutory limitations to liability. An example is the limitation of product liability in the European Union to personal injury and property damage (§ 15.5). Another example is the treaty limitations to the amount of damages to be awarded for cases involving aircrafts, space objects, nuclear energy (§ 16.9.1).

---

[39] An enforceable court decision has a prescription period of 30 years (§ 197 and 201 BGB).

[40] This would usually not be allowed in France (§ 1.6).

13
Strict liability in general

13.1   INTRODUCTION

In the previous chapters we have considered fault liability. In the following chapters we will look at another form of liability, one that does not require wrongful behaviour of the defendant. This is called *strict liability*.[1] An example is the Palsgraf case (§ 2.1), where it was presumed that the railway company was liable for the alleged negligence of its employees.

In this chapter we examine the concept of strict liability in general. We will begin by examining several ways in which fault liability can be applied to achieve results similar to strict liability (§ 12.2). These approaches are still used where there is no actual strict liability for a specific category of cases. We will continue with the arguments that justify imposing strict liability (§ 13.3). Subsequently we will look at several issues and questions of strict liability (§ 13.4), and introduce the two main categories of strict liability (§ 13.5).

13.2   FROM FAULT LIABILITY TO STRICT LIABILITY

While tort law starts from the principle that liability is based on a personal fault by the defendant, it is generally recognized that it is also possible to hold someone liable in the absence of a personal fault. This form of liability is called risk-based liability or *strict liability*.[2] An example is the liability of the employer for torts committed by his employees.

To introduce this topic, we should first consider whether strict liability is really necessary. Liability for other persons or objects could be achieved also with fault liability. For instance, if an employee committed a tort, the employer could be held liable if it was shown that the employer was negligent in supervising the employee, say by allowing the employee to work with a dangerous tool without proper instruction.[3] This approach upholds the principle of fault liability. An advantage of holding the employer liable besides the employee is that the victim has another venue for compensation, which is important if the employee is impecunious while the employer is sufficiently wealthy to pay the award of damages. The same approach

---

[1]   French: *responsabilité de plein droit*. German: *Gefährdungshaftung*.

[2]   Werro and Büyüksagis 2021.

[3]   The application of negligence also requires that the defendant actually did have a duty to supervise, a duty of care, but we can presume that here.

would work with the owner of an animal who injured another person, where liability of the owner as supervisor is necessary to obtain compensation, as a dog cannot be sued. A duty of supervision usually takes the form of a fairly high standard of care.

This approach, however, is not without problems. The victim must prove that the supervisor did not observe sufficient care. This can turn out to be an insurmountable obstacle, and the victim's claim would be denied as a result. It also seems unfair that the victim should have to prove the absence of due care, as the supervisor would be far better placed to prove the level of care. The position of the victim can be improved by readily assuming that the victim has provided prima facie evidence of the lack of care and setting the bar high for the disculpatory evidence by the supervisor that they did observe sufficient care. This amounts to a *rebuttable presumption* that the defendant exercised insufficient care. The defendant may provide evidence that this presumption is in fact unfounded. The next step is simply to *reverse the burden of proof* that sufficient care was taken. If courts subsequently make it very hard to prove sufficient care, the end result is very close to strict liability, as the defendant would be practically unable to escape liability.

The final step is to remove the possibility of disculpatory evidence altogether. That amounts to actual strict liability, as defendants are liable even if they can prove beyond any doubt that they were not negligent in supervision, nor otherwise at fault.

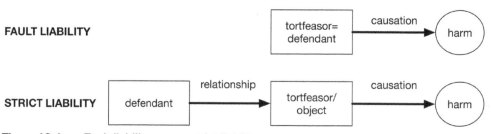

Figure 13.1   Fault liability versus strict liability

Whereas fault liability is fundamentally based on finding a wrongful action by the defendant, strict liability arises solely from the fact that an object or person caused harm in a certain way, and a specific kind of relation between the object or person and the defendant. This will become clearer in subsequent chapters.

All jurisdictions recognize the need to hold individuals liable for harm caused by other persons or things, and this often takes the form of strict liability. Nonetheless there is a large variety of ways in which this result is achieved: whereas some countries accept strict liability in many cases, others operate mostly with intermediate solutions like a rebuttable presumption of negligence or reversed burden of proof. Indeed, if concurrent actions are allowed, it may be possible to, for example, sue an employer on the basis of vicarious liability and simultaneously on the ground of negligence for not observing proper care. Strict liability and fault liability are not always clearly distinguishable.

13.3   JUSTIFICATIONS FOR STRICT LIABILITY

Once you understand what strict liability is, you may wonder why we should hold someone liable in the absence of a personal fault. Although the victim might consider it obvious that they should receive compensation from someone else, the defendant may have a different opinion and may point out that he did not do anything wrong. So what is the justification for strict liability? Legal scholars have argued this issue at length. Among the many reasons that have been proposed, three arguments stand out.[4]

First of all, the defendant may have been in a position to actually prevent the harm, or at least materially reduce the risk that the harm occurred. The employer could instruct his employee to drive safely, could impose restrictions on the use of dangerous tools. The owner of an animal could train the animal or hold it on a leash. In short, it seems reasonable to assume that the defendant had some form of *control* over the person or object.[5] Indeed, this is usually the case in the various forms of strict liability we will encounter. In the previous section the term 'supervisor' was used to express this presumption of control. The actual control over a person or object can provide ground for a legal obligation to supervise.

Secondly, the supervisor usually *benefits* or *profits* in some way from the activity in the course of which the risk of harm arose. Employers run a business for which they hire employees, and the possibility of harm due to employee actions is a risk that the business should bear. This line of reasoning can be extended to non-pecuniary benefits. The owner of a pet may not derive financial benefit from the animal but presumably decided to take a pet for emotional or psychological reasons. Benefit and control often go together, as the supervisor may be the person that brought the corresponding risk in the world, entered into the relationship with the person or object. The owner bought the dog, the employer hired the employee, the parent conceived the child. Even if there is no control over the risk at the moment of harm, the original choice was made by the supervisor. So there is a usually a form of choice involved (even if the choice itself was not wrongful), which does provide a further justification in favour of imposing strict liability. The choice, however, is not a separate justification, rather supports the argument from benefit or control.

A third justification of strict liability is found in the economic argument that the person in control of the risk should have an *incentive* to take precautionary measures to limit the risk. Liability is such an incentive. In the absence of strict liability, a business could increase its profits by foregoing cheap and simple precautionary measures if the business would not suffer from the harmful effects. The negative effects of the activity are devolved on parties who are external to the activity: in economic parlance these effects are called *externalities*. Strict liability internalizes these costs again. Companies may thereby be incentivized to properly balance the costs of safety measures against the entire social harm. Admittedly a similar result could theoretically be obtained by application of negligence, but as discussed earlier negligence requires

---

[4]   See also the case *Various Claimants v Catholic Child Welfare Society* [2012] UKSC 56, discussed in § 14.2.

[5]   Even if there was no actual possibility of control at the moment that the harm occurred, there usually was an earlier opportunity to take preventive measures.

that it can be established that the business was at fault, breached a duty of care. In cases where the lack of a certain safety measure cannot be qualified as an actual fault or negligent act, the victim may still suffer a significant injury that the company could easily prevent.

The various grounds for justification of strict liability have to be balanced against the reasons for restricting liability, just like we have seen for fault liability. Even if there are reasons to hold a person in a certain supervisory position liable, it may in specific instances seem unfair to actually impose liability. For instance, should a child who inherits a business be liable for fraud committed by an employee of the business, particularly if that employee is also the guardian of the child? If a couple's dog bites the woman, should the man be liable even though the woman is also co-owner? The specific and sometimes convoluted criteria in this area of the law can be understood as an attempt to balance the interests of both victim and supervisor.

13.4   THE THREE MAIN ISSUES OF STRICT LIABILITY

The need for balance underlines how important it is to set the precise limits of strict liability. There are three aspects whereby strict liability is limited, which can be phrased in the form of three questions that have to be answered.

- what is the *relation* between the person held liable and the actual cause of the harm (object or person)?
- to what *kinds of acts or events* does liability extend?
- which *defences* apply?

All legal systems have established criteria to resolve these issues, whereby the extent of strict liability is delimited. The justificatory reasons for strict liability can serve to interpret these criteria and make them comprehensible.

For the first question, we will encounter a variety of answers. If we believe that control is the paramount reason for strict liability, it seems logical to hold the supervisor liable (guardian in French law). If we focus rather on the benefit from the risk, we might look at the enterprise or business in which the object is used. Both approaches come together in the idea that the owner, keeper, employer, or parent is liable. It is also possible that there are several persons simultaneously liable, as we shall see in the case of motorized vehicles. This usually leads to joint and several liability (§ 9.3).

For the second question the easy answer in case of liability for persons is that the person must have committed a tort. But this approach does not work for objects such as animals and cars, as these cannot commit an actual tort. We are therefore left with the problem of finding another criterion to distinguish events that lead to liability from events involving the object where liability would be unjustified. If a dog bites a person, it seems right that the owner is liable, but what if the owner was assaulted by the victim and the dog sprang to his defence?

Finally, another way to avoid an overly large area of strict liability is to allow defences. In particular the defence of force majeure is a way to distinguish events that are simply due to bad luck, where external events are the real cause and not someone else's pet or vehicle.

13.5 TWO KINDS OF STRICT LIABILITY

Within strict liability we can make a further division between two kinds of strict liability that are fundamentally different in nature:

- liability for other persons, and
- liability for objects (and dangerous activities).

Liability for persons presumes that the other person committed a tort. If the tortfeasor was a very young child of a mentally disabled person, their behaviour may strictly speaking not fulfil the conditions for a tort because the lack of subjective wrongfulness (§§ 8.2–8.3), but the behaviour would at least need to be objectively tortious. That means that the behaviour would be a tort, if the condition of subjective wrongfulness would be fulfilled, it would meet all the criteria of a tort if the person would have been an adult of sound mind.

Liability for objects has to be regulated in a different way, as objects cannot commit torts. The problem is therefore to delineate the kind of harmful events involving the object for which the supervisor is liable. Is the owner of a dog liable for a broken window when a careless driver hit the dog which was then thrown through a window?

Another form of strict liability is liability for dangerous activities. We will discuss this group of cases together with liability for objects. The reason for doing so is that it is often quite difficult to separate cases of dangerous objects from cases involving dangerous activities. Is operating a nuclear plant a dangerous activity or does it involve a dangerous object? The issues involved are very similar, hence it makes sense to lump them together.

If we compare strict liability to fault liability, we see that strict liability uses different criteria to balance the need to protect the victim and the interest of individuals to limit their exposure to liability. Instead of the criterion of fault, there are various criteria tailored to the specific kind of strict liability. The other two elements of fault liability, causality and harm, in principle still apply to strict liability and may serve to further limit the extent of liability. The precise way in which these criteria – and the notion of damage – are applied may in specific jurisdictions be slightly different from the way fault liability is treated. For example, it is possible that remoteness of damage is applied more strictly or that pure economic loss is not compensated for strict liability. In an introductory text we cannot discuss these details: you should be aware of and actively check for such differences when researching strict liability in a specific jurisdiction.

In the following chapters we will examine liability for torts committed by other persons (Chapter 14), and liability for objects and activities (Chapter 15). As explained before, the actual rules we discuss are not all forms of strict liability, as that depends on the jurisdiction. The common thread is that someone can be liable for someone or something else, which may or may not be based on strict liability.

14
Liability for other persons

14.1 INTRODUCTION

This chapter is devoted to liability for other persons, which often is a form of strict liability.[1] We will start with vicarious liability, the liability for employees (§ 14.2). Subsequently we will consider other forms of liability for persons: extending liability to cover persons akin to employees (§ 14.3), children and mentally disabled persons (§ 14.4) and a more general rule for liability (§ 14.5). We will briefly examine the doctrine of non-delegable duties which provides a limited form of liability for the actions of independent contractors (§ 14.6). Finally we will look at organizational liability which supplements vicarious liability in a different way (§ 14.7).

14.2 LIABILITY FOR EMPLOYEES (VICARIOUS LIABILITY)

It has been accepted for a long time that employers may be liable for torts committed by their employees.[2] We start with a quick overview of the law in this regard in the three key jurisdictions considered in this text.

In England the liability for employees is called vicarious liability.[3] In the leading case *Various Claimants v Catholic Child Welfare Society*[4] the Supreme Court stated that the test for vicarious liability consists of two stages (at 21):[5]

- the relationship of employer and employee is one that is capable of giving rise to vicarious liability, and
- the connection that links the relationship and the tort.

These stages have to be examined in conjunction, they influence each other.

---

[1]   See also Giliker 2010, Van Dam 2013, paras 1606–07.

[2]   See Zweigert and Kötz 1998, pp. 643–5, Giliker 2010, pp. 227–54 on justification for this kind of liability.

[3]   In US law the liability of an employer for employees is referred to as the doctrine of *respondeat superior*.

[4]   [2012] UKSC 56.

[5]   Besides the requirement that the employee committed a tort.

In France the liability for subordinates (*préposés*) is found in art. 1242(5) Cc,[6] which states:

---

art. 1242(5) Cc
Les maîtres et les commettants, du dommage causé par leurs domestiques et préposés dans les fonctions auxquelles ils les ont employés …

art. 1242(5) Cc
The masters and the principals [are responsible] for the damage caused by their domestic servants and their subordinates in the functions in which they have employed them.

In Germany the liability for auxiliaries or vicarious agents (Verrichtungsgehilfen) is regulated in § 831 BGB:

---

§ 831 BGB
(1) Wer einen anderen zu einer Verrichtung bestellt, ist zum Ersatz des Schadens verpflichtet, den der andere in Ausführung der Verrichtung einem Dritten widerrechtlich zufügt. Die Ersatzpflicht tritt nicht ein, wenn der Geschäftsherr bei der Auswahl der bestellten Person und, sofern er Vorrichtungen oder Gerätschaften zu beschaffen oder die Ausführung der Verrichtung zu leiten hat, bei der Beschaffung oder der Leitung die im Verkehr erforderliche Sorgfalt beobachtet oder wenn der Schaden auch bei Anwendung dieser Sorgfalt entstanden sein würde.
(2) Die gleiche Verantwortlichkeit trifft denjenigen, welcher für den Geschäftsherrn die Besorgung eines der im Absatz 1 Satz 2 bezeichneten Geschäfte durch Vertrag übernimmt.

§ 831 BGB
(1) Whomever appoints someone else for a task is obligated to compensate the damage that the other caused to a third party in the performance of that task. The duty to compensate does not apply when the principal observed the care required in society in the choice of the appointed person and – insofar he had to procure devices or equipment or had to manage the execution of the task - in the procurement and management, or when the damage would also have occurred while observing this care.
(2) The same responsibility applies to the person who takes on the performance of the procurement or management meant in subsection 1, second sentence, on behalf of the principal on the basis of contract.

Note that this provision contains an exception if the employer proves they exercised reasonable care: this is therefore not a true form of strict liability.

Even though nominally these rules are all about employees, they use different concepts and criteria. Nonetheless they appear to cover by and large the same ground: an employer may be

---

[6]   For the sake of simplicity we leave out discussion of art. 1242(4) which imposes liability on teachers and artisans for students and apprentices.

liable for torts committed by their employees. That leaves out a number of details that we can now investigate. The issues identified in § 13.4 can serve as a guide, adapted to the circumstances of employer–employee relationships.

1. When is there an employer–employee relation, and can this liability also extend to similar relations?
2. For which acts by the employee is the employer liable?
3. Is the employee also personally liable and/or can the employer take recourse on the employee if they paid damages to the victim?

There are no specific defences for vicarious liability, as vicarious liability first requires that the employee fulfils the conditions of a specific tort. The employer can invoke the same defences that are available to the employee who is accused of having committed a tort.

14.2.1   The relationship

The starting point for vicarious liability is the presence of an employment relationship, a labour contract. However, in modern society there are numerous relationships which are similar to employment without there being an actual employment contract. Consider for instance independent contractors, temp workers, volunteers, platform workers[7] (Uber drivers, bicycle couriers). The justification for liability of the supervisor seems to apply also to some or all of those relationships. Many legal systems have therefore extended vicarious liability to apply also to certain relationships that are not an employment relationship in the strict sense of the word. An alternative approach is to establish additional forms of strict liability for non-employees (§§ 14.3–14.6). Here we discuss the extension of vicarious liability to encompass both employees and certain groups of non-employees.

In English law the doctrine of vicarious liability has been extended to all relationships 'akin to' an employment relationship. English law relies on a broad set of factors with a stress on an

---

[7]   Certain platform workes actually were found to be employees in several jurisdictions; there are currently numerous court cases about this issue.

actual employee relationship.[8] The leading case is *Various Claimants v Catholic Child Welfare Society*,[9] where the relationship is tested against five factors [35]:

> There is no difficulty in identifying a number of policy reasons that usually make it fair, just and reasonable to impose vicarious liability on the employer when these criteria are satisfied:
> (i) The employer is more likely to have the means to compensate the victim than the employee and can be expected to have insured against that liability;
> (ii) The tort will have been committed as a result of activity being taken by the employee on behalf of the employer;
> (iii) The employee's activity is likely to be part of the business activity of the employer;
> (iv) The employer, by employing the employee to carry on the activity will have created the risk of the tort committed by the employee;
> (v) The employee will, to a greater or lesser degree, have been under the control of the employer.

Hereby vicarious liability receives fairly wide application, compared to other systems. This is understandable as English law does not have many other grounds of liability for persons (see also § 14.3).

In German law, § 831 BGB requires that the tort has been committed by an auxiliary, a person used to perform a task for the principal (*Verrichtungsgehilfe*). In case law this has been interpreted as meaning persons who are dependent on instructions from the principal.[10] This may be an employee as well as similarly positioned non-employee, but not an independent contractor.[11]

In France, art. 1242(5) Cc establishes liability for faults of a subordinate (*préposé*). In case law this has been interpreted as comprising employees and independent contractors. The criterion is whether there is a 'relation of subordination' (control over the behaviour of the auxiliary).[12]

These approaches are quite similar as they extend also to certain independent contractors who are instructed by the principal and may sit at a desk doing the same work as an actual employee at the next desk. These are to be distinguished from fully independently operating professionals, such as an advocate who is hired by a company but does the work from their

---

[8] For instance, in *Cox v Ministry of Justice* [2016] UKSC 10 vicarious liability is extended to a prisoner who was put to work in the prison kitchen, and in *Armes v Nottinghamshire County Council* [2017] UKSC 60 to foster parents who abused their foster child.

[9] [2012] UKSC 56.

[10] Deutsch and Ahrens 2014, para 446, Wagner 2021, para 6.7: 'wer von den Weisungen seines Geschäftsherrn abhängig ist'. It suffices that the principal at any moment may limit or remove or determine in time and extent the conduct of the person who acted wrongfully.

[11] Deutsch and Ahrens 2014, para 446, Wagner 2021, para 6.11. Such contractors are hired for a fee and are independently responsible: they are not depending on instructions.

[12] 'Lien de préposition', Fabre-Magnan 2021, p. 441.

own office under their own control. The English approach appears to be broader by also including relationships such as inmates in a prison (§ 14.3). In Germany such cases might be resolved either by assuming a contractual relationship between victim and supervisor or by finding the violation of a *Verkehrspflicht*. In France the rule from the Blieck case (see § 14.5) would be applied.

14.2.2   The extent of liability

With regard to the extent of actions for which liability exists, there are again different approaches. To introduce the issue, it may be instructive to start with the so-called Salmond test that English law used in the past.[13] This test held that the employer was liable for two kinds of acts:

- wrongful acts authorized by the employer, and
- a wrongful and unauthorized mode of doing an authorized act.

An example of the first category would be an employer that ordered the driver of his car to ignore the speed limit in order to catch a flight.

An example of the second category could be the chauffeur making an inadvertent steering mistake, causing a traffic accident. However, this category also covers other kinds of mistakes that appear farther removed from the intentions of the employer.

To illustrate this, we can take a German case where the employer had asked his employee to pick up a freight load with a truck.[14] As the load was too large to fit into a single truck, the employer had instructed the employee to make two runs. Instead, the employee decided to take a lorry train[15] which would enable him to take the complete load in one run, even though the employer had told him not to do so. Unfortunately, the employee caused an accident with the lorry train. The German court found the employer liable under German law. Such a case would presumably fall within the second category of the Salmond test, thereby illustrating that this is a form of strict liability: the employer did not clearly do anything wrong as he had expressly forbidden the use of the lorry train that occurred.

The justification for holding the employer liable in these cases may be found in considering that the employee acted solely for the benefit of the employer, even if the employee made an error in judgement as to the proper way to execute the acts.

Over time the Salmond test was found to be too restrictive. A third category of acts, outright unauthorized acts, would not be compensated on the basis of vicarious liability. The English House of Lords finally decided to broaden the scope of vicarious in the leading case *Lister*

---

[13]   By John Salmond in his *Law of Torts* (London: Steven & Haynes 1907), § 29: 'a master is not responsible for a wrongful act done by his servant unless it is done in the course of his employment. It is deemed to be so done if it is either (a) a wrongful act authorised by the master, or (b) a wrongful and unauthorised *mode* of doing some act authorised by the master'.

[14]   BGH 6 October 1970, NJW 1971, 31 (lorry-train).

[15]   Two connected trailers making one long vehicle.

v Hesley Hall.[16] This case involved sexual abuse by the warden of a school for children with emotional and behavioural difficulties. Evidently the abuse was completely unauthorized and did not benefit the employer in any way. Nonetheless the House of Lords decided that the employer should also be liable for unauthorized acts if the acts had a sufficiently 'close connection with the employment'.

It appears that the relevant aspect of such cases is that the employment provided the employee with means and/or opportunity to commit the tort. Actions that were undertaken by the employee purely for their own benefit[17] and completely outside the work environment and work hours, without use of any object from work, are probably not sufficiently closely connected to lead to vicarious liability. But the precise boundaries may be hard to determine. An example is an employee who bears a grudge and who deliberately leaks personnel data from the employer on the internet.[18] The court of first instance found the employer liable, but the Supreme Court decisively declared that this specific case lies outside the scope of vicarious liability.

The gradual extension of the actions for which the employer is liable can be observed in other jurisdictions as well.[19] In French law, the employer is liable for all acts by the employer unless the employee was acting 'outside the functions for which he was employed, without authority and for purposes alien to his role'.[20] The effect of these cumulative criteria is that liability may exist for unauthorized acts.

In German law the criterion is whether the employee acted in the exercise of function assigned to him, which also covers a prohibited way of performing this function.[21] This may include intentional acts when the employment gave the possibility of harming others. The upshot is that the transfer of the task increased the risk of harming interests of others.[22] The liability of § 831 BGB is not completely strict liability, it is merely a presumption of lack of care: § 831 BGB allows the employer to escape liability if the employer 'exercises reasonable care when selecting' the employee. However, due to the possibility of the employee taking recourse on the employer when the employee himself is sued (see below), this limitation of § 831 BGB has become mostly ineffective and the employer is usually strictly liable.[23]

---

[16]   *Lister and Others v Hesley Hall Limited* [2001] UKHL 22.

[17]   In case law one may encounter the phrase 'a frolic of their own'.

[18]   This is the case of *WM Morrison Supermarkets plc v Various Claimants* [2020] UKSC 12, where vicarious liability was ultimately rejected.

[19]   See also the comparative study Giliker 2010.

[20]   Cass. (plén.) 19 May 1988, D. 1988.513. The case involved an insurance salesman who ran a fraudulent financial scam on the side, without the knowledge of the insurance company, that nonetheless was found to be liable. The facts of the case resemble those of *Frederick and ors v Positive Solutions (Financial Services) Ltd*, [2018] EWCA Civ 431, where the Court of Appeal found that the scam was entirely a frolic of his own. The case is as of October 2021 still before the UKSC (case UKSC 2018/0067).

[21]   BGH 6 October 1970, NJW 1971, 31 (lorry-train).

[22]   Wagner 2021, para 6.15.

[23]   Deutsch and Ahrens 2014, para 457, also noting the effect of insurance.

The extension of vicarious liability to unauthorized acts is still contentious. For example, in Islamic law liability of the employer is apparently limited to authorized acts.[24]

14.2.3   Recovering damages from the employee

If the employer is liable under vicarious liability, the employee is in principle also personally liable, as the employee did commit a tort. In practice it is usually the employer who is sued instead, as there is a better chance that the employer can actually compensate the entire damage (has 'deeper pockets'). Now there may be rules that allow the employee to obtain compensation from the employer if the employee was personally sued. And there may be rules that allow the *employer* to sue the employee, in order to *recover* the damages that the employer had to pay on the basis of vicarious liability. Such an action is also called 'taking recourse against' the employee, or 'indemnity' (the employee has to *indemnify* the employer). Rules about recovery of damages can be located in the provisions of tort law, but they may also be found in other parts of the code, for example in the general rules on joint and several obligations, or in labour law.

At first sight it may seem logical that the person who actually committed the tort should ultimately have to bear the damages. On closer consideration there is good reason to have the employer instead bear the costs, if the tort is a common risk that may occur unintentionally in the course of the employment. For example, if a driver unwittingly makes a steering error while driving their employer's truck, thereby damaging another vehicle, it does not seem fair to let the driver pay the damage, as it is the employer who benefits from the truck rides.

Generally speaking, jurisdictions seem to prefer a rule whereby the employer cannot recover the damages that he paid from the employee, except when the employee committed the tort intentionally. This is no undue burden for businesses, as businesses are usually insured for vicarious liability.[25]

The aforementioned result is achieved in different ways. In German law originally § 840 II BGB allowed the employer to take recourse against the employee for any damages paid on the basis of § 831 BGB. However, the courts have turned this rule on its head and allow the employee to take recourse against the employer when the employee has to pay damages for negligently caused damage to third parties.[26] The employer cannot obtain compensation from the employee in the reverse case. Only in the case of intentional torts is the employee barred from compensation by his employer.

In French law the employee/subordinate is immune to a claim from the victim of their tort when the subordinate acted without exceeding the limits of the task which had been entrusted

---

[24]   Basir Bin Mohamad 2000.

[25]   This may even be compulsory, as under the English Employers' Liability (Compulsory Insurance) Act 1969.

[26]   Wagner 2021, para 6.28, referring to BGH 10 January 1955, III ZR 153/53, BGHZ 16, 111.

to them by their principal (the employer).[27] Consequentially the principal is also barred from taking recourse against the subordinate.[28]

In English law the employer is legally entitled to recover damages from the employee if the employer has paid compensation on the basis of vicarious liability for a tort committed by the employee.[29] However, this rule was controversial, and English insurance companies entered into a gentleman's agreement not to effect this rule.[30] As a result employees are normally not sued by their employers, as most employers are insured and the insurance company will then pay the damages. The legal situation becomes more complicated when the employer is also at fault (for its own negligence or for a tort by another employee), in which case the rules for joint and several liability apply and not the rule of *Lister v Romford*.[31]

14.3   LIABILITY FOR PERSONS SIMILAR TO EMPLOYEES

Vicarious liability has been explained as strict liability for employees and other persons in a similar position as employees. This generally includes temporary workers who may not have an employment contract but otherwise are nearly indistinguishable from regular employees. Usually the principal (as is the name of the person ordering the services of another person without an employment contract) is also liable for such workers under vicarious liability. If we move even further away from the employee relationship, the approaches diverge.

In England, vicarious liability can also be assumed where there is no employment contract.

> Where the defendant and the tortfeasor are not bound by a contract of employment, but their relationship has the same incidents, that relationship can properly give rise to vicarious liability on the ground that it is 'akin to that between an employer and an employee'.[32]

Recent English precedents have extended vicarious liability to relations that are progressively harder to qualify as similar to employment, such as foster parents and prisoners who were put to work.[33] The justification of these extensions was found primarily in the *control* that the defendant exercised over the activities of the tortfeasor. Vicarious liability does not, however, extend to independent contractors.[34]

---

[27] Cass. 25 February 2000, JCP 2000, I, 2141 (Costedoat), see Viney, Jourdain and Carval 2013, p. 1084, Fabre-Magnan 2021, p. 454.

[28] Viney, Jourdain and Carval 2013, p. 1087, referring among others to Cass., 2, 2 December 2007, no. 07-13403.

[29] *Lister v Romford Ice and Cold Storage Co* [1957] A.C. 555.

[30] Winfield and Jolowicz 2020, para 21-039.

[31] Winfield and Jolowicz 2020, para 21-040.

[32] *Various Claimants v Catholic Child Welfare Society* [2012] UKSC 56, nr. 47.

[33] *Cox v Ministry of Justice* [2016] UKSC 10: a prisoner accidentally dropped two sacks of rice on Cox (catering manager in prison), *Armes v Nottinghamshire County Council* [2017] UKSC 60: foster parents abused child.

[34] *Barclays Bank Plc v Various Claimants* [2020] UKSC 13, a case involving sexual assault by an independently practising doctor who was hired by Barclays to conduct medical examinations on prospective employees.

In civil law jurisdictions the primary way of extension is by using a broader term than 'employee'. For instance, in Germany the concept of 'Verrichtingsgehilfe' (auxiliary) can encompass certain actions of an (independent) advocate. In France the notion of 'préposé' (subordinate) similarly abstracts from the formal requirement of an employment contract.

Alternatively, a codification may contain separate grounds of liability for other persons which provide a supplementary ground of liability next to vicarious liability.

The French art. 1242 Cc lists several other relationships:

Art. 1242 Cc
(6) Les instituteurs et les artisans, du dommage causé par leurs élèves et apprentis pendant le temps qu'ils sont sous leur surveillance.
(7) La responsabilité ci-dessus a lieu, à moins que les père et mère et les artisans ne prouvent qu'ils n'ont pu empêcher le fait qui donne lieu à cette responsabilité.
(8) En ce qui concerne les instituteurs, les fautes, imprudences ou négligences invoquées contre eux comme ayant causé le fait dommageable, devront être prouvées, conformément au droit commun, par le demandeur, à l'instance.

Art. 1242 Cc
(6) The teachers and artisans [are liable] for the damage caused by their pupils and apprentices during the time that they are under their supervision.
(7) The above responsibility applies unless the father and the mother and the artisans prove that they could not have prevented the action that gave rise to their liability.
(8) Regarding teachers, the faults, imprudent or negligent acts held against them as having caused the harmful act, must be proven, according to the general rules, by the claimant in the proceedings.

The liability of teachers and artisans is an oddity, and not usually found elsewhere. Art. 1242(7) Cc contains an exception to the liability for parents and artisans (similar to the German exception for vicarious liability), but for parental liability this exception is ineffective (see § 14.4). Probably the same regime applies to the artisan.[35] As regards teachers, the law used to be fairly strict. The legislator tried to restrict the liability by adapting art. 1242(8) Cc. More importantly, art. L911-4 of the Education Code (Code de l'éducation) declares that victims cannot sue the teachers for wrongful acts by their pupils, but need to sue the State instead. Teachers are thereby largely protected from the apparent consequences of art. 1242(6) Cc.

Some jurisdictions have a specific rule for liability of principals for the *independent contractors* or agents they employ insofar these are not covered by the liability for employees.[36] However, the extent of this form of liability is rather restricted. Most jurisdictions (including England) do not generally hold a principal liable for torts by independent contractors. This is

---

[35]   Viney, Jourdain and Carval 2013, p. 1223.

[36]   In The Netherlands there is a specific provision for independent contractors (art. 6:171 BW), similarly in Albania (art. 619 Civil Code) and Lithuania (art. 6.265 Civil Code). Furthermore art. 6:172 Dutch BW establishes liability of principals for certain actions of their representative agents.

reasonable as an independent contractor is usually not controlled by the principal and runs their own business. As a patient you hardly expect to be held liable if for example your surgeon negligently injures a nurse during your operation, even though you legally are the surgeon's principal for the operation.

If a particular relationship is not covered by vicarious liability or a similar rule for strict liability, the victim may still have other options to obtain compensation from the principal. Courts may apply negligence, and hold the principal liable for violating a duty to give proper instruction or to provide adequate supervision.[37] Alternatively, the facts of the case might be covered by some form of organizational liability (§ 14.7).

14.4 LIABILITY FOR CHILDREN AND MENTALLY DISABLED PERSONS

Another category of strict liability for other persons is found mostly outside a commercial or economic context. This is the liability of parents (and wardens) for their children, and guardians for mentally disabled persons. The justification for strict liability in this case cannot be found in economic benefit (except where the guardianship is on a professional basis). This form of liability can be better understood from a responsibility to supervise persons under your care. An added systematic justification is that many jurisdictions have rules that exclude or limit liability for children and mentally disabled persons (§ 8.3): in order to provide the victim with compensation, the supervisors may be held liable instead.

Civil law jurisdictions usually have several detailed provisions regulating liability for children and mentally disabled persons (who need to be under supervision). The general approach is that the parent, guardian or supervisor is liable, and that there is an exclusion of liability of the child or person under supervision. See for instance § 832 BGB for the liability of parents or guardians of children (with an exception if the parent proves he or she observed sufficient care).

---

§ 832 BGB
(1) Wer kraft Gesetzes zur Führung der Aufsicht über eine Person verpflichtet ist, die wegen Minderjährigkeit oder wegen ihres geistigen oder körperlichen Zustands der Beaufsichtigung bedarf, ist zum Ersatz des Schadens verpflichtet, den diese Person einem Dritten widerrechtlich zufügt. Die Ersatzpflicht tritt nicht ein, wenn er seiner Aufsichtspflicht genügt oder wenn der Schaden auch bei gehöriger Aufsichtsführung entstanden sein würde.
(2) Die gleiche Verantwortlichkeit trifft denjenigen, welcher die Führung der Aufsicht durch Vertrag übernimmt.

§ 832 BGB
(1) Whomever on the basis of a statute has a duty to supervise a person who, because of being a minor or his mental or physical condition requires supervision, is obligated to

---

compensate damage that this person causes unlawfully to others. The duty to compensate does not apply if he has fulfilled his duty to supervise or if the damage would also have occurred with proper supervision.
(2) The same responsibility applies to the person who takes on the supervision on a contractual basis.

The child is not liable (§ 828 BGB), nor is a mentally disabled person (§ 827 BGB). See § 8.3.
   In French law, art. 1242(4) Cc provides a general liability of parents for their children.

art. 1242(4) Cc
Le père et la mère, en tant qu'ils exercent l'autorité parentale, sont solidairement responsables du dommage causé par leurs enfants mineurs habitant avec eux.

Art. 1242(4) Cc
The father and the mother, insofar they exercise their parental authority, are jointly and severally liable for the damage caused by their underaged children who live with them.

Importantly, for parental liability it is not necessary that the child acted wrongfully (a *faute*), rather it suffices that there was an 'act' (*fait*) of the child.[38] Thereby the liability of the parents may arise even where the child itself is not liable. Originally there was an exception to the parental liability in art. 1242(7) Cc if the parents prove that they could not have prevented the action of the child, but this exception has been declared without effect by the Cour de Cassation,[39] leaving only force majeure or contributory negligence as a possible defence.
   You may wonder what the position is of persons who effectively take over the parental role. The French Cour de Cassation has steadfastly refused to extend the application of the above provision to other persons than the parents.[40] Since the Blieck decision (§ 14.5) such persons can be liable on a different ground, therefore extending art. 1242(4) Cc is no longer needed. Similarly, the liability for actions by mentally disabled persons is covered by the Blieck decision.

---

[38]   Cass. (plén.) 9 May 1984, no 79-16612, D. 1984, 525 (Fullenwarth), about a seven-year-old boy shooting an arrow in the eye of a playmate: it suffices that the child committed an act that was the direct cause of the harm. Although not entirely clear, the decision has been affirmed, for instance in Cass., 2, 10 May 2001, no. 99-11287 (Levert) about an injury by a tackle during a rugby match: the liability of parents does not require the presence of a fault of the child, and clearly Cass. (plén.), 13 December 2002, no. 00-13787: it suffices that the damage of the victim was directly caused by the act, even if not wrongful, of the minor. Critical on this line of cases: Le Tourneau 2020, paras. 2233.71–2233.74.

[39]   Cass., 2, 19 February 1997, no. 94-21111 (Bertrand), about a 12-year-old boy colliding with his bike into a motor cycle.

[40]   Viney, Jourdain and Carval 2013, pp. 1188–9. This may partly be explained by the fact that art. 1242 also provides liability for specific other categories, such as teachers for their pupils.

In common law, the opposite approach prevails. Unless specific statutes have been enacted,[41] the parent or guardian can only be held liable on the basis of another tort, in particular the tort of negligence.[42] Parents do have a duty to supervise their children, but they are only liable for negligence in the execution of that duty. The child or mentally disabled person can also be personally liable, although courts may take into account the lack of discernment when assessing the liability of such persons.[43] Thereby the personal liability of children is limited, albeit at the expense of the victim of harm caused by children. Similarly, common law does not have a specific ground of liability for guardians of persons of unsound mind. Barring specific statutes, a victim would need to base an action on negligence.

This area of the law needs careful study when encountered in practice, due to the frequent occurrence of very specific rules and limitations.

14.5   A GENERAL RULE OF LIABILITY FOR OTHER PERSONS?

By now you might wonder whether it is not preferable to adopt a general rule of liability for other persons instead of the fragmentary approach we have seen in the previous sections.[44] Such a rule would, however, run into difficulties when it comes to defining the connection between the actions for which the supervisor is liable, and the relationship in question. There are simply too many different kinds of relationships involving too varied circumstances to make a simple, easily applicable rule feasible. Nonetheless there are some developments which seem to go in the direction of a more general approach.

One such development is the Blieck decision in France.[45] In this leading case the Cour de Cassation took the introductory paragraph of then art. 1384 Cc (nowadays art. 1242 Cc), which is only a preface to the specific forms of strict liability listed after the first sentence.

Art. 1242 Cc
(1) On est responsable non seulement du dommage que l'on cause par son propre fait, mais encore de celui qui est causé par le fait des personnes dont on doit répondre, ou des choses que l'on a sous sa garde.

Art. 1242 Cc
(1) One is responsible not only for the harm one causes by one's own acts, but also for the harm that is caused by the acts of persons for which one is responsible, or the things that are under one's custody. ...

---

[41]   Quite a few US states have in fact specific statutes to regulate parental liability.

[42]   Winfield and Jolowicz 2020, para 25-025.

[43]   This could be considered as assuming a requirement of culpability for fault, or as applying a subjective test to the tort of negligence (reasonable child of the respective age, instead of reasonable person).

[44]   Arguing for such a rule: Beuermann 2019.

[45]   Cass. (plén.) 29 March 1991 (Blieck), JCP 1991.II.21673.

The Cour de Cassation declared that this paragraph actually establishes a general liability for other persons. An association was held liable for a mentally disabled boy, because it had 'accepted the burden of organizing and controlling, on a permanent basis, the way of life of this disabled person'. In later case law the criterion became that liability rests on the person or organization that has the power to 'organize, direct and control'. The effect is that there is a form of liability for other persons in certain cases where no employment relationship can be found, such as a sports club for its members.[46]

The Blieck rule can be viewed as a step towards a general rule of liability for other persons. It may cover children (outside parental supervision), mentally disabled persons and adults outside an employee relationship (such as volunteers, members of sports clubs). The notion of *control* resembles the way in which English law has extended vicarious liability.

14.6   NON-DELEGABLE DUTIES

English law contains another doctrine that is related to vicarious liability: *non-delegable duties*. This means that you have a certain kind of duty which, if you assign someone else to fulfil that duty for you, will result in liability for yourself if that other person is negligent in the fulfilment of the duty. This has an effect quite similar to vicarious liability. An important difference is that it is irrelevant what the relationship is between the person on whom the duty rests and the person that actually fulfils the duty: it does not have to be an employee or someone in a similar position as an employee. Hence the doctrine of non-delegable duties may provide a form of liability for independent contractors under common law.

The leading case in England is *Woodland v Essex County Council* [2013] UKSC 66 regarding the liability of the education authority for swimming lessons that were delegated to swimming instructors. In this case, where a child was injured due to negligence of the instructors, the Supreme Court decided that there are five defining features that typically are involved in a case where there is a non-delegable duty:

1. the claimant is a patient or child or some otherwise vulnerable or dependent person;
2. there is an antecedent relationship between the claimant and the defendant which puts the claimant in the care of the defendant and from which it is possible to assign to the defendant a positive obligation actively to protect the claimant from harm (as opposed to a duty simply to refrain from harmful conduct);
3. the claimant has no control over how the defendant chooses to perform those obligations;
4. the defendant has delegated some part of its function to a third party, and the third party is exercising, for the purpose of the function delegated to it, the defendant's custody or care of the claimant and the element of control that goes with it; and
5. the third party has been negligent in the exercise of that delegated function.

---

[46]   Cass., 2, 22 May 1995, JCP 1995.II.22550.

As can be seen from this list of rather specific criteria, the doctrine of non-delegable duties does not amount to a general rule for independent agents.

In civil law systems, the cases that fall under the doctrine of non-delegable duties may be dealt with at least partly under other forms of liability for persons, such as liability for independent contractors (§ 14.3). In Germany there also exists liability for negligent delegation of *Verkehrspflichten*.[47]

14.7 LIABILITY IN ORGANIZATIONS

By now you may have noticed the fragmented state of the law that regulates the liability for other persons. This may leave gaps in protection, where the facts of the case do not match the exact criteria of the rule. Furthermore the application of vicarious liability might be restricted by an exception, such as in German law if the employer proves that he observed reasonable care. In order to patch up liability in this area, there is a related doctrine that focuses not so much on individuals as well as on *organizations*. Such an approach ties into the relevance of economic profit and control for justification of strict liability. As this is a complex area that is the domain of business law rather than general tort law, we will only discuss a few instruments that particularly pertain to tort liability,[48] by way of example and not covering all three key jurisdictions.

14.7.1 Liability of a corporate body for actions by the board

A corporation is only a legal person, not a real person. In order for a corporation to act, the actions of specific individuals have to be attributed to the corporation. In this way a corporation may sign a contract, even though in fact the CEO wrote her signature under the contract. As a counterpart of the representation of the organization by board members and directors, corporations may also be held liable for wrongful acts by the CEOs and other members of the board while in function. An example is a fraudulent statement by a director that benefits the company.[49] Such an act can be considered to be an act of the corporation itself for which it is itself liable. This kind of liability may be laid down in a codified rule. An example is § 31 BGB, which states:

§ 31 BGB
Der Verein ist für den Schaden verantwortlich, den der Vorstand, ein Mitglied des Vorstands oder ein anderer verfassungsmäßig berufener Vertreter durch eine in Ausführung

---

[47]   Wagner 2021, para 6.12, giving the example of failing to check whether the company to which the duty was delegated did actually exist as a real company.

[48]   See also Van Dam 2013, 1606-2 and 1608, Clerk and Lindsell 2020, paras 5-75 through 5-84, Winfield and Jolowicz 2020, para 25-027 through 25-034, Wagner 2021, para 6.36-6.48.

[49]   Winfield and Jolowicz 2020, para 25-032.

der ihm zustehenden Verrichtungen begangene, zum Schadensersatz
verpflichtende Handlung einem Dritten zufügt.

§ 31 BGB
The association is liability for damage by that the board, a member of the board, or
another representative appointed according to the bylaws caused in the performance
of the tasks within his purview when that damage was caused to another by an act that
obliges to compensation of damage.

Note that such a rule supplements vicarious liability, since board members need not be
employed by the corporation. Board members are furthermore usually not instructed by the
corporation. The relation may rather be the opposite: it is the board that directs the company.
Vicarious liability may therefore not apply to torts committed by board members. Hence
the need for a different ground of liability. Incidentally, the rule by which actions of board
members may be attributed to the company does have its limitations. If the CEO punches
a personal enemy when leaving the office, that may not be considered a tort by the company.

14.7.2 Negligence of directors and majority shareholders that direct the actions of the corporation

If a corporation acts wrongfully, it can be argued that the directors (or majority shareholders,
who effectively own the company) were in a position to intervene and to avoid the harm
caused by those actions. Neglecting to intervene may thereby give rise to an action on the basis
of negligence against the directors or majority shareholders.

This is the principal way in which multinational corporations may be subject to claims for
abuses by national subsidiaries. An example is the English case *Vedanta Resources Plc and
Konkola Copper Mines Plc v Lungowe and Ors.*[50] Formally the case is only about the issue of
whether the English courts have jurisdiction, but the decision already provides indications
about the criteria under which the parent company could be liable.

49. ... Direct or indirect ownership by one company of all or a majority of the shares of
another company (which is the irreducible essence of a parent/subsidiary relationship)
may enable the parent to take control of the management of the operations of the business
or of the land owned by the subsidiary, but it does not impose any duty on the parent to
do so .... Everything depends on the extent to which, and the way in which, the parent
availed itself of the opportunity to take over, intervene in, control, supervise or advise the
management of the relevant operations (including land use) of the subsidiary. All that the
existence of a parent subsidiary relationship demonstrates is that the parent had such an
opportunity.

---

[50]   [2019] UKSC 20 and also *Okpabi and ors v Royal Dutch Shell Plc* [2018] UKSC 68.

However, it may not be presumed too easily that a director is personally responsible for torts due to the company, as that would destroy the protection offered by a limited liability company. In English law the requirement is that there 'must have been an assumption of responsibility such as to create a special relationship with the director or employee himself'.[51] The topic of personal liability of directors is fascinating, but too complicated to discuss here at length.

14.7.3   Organizational duty

A corporation may also be liable in negligence for not organizing its business appropriately. In Germany this is the category of *Organizationsverschulden* (liability for inadequate organization, organizational negligence), which is a subcategory of fault liability invented by German courts as an application of § 823 BGB. Organizational negligence focuses on general organizational issues. For example, an organization may have neglected to set up an adequate information structure to ensure that customer requests are processed quickly and forwarded to appropriate departments. The organization may be held liable on the basis of organizational negligence because it should have acted differently if the responsible department would have known about certain information.

---

[51] *Williams v Natural Life Health Foods Ltd* [1998] UKHL 17. See further Clerk and Lindsell 2020, paras 5-81 through 5-83.

15
Liability for objects and activities

The second category of strict liability is the liability for objects and activities. Historically, legal systems tended to use strict liability primarily for certain kinds of tangible objects. However, over time some jurisdictions have established liability for dangerous activities as well, which are not tangible objects. For the sake of simplicity, I will in the following often just speak of 'strict liability for objects' as shorthand for strict liability for objects and activities. It should be noted that not all forms discussed below are actual strict liability rules: we discuss the general landscape of liability for objects.

The justification for strict liability can be found in the fact that the person who is held liable has control over the object and can thereby limit the risks that it causes to others. Holding this person liable provides a powerful incentive to take sufficient precautionary measures. Furthermore, the person in control usually also benefits from the existence and activity of the object. Nonetheless there is hesitation in many jurisdictions to broadening the categories of objects for which strict liability exists.

An overview of objects and activities that have been regulated in particular results in the following division: animals (§ 15.1), motorized vehicles (§ 15.2), immovable objects, in particular buildings (§ 15.3), other dangerous objects and activities (§ 15.4), and products (§ 15.5). Finally, a brief discussion of intangible objects (§ 15.6) is useful as these are becoming more and more prominent.

15.1   ANIMALS

It is instructive to start with the liability for animals, as this is quite broadly accepted across the globe and demonstrates several issues. It is well known that animals may on occasion harm human beings or cause other kinds of damage, because animals have a mind of their own and are not completely predictable. Hence it seems justified to provide victims of harm caused by animals with a means of recourse.

15.1.1   The kind of animals

English law provides a useful starting point. In English law liability is governed by the Animals Act 1971. This act holds the *keeper* liable for dangerous animals,[1] for damage caused by dogs

---

[1]   S. 2 Animals Act 1971: dangerous animals are animals that are not domestic to the British Islands and when fully grown are (briefly put) likely to create severe damage if unrestrained.

to livestock,[2] and for damage by trespassing livestock.[3] The keeper is defined as the owner or possessor[4] of the animal (s. 6(3) Animals Act 1971). In case of trespassing livestock or horses the liable person is the person to who the livestock or horse 'belongs', which is the person in whose possession the animal is (art. 4 and 4A Animals Act 1971). If the Animals Act 1971 does not apply, liability for an animal may be based on negligence.

We can learn several things about strict liability for objects from this description. First of all, you cannot assume that the law follows the natural language as regards the *kind of objects* to which liability extends. The Animals Act only applies to specific kinds of animals, which are not clearly defined. Dangerous animals is not a clear-cut category. The act speaks of 'an animal which belongs to a dangerous species' (art. 2(1)). In art. 6(2) this is further explained as a species which is not commonly domesticated in the British Islands; and 'whose fully grown animals normally have such characteristics that they are likely, unless restrained, to cause severe damage or that any damage they may cause is likely to be severe'. Lawyers quite often need to look at boundary cases where there is considerable discussion on what objects fall within the limits of the rule.

For French law, art. 1243 Cc imposes strict liability on the owner or user of an animal. However, there is also strict liability for movable and immovable objects based on art. 1242(1) Cc, which includes all animals (§ 15.4). Therefore art. 1243 Cc is superfluous, although there are still cases based on art. 1243 Cc, which in practice leads to the same results as an action based on art. 1242(1) Cc.[5]

German law makes a distinction between strict liability for what are called 'luxury animals' (*Luxustiere*, primarily pets) and a heightened fault-based liability for 'useful animals' (*Nutztiere*, particularly farm animals), see § 833 and 834 BGB.

---

§ 833 BGB
Wird durch ein Tier ein Mensch getötet oder der Körper oder die Gesundheit eines
Menschen verletzt oder eine Sache beschädigt, so ist derjenige, welcher das Tier
hält, verpflichtet, dem Verletzten den daraus entstehenden Schaden zu ersetzen. Die
Ersatzpflicht tritt nicht ein, wenn der Schaden durch ein Haustier verursacht wird, das dem
Beruf, der Erwerbstätigkeit oder dem Unterhalt des Tierhalters zu dienen bestimmt ist, und
entweder der Tierhalter bei der Beaufsichtigung des Tieres die im Verkehr erforderliche
Sorgfalt beobachtet oder der Schaden auch bei Anwendung dieser Sorgfalt entstanden sein
würde.

§ 834
Wer für denjenigen, welcher ein Tier hält, die Führung der Aufsicht über das Tier durch

---

[2]   S. 3 Animals Act 1971.

[3]   S. 4 Animals Act 1971. S 4A Animals Act 1971 imposes liability for horses causing damage due to being on land in England without legal authority. This is not precisely the same as trespassing (due to the more lenient rules that allow horses to be present on another's land) but is quite close.

[4]   Or head of the household of which the possessor is a member or owner.

[5]   Le Tourneau 2020, paras 2222.12 and 2222.55, and in detail paras 2222.13ff.

> *Vertrag übernimmt, ist für den Schaden verantwortlich, den das Tier einem Dritten in der im § 833 bezeichneten Weise zufügt. Die Verantwortlichkeit tritt nicht ein, wenn er bei der Führung der Aufsicht die im Verkehr erforderliche Sorgfalt beobachtet oder wenn der Schaden auch bei Anwendung dieser Sorgfalt entstanden sein würde.*
>
> § 833 BGB
> If an animal kills a human being or injures the body or health of a human being or damages an object, the person who keeps the animal is obligated to compensate to the victim the resulting damage. The duty to compensate does not apply when the damage was caused by a domestic animal that serves the profession, the gainful employment or the maintenance of the keeper of the animal, and the keeper observed the care required in society in the supervision of the animal or if the damage would also have occurred when observing such care.
>
> § 834
> Whomever takes on the supervision of an animal on behalf of the keeper of the animal on the basis of contact, is responsible for the damage that the animal causes to another in the way meant in § 833. The responsibility does not apply when he has performed the supervision with the care required in society or when the damage would also have occurred if he would have observed such care.

These rules all presume that the animal has an owner (this is also implied by the notion of a keeper, discussed in the following subsection). Wild animals are usually not covered, as it is not clear who should be liable.[6] In Germany there is a specific rule for wild animals that are hunted: the hunting company is liable for certain kinds of damage to land.[7]

15.1.2   The liable persons

Secondly, the *person who is liable* can be defined in a variety of ways. Generally the law uses the term 'keeper' or a close synonym. This is usually defined in reference to categories from property law (relating to the owner), but the justification of this concept lies rather in the actual physical control over the object. It makes sense that the person who should be liable is the person who could actually contain the risks that the animal caused harm. We have seen that English law vacillates between keeper and possessor. In case of negligence, the person held liable would be the person who actually did have a duty of care and breached that duty, which again implies the actual possibility of preventing harmful behaviour by the animal.

In French law a general term is used: *gardien*, meaning guardian, custodian.[8] This term can, depending on the precise circumstances of the case, encompass either the owner or the keeper,

---

[6]   In France there have been attempts to hold the owner of the land on which the wild animal was resident liable, but those have failed (Viney, Jourdain and Carval 2013, p. 789, para 635).

[7]   § 29 *Bundesjagdgesetz* (Federal Hunting Act), see also § 30 and 31. Originally this rule was found in § 835 BGB, but this provision has been repealed and the rule was moved to the *Bundesjagdgesetz*.

[8]   Art. 1243 Cc.

or both, or even another person (such as a thief). You remain *gardien* when the object/animal escaped out of your control.[9]

In German law the keeper (*derjenige welcher das Tier hält*) is liable for the animal, but if he contractually hired someone else to supervise the animal, the supervisor is liable instead (§ 834 BGB).[10] Hence German law requires you to look carefully at the role of the defendant as that determines the applicable norm for liability. German law uses various indications to determine whether someone is a keeper. Important are mainly who benefits from the animal (in particularly over a longer period of time), and the actual control over the animal. A keeper remains keeper if he lends the animal only for a short period to someone else.

Hence there is a variety of concepts to indicate the persons who may be liable: the main indicators are legal ownership and factual control over the object.

15.1.3   The kind of events

The third relevant question is *what kinds of events* the person is liable for. The English Animals Act 1971 is admirably clear as to the kind of behaviour that leads to liability, speaking of damage 'caused', injury by dogs to livestock, trespassing livestock and horses. Notice that s. 5 of the Animals Act 1971 contains some exceptions, such as complete contributory negligence, acceptance of risk and liability to trespassers. You should always check for a given case whether one of these exceptions applies. A disadvantage of the Animals Act is that it is limitative, there are numerous other kinds of behaviour which do not give rise to liability under the Animals Act but for which liability would seem appropriate. Such behaviour can only lead to compensation on the basis of another tort, in particular negligence.

For civil law systems there is usually a general rule, which may however not be easy to interpret.

In German law the liability for animals extends only to personal injury or property damage caused by the animal (§ 833 BGB). This does provide an indication in that the animal is supposed to have acted.

The French law liability for animals requires a 'fait de l'animal', an act of the animal.[11] The animal must have had an active role (*rôle actif*). This requirement has been interpreted in line with the general liability for objects on the basis of art. 1242 Cc (see § 15.4).[12]

---

[9]   Some jurisdictions have different rules when an animal has been stolen (art. 1669 Código Civil Guatemala), or when an object has been given in the custody of another (art. 152 Slovenian Obligations Code).

[10]   This provision has an exception if the supervisor observed due care; in that case the supervisor is not liable, only the keeper.

[11]   The official phrase is 'fait de la chose ou de l'animal', Viney, Jourdain and Carval 2013, p. 818, referring to Cass. 6 February 1929, Gaz. Pal. 1929, 1, p. 801.

[12]   Cass., 2, 17 January 2019, no 17-28861. The case involved two dogs running towards two horses, scaring them and leading to a fall and injury of one of the riders. The Cour de cassation considered that the dogs acted 'abnormally', which is one of the ways in which liability for objects may arise.

15.1.4   Defences

Finally, strict liability for objects is usually limited by allowing certain *defences*, such as force majeure or contributory negligence. Whether such defences apply requires research: they may be explicitly stated in the provisions on strict liability, or they may be implicit (and recognized in case law). See for instance s. 5 of the Animals Act 1971.

15.2   MOTORIZED VEHICLES

Another common form of liability is liability for motorized vehicles. Motorized vehicles are, regrettably, a major cause of death and injury. They pose a particular danger as cars are large, heavy and move at considerable speed. The risk of accidents can furthermore materialize even when there is only the tiniest bit of negligence by the driver. Victims would be at a disadvantage to obtain compensation if they could only act on the basis of negligence. Legislators all around the world have therefore enacted rules that impose specific forms of liability.

In France there is the *Loi Badinter* (the Badinter Act)[13] which created a form of strict liability for accidents where a motorized vehicle was involved.

LOI BADINTER[14]

Article 1
The provisions of the present chapter apply to victims (even if the victims were transported on the basis of a contract) of a traffic accident in which a terrestrial motorized vehicle was involved, including trailers and semi-trailers, but excluding trains and trams that move on their own tracks.

Article 2
The driver or the keeper of a vehicle as meant in art. 1 cannot invoke the defence of force majeure or an act of a third party against victims, including drivers.

Article 3
The victims, outside the drivers of the motorized vehicles, are compensated for damage resulting from injury to their person, without application of contributory negligence, except in case of inexcusable fault if that is the sole cause of the accident.
The victims designated by the previous paragraph, if they are less than 16 years old or over 70 years, or if, regardless of their age, are at the moment of the accident legally qualified as being permanently incapacitated or invalidated at least 80 percent, are always compensated for damage resulting from personal injury.
Nonetheless, in the cases as intended by the two preceding paragraphs, the victim is not

---

[13]   *La loi nº85-677 du 5 juillet 1985 tendant à l'amélioration de la situation des victimes d'accidents de la circulation et à l'accélération des procédures d'indemnisation.* Badinter was the Minister of justice who proposed the act.

[14]   The original French is not quoted, for considerations of space.

compensated by the instigator of the accident for the damages resulting from their injury if the victim has voluntarily sought the damage suffered.

Article 4
The fault committed by the driver of a motorized vehicle has as effect to limit or exclude compensation of damage that he has suffered.

Article 5
The fault committed by the victim has as effect to limit or exclude compensation of damage to his goods. … When the driver of a terrestrial motorized vehicle is not the owner, the fault of the driver can be opposed to the owner for the compensation of damages caused by his vehicle. The owner can take recourse on the driver.

In Germany there is the Road Traffic Act.[15] This act imposes liability on both the driver and the keeper. The relevant provisions are as follows

STRASSENVERKEHRSGESETZ[16]

§ 7 Liability of keeper, joy-riding
(1) If, during the use of a motorized vehicle, a person is killed, the body or health of a person is injured or property is damaged, the keeper is obliged to compensate the damage caused thereby.
(2) The duty to compensate is excluded if the accident is caused by force majeure.
(3) If someone uses the motorized vehicle without knowledge or consent of the keeper of the vehicle, that person is liable instead of the keeper. The keeper remains liable of the use of the vehicle was made possible by his negligence. The first sentence is not applicable if the user of the vehicle was hired for operating the vehicle or if the vehicle was entrusted to him.

§ 8 Exceptions
The provisions of § 7 do not apply
1. if the accident was caused by a motorized vehicle that can drive on a level road not faster than 20 kilometres per hour, unless it is a motorized vehicle with autonomous driving function in the meaning of § 1d part 1 and 2 that was in autonomous operation,
2. when the victim was involved in the operation of the motorized vehicle or
3. when an object was damaged that was transported by the vehicle, except if it was carried by a transported person (passenger) or that person has the object with him.

§ 9 Contributory negligence
If negligence by the victim has also caused the damage, the provisions of § 254 BGB find application, with the addition that in case of property damage the negligence by the person

---

15 *Straßenverkehrsgesetz.*

16 The original German is not quoted, for considerations of space.

who exhibited factual control over the object is equivalent to negligence by the victim.
…

§ 18 Liability of driver
(1) In the case of § 7 (1) the driver of the vehicle is also liable according to the provisions §§ 8 through 15. The duty to compensate is excluded when the damage was not caused by negligence of the driver.
(2) …

The Road Traffic Act contains several further provisions that regulate details, for instance regarding the kind of damage that may be compensated.[17]

English law is an outlier in that it does not have a specific act or other statutory rule regarding liability for motorized vehicles. Victims need to invoke the tort of negligence to obtain compensation. The mere fact that a collision has occurred does not provide evidence of negligence,[18] but courts do require a high level of care from road users (not limited to drivers of motorized vehicles).[19]

We can analyse these arrangements in a manner similar to how we analysed liability for animals.

First of all, what kind of vehicles are covered? We generally understand what is meant by motorized vehicles: normal automobiles, including three-wheel vehicles are covered, whether powered by gasoline or electricity. Motors would also be covered. However, it is not immediately clear whether an electric bicycle or an e-scooter is also a motor vehicle in the meaning of the law. Similarly, is a forklift on a private factory terrain a motor vehicle in the meaning of this form of strict liability? The *Loi Badinter* explicates that only terrestrial vehicles are covered (therefore does not extend to airplanes); this is implied in the German Road Traffic Act, as it refers to the road which is terrestrial.

Secondly, *who* is liable? The French liability for motor vehicles extends to both the driver (*conducteur*) and the custodian (*gardien*).[20] In German law, for motorized vehicles the rule is that the keeper is strictly liable (§ 7 *Straßenverkehrgesetz*), while the driver is liable on the basis of negligence with a reversed burden of proof (§ 18 *Straßenverkehrgesetz*). Hence German law requires you to look carefully at the role of the defendant as that determines the applicable norm for liability. In English law the liability is based on negligence, and therefore can only aim at the person who was actually in a position to prevent the accident by observing due

---

[17] See further Wagner 2021, paras 8.45–8.68.

[18] However, the court may apply the doctrine of *res ipsa loquitur* for the breach of a duty of care, which means that the claimant managed to prove the breach (without proving a particular act or omission) and the defendant needs to rebut that. This is particularly so if the occurrence would normally only happen due to negligence and there is no other likely cause. See more extensively Clerk and Lindsell 2020, paras 7-203 through 7-208.

[19] Clerk and Lindsell 2020, paras 7-209 through 7-214. For instance, a learner driver is judged by the standard of a reasonable experienced driver, although the claimant was her instructor (*Nettleship v Weston* [1971] 2 QB 691). Incidentally the Court of Appeal did reduce damages due to contributory negligence on the part of the instructor.

[20] Art. 2 Loi Badinter.

care. This will usually be the driver or (in case of insufficient maintenance) the owner. At first sight you may wonder why French and German law hold the owner or keeper strictly liable instead of starting with the driver who seems the obvious candidate for liability. An underlying reason for doing so is that these countries have a system of mandatory insurance for owners of motorized vehicles.[21] The owner therefore will usually be insured and the insurance company will actually bear the damages. Thereby the victim is assured of proper compensation, which is indirectly paid for by the collective of all owners of vehicles through the insurance fees paid by all owners together.

Thirdly, for what events is the defendant liable? This can be regulated in a positive manner, for example in the German reference to personal injury or property damage. It is not necessary that the vehicle was moving; the liability also extends to a fire caused by a defect in the car.[22] But liability can also be constrained by allowing certain defences. In German law the *Straßenverkehrgesetz* holds the keeper responsible for all personal injury and property damage caused by the vehicle, except in case of force majeure (§ 7(1) and (2)) and a few very particular exceptions in § 8. Contributory negligence applies as well (§ 9).

The French liability for motorized vehicles applies similarly: the vehicle was involved in the accident and was not wholly passive. Liability is only limited in case of an inexcusable fault by the victim or intention to seek the damage (art. 3 Loi Badinter).

For English law again the general rules of negligence apply.

The systems discussed above are similar to arrangements elsewhere. Many jurisdictions have adopted separate statutes for regulating liability for motorized vehicles. For instance, in Japan there is the Automobile Liability Security Act, No. 97, 1955. More recent codifications fairly often regulate liability for motorized vehicles as part of the rules on tort law in the code.[23]

In codes influenced by the Russian civil code there is often a provision providing strict liability for dangerous activities that mentions driving motorized vehicles as a specific dangerous activity.[24]

15.3   IMMOVABLE OBJECTS

Another common form of liability is liability for immovable objects, such as land or buildings.[25] Note that we are not discussing property torts like trespass to land where someone infringes a property right. The situation is the converse: someone else is being harmed by the land or building.

An example that goes back to ancient times is the liability for collapsing buildings.[26]

---

[21]   Also, the owner is easy to establish by the license plate.

[22]   BGH 21 January 2014, VI ZR 253/13, NJW 2014, 1182, BGH 26 March 2019, VI ZR 236/18.

[23]   An example is art. 1388 of the new Civil code of Seychelles (2020, which entered into force on 1 July 2021).

[24]   For instance, art. 948 of the Belarus Civil code, art. 1187 Civil code of Ukraine.

[25]   The rules for liability for immovable objects may also be found in specific statutes.

[26]   A form of presumption of liability of the builder could already be found in art. 229 of the code of Hammurabi, around 1750 B.C.

In Roman law there was an action for liability for things falling or thrown out of buildings (the *Actio de Effusis vel Dejectis*).[27] Many South American countries have maintained such a rule about objects that fall off or are thrown from buildings.[28] See for instance the Chilean civil code, which served as a model for most other South American codes.

CÓDIGO CIVIL DE LA REPÚBLICA DE CHILE (1857)

Art. 2328.

El daño causado por una cosa que cae o se arroja de la parte superior de un edificio, es imputable a todas las personas que habitan la misma parte del edificio, y la indemnización se dividirá entre todas ellas; a menos que se pruebe que el hecho se debe a la culpa o mala intención de alguna persona exclusivamente, en cuyo caso será responsable esta sola. ...

Art. 2328.

The damage caused by a thing that falls or is thrown from the top of a building is attributable to all persons who inhabit that part of the building, and compensation will be divided between all of them; unless it is proven that the fact is due to the fault or bad intention of one person exclusively, in which case that person will solely be responsible. ...

In French law there is also a specific provision for liability for collapsing buildings.

Article 1244 Cc

Le propriétaire d'un bâtiment est responsable du dommage causé par sa ruine, lorsqu'elle est arrivée par une suite du défaut d'entretien ou par le vice de sa construction.

art. 1244 Cc

The owner of a building is responsible for the harm caused by its collapse if this has happened due to negligent maintenance or a defect in its construction.

However, due to the general rule in French law for objects (see § 15.4), there is no reason to use this provision anymore: art. 1242(1) Cc can be applied to objects such as trees, elevators, stairs, roofs, ponds.[29]

The German BGB has three provisions regarding liability for damage caused by collapsing buildings (or other structures) or by objects falling off of buildings. Liable are respectively the possessor of land on which the building stands (§ 836), the possessor of the building on the land (§ 837), and the person with a duty of maintenance of the building (§ 838). The liability also applies when for example a brick falls off due to a hurricane or lightning, as these are not

---

[27] Digests 9.3.1pr.

[28] Similarly § 1318 of the Austrian BGB.

[29] Viney, Jourdain and Carval 2013, p. 787.

considered uncommon influences.[30] These provisions follow the, by now familiar, German pattern of a liability that can be averted by proving that the defendant exercised due care.

You can read and analyse these provisions on your own, following the pattern used in the previous sections on animals and motorized vehicles.

Finally we can briefly discuss English law, which has two specific statutes that impose a stronger duty of care for the application of negligence in this area. In English law there is a strict distinction between persons who were invited onto the premises (visitors), and uninvited persons (trespassers or others).[31] The occupier of the land has a duty of care[32] towards visitors under the Occupiers' Liability Act 1957 for 'dangers due to the state of the premises' (s. 1(1)). The occupier is the person who 'has a sufficient degree of control over premises that he ought to realize that any failure on his part to use care may result in injury to a person coming lawfully there'.[33] The owner in possession of the premises is an occupier, but others may be in such a position as well. The act applies to visitors, a person who was given permission to enter (s. 1(2)). The occupier has a duty of care to all visitors, as laid down in s. 2(2). The act has detailed rules for various types of visitors and different kinds of damage.

Individuals that were not authorized by the occupier to enter the land can invoke the Occupiers' Liability Act 1984. That act provides for a duty of care only where the occupier of the land is, simply put, aware of a danger for which it is reasonable that the occupier protects trespassers.[34] In that case a duty arises 'to take such care as is reasonable in all the circumstances of the case to see that he does not suffer injury on the premises by reason of the danger concerned' (s. 1(4) Occupiers' Liability Act 1984), which may also be achieved by warnings. The Act provides further details.

15.4 OTHER FORMS OF LIABILITY FOR OBJECTS OR ACTIVITIES

Besides animals and cars there are many other kinds of objects for which strict liability may exist in various legal systems. I will only provide an overview to give you some idea of the kinds of objects and activities for which liability may exist.[35]

Several jurisdictions have specific rules for certain objects, or related activities. An example is the German rule imposing liability for mining activities (§ 114 *Bundesberggesetz*, BBergG).[36] This shows that you may need to look outside the civil code to find rules for specific objects. In Dutch law there are several provisions that impose liability on the professional user of

---

[30] Bamberger Kommentar 2019, § 836, para 20.

[31] Such as persons who exercise a private right of way.

[32] The cause of action would therefore be negligence based on breach of duty of care, where the Occupiers' Liability Act 1957 determines whether the occupier owes a duty of care and what the standard of care is.

[33] *Wheat v Lacon & Co Ltd* [1966] AC 552, at 577, see Winfield and Jolowicz 2020, para 10-007.

[34] Paraphrasing s. 1(3) Occupiers' Liability Act 1984, see Winfield and Jolowicz 2020, para 10-037.

[35] A more extensive overview can be found in Oertel 2010.

[36] Deutsch and Ahrens 2014, para 578.

a dangerous substance (art. 6:175 BW), the manager of a garbage dump for environmental pollution caused by substances that were dumped (art. 6:176 BW), the manager of a mine for certain dangers consequent on the mining operation (art. 6:177 BW). As these examples show, the liability for objects cannot be completely separated from activities. Indeed, a connection between activity and object was arguably already implied in the German distinction between useful animals and luxury animals.

France has a general liability for the guardian of objects, regardless of whether these objects are particularly dangerous or not. This has been developed in a way similar to the Blieck case, by an extensive interpretation by the Cour de Cassation of art. 1242(1) Cc.[37] This form of liability requires an 'act of the thing' (*fait de la chose*).[38] This phrase implies that the object was the cause of the harm, it intervened in the realization of the damage.[39] The case law about this criterion is not easily summarized; it appears that the courts require an *active role* of the object, and that the object is in some way *abnormal*.[40] Abnormality means that the object is defective, behaving differently from what is normatively expected or socially desirable: while it may be 'normal' for a wild bear to bite humans who approach too closely, this is 'abnormal' in the sense of this form of liability. On the other hand, a curb of ten centimetre high, clearly visible painted white, is not abnormal.[41] The guardian of the object is the person who has the use, control and management of the object.[42]

The 2018 Djibouti Code civil codifies the main outline of the French development:

DJIBOUTI CODE CIVIL (2018)

Article 1392
Tout fait dommageable d'une chose engage de plein droit la responsabilité de celui qui en a la garde.
Le gardien est celui qui a l'usage, le contrôle et la direction de la chose au moment du fait dommageable. Le propriétaire est présumé gardien de la chose.
Le fait de la chose et son rôle causal sont présumés lorsque celle-ci, en mouvement, est entrée en contact avec le siège du dommage. Dans les autres cas, il appartient à la victime de prouver le fait de la chose, en établissant soit le vice de celle-ci, soit l'anormalité de sa

---

[37]   Cass. (Chambre réunie) 13 February 1930, DP 1930.I.57 (Jand'heur II).

[38]   Viney, Jourdain and Carval 2013, p. 813ff , Fabre-Magnan 2021, p. 301. In case of fault liability a human act (*fait de l'homme*) is required.

[39]   Viney, Jourdain and Carval 2013, pp. 817–18, Fabre-Magnan 2021, p. 301, refering to Cass., 19 February 1941, DC 1941, p. 85.

[40]   Viney, Jourdain and Carval 2013, pp. 818 and 829, Fabre-Magnan 2021, p. 302.

[41]   Cass., 2, 29 March 2012, no 10-27553.

[42]   '[L]'usage, la direction et le controle', from Cass. 2 December 1941, DC 1942, 25, JCP 1942, II, 1766, see Fabre-Magnan 2021, p. 305.

position, de son état ou de son comportement, et son rôle dans la réalisation du dommage.

Art. 1392

Every harmful event of an object leads by law to the liability of its custodian.

The custodian is the person that has the use, control and direction of the object at the moment of the harmful event. The owner is presumed to be custodian of the object.

The event of the object and its causal role are presumed when it came into contact during movement with the place where the harm occurred. In other cases, the victim has the burden of proof of the event of the object, while establishing either a defect of the object, or the abnormality of its position, its state or its behaviour, and its role in the realization of the harm.

Similar provisions (albeit not always completely strict, rather a presumption of negligence or reversed burden of proof) can be found elsewhere.[43]

In England there is a particular form of strict liability that is called the Rule in *Rylands v Fletcher*, after the precedent of the same name.[44] This 'rule' amounts to a form of strict liability for water flooding from one terrain to another. In civil law systems such cases are often dealt with on the basis of neighbour law (§ 6.3). Roman law already had an action to prevent water flooding towards a neighbour, and the French Code civil still contains a (limited) provision to this effect.[45] The rule of *Rylands v Fletcher* has received a lot of attention as it was one of the few forms of strict liability in English law. Nowadays the scope of its application has been restricted: it is viewed simply as a sub-species of private nuisance,[46] albeit that it does take the form of strict liability with specific requirements. However it did form the basis for an extensive form of strict liability in India,[47] as well as a form of strict liability in the US Restatement of Torts, which we will turn to next.

In several modern civil codes there are rules for dangerous objects or activities. This may be inspired by § 519 and § 520 of the US Restatement on Torts (Second).[48] According to these provisions, an individual who carries out an 'abnormally dangerous activity', is liable for the

---

[43]   Art. 493(1) Portuguese Codigó Civil, art. 2051 Italian Codice Civile, art. 6:173 Dutch BW, and outside Europe art. 427 East Timor Código Civil.

[44]   *Rylands v Fletcher* [1868] UKHL 1.

[45]   Art. 681 Cc: every owner must establish roofs in such a way that rain water will flow on his own land or onto public road; he may not let it flow on the land of his neighbour (*Tout propriétaire doit établir des toits de manière que les eaux pluviales s'écoulent sur son terrain ou sur la voie publique; il ne peut les faire verser sur le fonds de son voisin*). See also art. 640 Cc.

[46]   Clerk and Lindsell 2020, para 19-44, In *Transco plc v Stockport Metropolitan Borough Council* [2003] UKHL 61 the rule was called 'a sub-species of nuisance' (Lord Bingham, nr. 3). In Australia the rule has been abolished (*Burnie Port Authority v General Jones Pty Ltd* [1994] HCA 13).

[47]   In the case *M.C. Mehta v Union of India (UOI) and Ors.* 1987 SCR (1) 819, AIR 1987 965, discussed later in this section.

[48]   These provisions actually were inspired by the English case *Rylands v Fletcher* (§ 14.4). See about the influence of these provisions Büyüksagis and Van Boom 2013, at p. 627. Incidentally they refer to the Third Restatement.

resulting personal injury and property damage. The liability arises regardless of whether the defendant exercised utmost care. Furthermore, the liability is restricted to the kind of harm typical of the danger of the activity. § 520 provides several guidelines to what is abnormally dangerous, such as the likelihood and extent of harm, possibility to reduce or eliminate risk, whether it is a common activity or is important for society, and whether the activity was exercised at an inconvenient location. Application in practice is restricted to explosives in blasting operations, vicious animals, and large volume of water escaping from a reservoir.[49]

A rule of strict liability for dangerous activities is frequently found in more recent codifications.[50] Such a general provision is useful: instead of many very specific rules as in the Dutch civil code, there is only one provision, which the courts can interpret to also apply to dangerous activities that were hitherto not recognized. A disadvantage is that such a provision may lead to legal uncertainty as businesses that start new activities may wonder whether they are strictly liable for those. The uncertainty is, however, limited to the extent that these forms of liability typically appear to aim only at physical dangers, that is, to personal injury and property damage, and not to pure economic loss.

In common law systems there is generally hesitation to accept strict liability. Specific statutes may impose liability, but there are few precedents that establish new forms of strict liability. Nonetheless in India a strict form of liability has been accepted for dangerous activities in the case *M.C. Mehta v Union of India (UOI) and Ors. 1987.*[51]

15.5   PRODUCT LIABILITY

Product liability is a fairly recent, but nowadays well accepted, form of liability for objects.[52] It is essentially a form of strict liability, with a few peculiarities, but it is also restricted in a way which makes it approximate fault liability again.

The background of product liability is the rise of industrially produced consumer goods, which had the potential of causing widespread damage while for many victims it might be hard to prove a fault of the actual producer. This is strengthened by the fact that products often are assembled from parts which themselves are supplied by other manufacturers. Furthermore, the manufacturer might be located in a different country than the consumer, creating further obstacles for consumer to successfully claim damages in court.

The solution to these issues was created in the 1960s in the United States, where a California court established liability of a manufacturer for defects in a product, even in the absence of

---

[49]   Goldberg and Zipursky 2010, p. 259.

[50]   For instance, art. 493 Código Civil of Portugal, art. 601 Bộ Luật (Civil Code of Vietnam 2015), art. 1757 Argentine Código Civil y Comercial de la Nación (2015), art. 927 Código Civil Brasileiro (2002), art. 752 Camodian Civil Code (2007), art. 1058 Estonian Võlaõigusseadus (Law of Obligations Act 2002). The approach is also followed in the Russian civil code (art. 1065) and codes inspired by the Russian code. See also the discussion in Lee 2014.

[51]   Decision of the Supreme Court of India in the case *M.C. Mehta v Union of India (UOI) and Ors.* 1987 SCR (1) 819, AIR 1987 965. About this case: Raj, Mookherjee and Borthakur 2021, at 430–33.

[52]   Koziol et al. 2017, Reimann 2021.

negligence.[53] The resulting strict liability for defective products was taken over in the Second Restatement of Torts, and adopted by American courts over the following years. The American approach spread over the world and can by now be found in many if not most jurisdictions.[54]

In the USA there currently is no uniform regulation for product liability. Individual states have diverging rules and case law. Nonetheless the Restatement (Third) of Torts: Product Liability describes the commonalities between the various rules. In the European Union the rules on product liability are based on the Product Liability Directive 85/374/EEC, which has been transposed in the national laws of the European Union member states.[55] Other countries have enacted similar rules, usually based on the American and European models.[56] Quite often product liability is not found in the civil code but rather in specific consumer protection acts.[57] Consider the example of a common law system like Malaysia (Consumer Protection Act 1999),[58] a mixed legal system like South Africa (s. 61 Consumer Protection Act (CPA) of 2011),[59] and a civil law system like Georgia (arts. 1009–1011 Civil code Georgia 1997).

To understand how product liability works, we will focus on the European Union rules. As stated above, product liability has been harmonized by the Product Liability Directive 85/374/EEC which all European Union member states had to transpose (or implement) into their own legal system, usually either in the code or with a specific act. While the exact wording of these implementations may differ, the actual interpretation should be identical in every member States, baring a few minor details that are allowed by the directive as being left to the discretion of the member state. The uniform interpretation of those rules is in the EU realized by the instrument of prejudicial questions to the European Court of Justice. Hence for studying the general rules of product liability in the EU we could suffice with looking solely at the rules of the Directive, but if we have to describe the law in a member state we should actually refer to the local implementation of the Directive, and only refer to the Directive for authoritative interpretation of the national provisions.

The typical elements of product liability are the following:

— There is a product,
— The product has a defect,[60]
— The defect caused harm to a consumer.

---

[53]   Goldberg and Zipursky 2010, p. 270, referring to *Greenman v Yuba Power Products, Inc.* (1963) 59 Cal.2d 57.

[54]   Reimann 2021.

[55]   In England the Consumer Protection Act 1987 (before Brexit, but remained in force thereafter), in Germany the *Produkthaftungsgessetz* (Product liability act), in France in art. 1245 ff. Cc.

[56]   Reimann 2021. Reimann 2003 is critical about the effect the formal harmonization of rules has had in legal practice, in particular court decisions.

[57]   For example, in Argentina the rules are not found in the Código Civil y Comercial, but rather in the Consumer Protection Law 24240 (*Ley 24240 de Defensa del Consumidor) of 1993*.

[58]   Act no 599 Laws of Malaysia.

[59]   www.gov.za/documents/consumer-protection-act.

[60]   Art. 6 Product Liability Directive.

- If these elements are present, the producer or manufacturer of the product is in principle liable.[61] However, a defence may apply.

These elements require some explanation. As an example we will refer to the rules of the European Product Liability Directive.

Product liability is usually restricted to *products*, by which is understood tangible goods.[62] This excludes for instance software, except where the software is part of a product. Some jurisdictions extend product liability to cover both defective goods and *services*.[63]

The *defect* may consist of a design defect (an incorrect design, which therefore applies to all the products), a manufacturing defect (a defect caused during the manufacturing process, which may only apply to a single product), or a marketing defect (which covers insufficient information or warnings). The notion of a marketing or information defect is an extension of what you would normally conceive of a defect, as it is not about the product itself as well as the surrounding materials and information. However, this extension is justified as a product must be understood in connection with any warnings or operating instructions in the manual and other materials.

The requirements of causation and harm are familiar from the general rules on tortious liability. Product liability is often restricted to harm suffered by consumers, excluding professional users.[64] The consumer is principally the person who actually bought the product, but it can also be a third party. The compensable damage is usually restricted to personal injury or property damage and does not encompass pure economic loss. There may be additional restrictions to the kind or amount of damage that can be recovered.

The *producer* or *manufacturer* is liable, which is relevant as this provides a direct claim on the producer even if there is no contract between consumer and producer. By producer is normally meant the company or person that put the product in circulation (by sale or otherwise), to exclude cases where an unsafe product in development is stolen.[65] Usually there is a so-called *distribution chain*, a chain of companies through which the product ends in the hands of the consumer. For instance, a foreign producer manufactures the product, sells a batch to a wholesale company who imports the goods in the country, who sells smaller sets to a retailer (shop), and the consumer buys one product in the shop. Product liability rules may help the consumer by placing one or more parties in the chain in the same position as the foreign producer:[66] this makes it easier for the consumer to obtain damages as he does not have to start a procedure in a foreign country. For instance, the importer can be treated like the producer. Furthermore, the concept of producer may be extended to include manufacturers

---

[61]   Art. 1 Product Liability Directive: The producer shall be liable for damage caused by a defect in the product.

[62]   Art. 2 Product Liability Directive: 'product' means all movables even if incorporated into another movable or into an immovable. 'Product' includes electricity.

[63]   For example, art. 1112 Civil Code Of The Republic Of Tajikistan Part One (1999) and other codes inspired by the Russian civil code, also art. 931 of the Brazilian Civil Code 2002 (CC/02), about which Celli 2021, at 547.

[64]   For this and the following see art. 9 Product Liability Directive.

[65]   See art. 7(a) Product Liability Directive.

[66]   See art. 3 Product Liability Directive.

of component parts of the product.[67] There is no consensus outside Europe on whether other parties than the actual producer can be held liable.

Although at first it may look as if the consumer receives considerable protection from product liability, on closer inspection the actual protection is fairly limited. Not only is the kind of damage that is recoverable restricted to personal injury and property damage, but product liability is further restricted by several defences. Again taking the Product Liability Directive as an example, we can see the following defences:

Article 7 Product Liability Directive 85/374/EEC after Directive
The producer shall not be liable as a result of this Directive if he proves:
(a) that he did not put the product into circulation; or
(b) that, having regard to the circumstances, it is probable that the defect which caused the damage did not exist at the time when the product was put into circulation by him or that this defect came into being afterwards; or
(c) that the product was neither manufactured by him for sale or any form of distribution for economic purpose nor manufactured or distributed by him in the course of his business; or
(d) that the defect is due to compliance of the product with mandatory regulations issued by the public authorities; or
(e) that the state of scientific and technical knowledge at the time when he put the product into circulation was not such as to enable the existence of the defect to be discovered; or
(f) in the case of a manufacturer of a component, that the defect is attributable to the design of the product in which the component has been fitted or to the instructions given by the manufacturer of the product.

The first three defences are understandable; only products that were intended to be used by consumers and that were originally defective should lead to liability. The other three defences are, however, significant restrictions. In particular the fifth defence, also referred to as the risk development defence, means that the produced is not liable for risks that were not known at the time.

For cases that do not fulfil all elements of product liability the victim may base an action on negligence or some other form of fault liability (provided of course that the conditions for fault liability are fulfilled). Given the various restrictions to product liability, this is an important option in practice. The English case of *Donoghue v Stevenson*[68] is an early example where a manufacturer was held liable for a defective product.

---

[67] As is the case in art. 3 Product Liability Directive 85/374/EEC.
[68] [1932] AC 562.

15.6   INTANGIBLE OBJECTS

At this point a brief remark is in order regarding intangible objects. Liability for objects is primarily concerned with tangible objects, such as animals, cars, and immovable goods like houses. Given the rapid development of digital technology, there is a growing interest in forms of liability specifically tailored to phenomena such as data, software, and AI.[69] Currently tort law addresses harm caused by intangibles with the existing rules of fault liability, in particular negligence and other torts like infringement of intellectual property (IP), defamation, malicious falsehood. In § 7.5 we briefly looked at the liability for information and content.

---

[69]   Tjong Tjin Tai 2018, Wendehorst 2020.

16

Tort law in the world

16.1   INTRODUCTION

In the previous chapters we discussed many different torts and related doctrines in English, French and German law. These provide a basis for further research into other tort law systems. Concepts and terminology found elsewhere will usually appear familiar and can be readily understood, even if additional research is needed to ascertain the exact content of foreign legal concepts. Nonetheless you may easily be led astray if you presume too quickly that you understand a new common law or civil law system, as a system may have its own idiosyncrasies that you might not immediately be aware of and which can be confusing. And there are also systems which cannot really be classified as common law or civil law.

This chapter consists of an extremely brief overview of the varieties in tort law that you may encounter in comparative research.[1] Limited and sketchy though these notes are, they are hopefully useful for gaining a first impression of the different tort law systems found across the globe.

16.2   THE NATIONAL SYSTEMS OF TORT LAW

The tort law systems of the world can be divided into several groups or families.[2] The vast majority of these tort law systems is either a common law system (§ 16.3) or has a codified form of civil law (§ 16.4).[3] But there are also several systems that do not fit into these two categories (§§ 16.5–16.8).

---

[1]   An excellent resource of English translations of provisions of codes around the world is Kadner Graziano 2018.

[2]   Siems 2014. Chapter 4 is particularly insightful on classification of legal systems, see further Zweigert and Kötz 1998, Glenn 2010. Note: this overview only describes to what kind of system the *tort law* belongs, which need not apply to the whole legal system of that country. In particular family law is often regulated differently. If a country like, say, India, is listed as common law as regards it tort law system, this does not mean that all aspects of civil law are regulated by common law (instead Hindu law may apply for family law).

[3]   This focuses on countries, and ignores specific regional jurisdictions within such countries such as Scotland, Quebec and Louisiana, which have legal systems that differ fundamentally from the rest of the country (§ 16.9.2).

Figure 16.1   Map of tort law systems around the world (created with mapchart.net)

16.3 COMMON LAW SYSTEMS

The general structure of torts in English law has served as a model for other common law jurisdictions. However, these jurisdictions have over time distanced themselves from their origin.

16.3.1 Common law in the USA

A special case is the United States of America. As the USA gained independence from England and English common law a long time ago, there are nowadays numerous differences between the two systems. For instance, vicarious liability is called *respondeat superior* in US law; instead of legal causation (remoteness and 'scope of the rule') US law has the requirement of *proximate cause*. Despite such differences, the terminology and categorization of US tort law is still very similar to English law. A working knowledge of English common law is therefore a good starting point to understand US tort law.

A complication to studying tort law in the US is that there is no federal US common law system. Tort law (and contract law) is principally within the competence of each US state. Courts and legal scholars therefore tend to describe only the tort law within an individual state: a Delaware court case focuses primarily on Delaware precedents, a California court will refer to the relevant Californian provisions and precedents. To be true, courts may also cite case law of other US states, but such cases do not have binding force.

Most of the US has a common law system of tort law, although some states have actually codified (parts of) tort law by regulating common law torts like trespass and negligence in the state code.[4] An exception is Louisiana, which has a civil law system based on French and Spanish law, although there are common law elements as well. The development of tort law is mainly in the hands of the state courts, although there are also many specific statutes in each state that regulate tort law, more so than in England.

The large variety among US states gave rise to a movement to promote uniformity, culminating in the drafting of so-called Restatements of Law. Restatements are treatises created and published by the American Law Institute (ALI) and essentially are a compilation and summation of case law on a particular subject. The compilation not only orders case law, but more importantly summarizes the main principles in the form of rules that resemble civil law codified rules. Although the Restatements do not have legal authority, in practice they tend to be cited often by US courts to support their decisions. However, individual US states may have case law and legislation which deviate from the principles stated in the Restatement, in which case the actual sources of law prevail.

At present the Restatement (Second) of Torts[5] (four volumes, published between 1965 and 1979), is the most recent complete set. A few specific volumes of the Restatement (Third) of Torts have been published (covering Products Liability, Liability for Physical and Emotional Harm, and Apportionment of Liability), superseding the corresponding parts of the

---

[4]   An example is California: arts. 1708–1725 California Civil Code provide the main rules regarding tort law.

[5]   This is the second version, hence the (Second).

Restatement (Second) of Torts. The ALI is in the process of revising the remaining parts of the Restatement (Second) of Torts.[6]

Although the Restatement of Torts does provide guidance and a semblance of uniformity, the actual tort law rules may on occasion vary quite a lot amongst states.[7] Liability for animals, for instance, is not regulated in a uniform manner. Some states have strict liability imposed by statutory law, others only have negligence available as a cause of action for injury caused by animals (besides the liability for abnormally dangerous activities, see § 15.4). The need to examine the specifics of state law makes US tort law hard to study.[8]

16.3.2 Common law systems in the Commonwealth

Countries with a common law system are mainly former English colonies.[9] England, as colonizing power, imposed its law in its colonies by decrees or other legal acts. When the former colonies regained independence, they usually chose to keep the framework of common law as a source of law, for the sake of continuity. In order to do so, the new state needed to proclaim its sovereignty over legal matters, while simultaneously establishing common law as a source of law.

See for example Zambia: chapter 11(2) English Law (Extent of Application) Act states:

---

2. Extent of application of English law
Subject to the provisions of the Constitution and to any other written law—
(a) the common law;
(b) the doctrines of equity;
(c) the statutes which were in force in England on 17th August, 1911, being the commencement of the Northern Rhodesia Order in Council 1911; and
(d) any statutes of a later date than that mentioned in paragraph (c) in force in England, now applied to the Republic, or which shall apply to the Republic by an Act of Parliament, or otherwise;
shall be in force in the Republic.

Therefore it is the choice of the state itself to maintain common law as a source of law. This means: common law as it is at the moment of independence. Later developments are not automatically taken into account anymore, as that would mean relinquishing legal sovereignty, which would be at odds with the hard-won independence. If a country would like to take over a new development that occurred in the common law of England and Wales, it would have to consciously adopt it in its own laws, by statute or by precedent. When considering common

---

[6]   See www.ali.org/publications/show/torts/.

[7]   An important singular exception is the state of Louisiana which, as a former French colony, continues to have a civil law system.

[8]   An introductory book is Goldberg and Zipursky 2010, which provides a good overview of the main outlines.

[9]   An exception is Ireland.

law in a former colony you typically need to discount all developments in English law after independence.

Nonetheless there is one way in which independent countries did maintain a link with later developments in English law. For a long time, many former colonies (part of the so-called Commonwealth of Nations) continued to allow appeal for their national court cases to the English Privy Council. In this way countries could keep their legal development in line with English common law and with other countries in the Commonwealth. An important case decided by the Privy Council was *The Wagon Mound (No. 1)*,[10] which is still the leading case on remoteness of damage in English common law.[11]

The position of the Privy Council has eroded over the years. One by one, countries abolished appeal to the Judicial Committee of the Privy Council, thereby gaining complete independence and control over their own legal destiny. The usual way to do so is to set up a national Supreme Court. In the Caribbean a group of countries has established the Caribbean Court of Justice to replace the Privy Council for developing their common law. In 2021 only a few Commonwealth countries still allow appeal to the Privy Council: Antigua and Barbuda, The Bahamas, Brunei, Cook Islands and Niue (Associated States of New Zealand), Grenada, Jamaica, Kiribati, Mauritius, St Christopher and Nevis, Saint Lucia, Saint Vincent and the Grenadines, Trinidad and Tobago, Tuvalu.[12]

Despite the formally independent development of common law, many commonwealth countries still tend to consult each others' precedents, in particular where new developments or difficult issues are involved. Hence we can observe an Australian court cite Canadian case law; although formally not binding, such decisions may have 'persuasive authority'. English courts also take notice of other common law jurisdictions. An example is the references by the House of Lords to the Supreme Court of Canada in *Lister v Hesley Hall*.[13]

For common law systems other than England and Wales, the basic outline of tort law has mostly been inherited from English law, but the national courts may have given their own interpretation by newer national precedents. A few states have opted to codify their tort law system, while keeping the conceptual framework of English tort law. In Israel, for instance, many common law torts have been codified in the Civil Wrongs Ordinance, while others have been codified in various statutes.[14] The details of the torts, however, are still regulated by the case law.

When examining a common law system, you can start with the presumption that the general torts from English law are also recognized, and that they follow the same general outline. However, this is only a presumption: you should be prepared for surprises and differences from divergent precedents and specific acts.

---

[10] *Wagon Mound (No. 1)* [1961] UKPC 2, [1961] AC 388.

[11] Privy Council decisions are not always binding to English courts, see the rule in *Willers v Joyce* [2016] UKSC 44.

[12] www.jcpc.uk.

[13] [2001] UKHL 22, at 70 and 82.

[14] Barak 1990, Perry 2019.

An example of an extension through precedent is the extension in Indian law of the strict liability rule of *Rylands v Fletcher* to a more extensive rule of strict liability.[15] The opposite is also possible: a precedent which limits the extent of a tort. A striking example can be found in Canada where the tort of breach of statutory duty has been abolished in the decision *The Queen (Can.) v Saskatchewan Wheat Pool.*[16] An example of an extension through a specific act is the Accident Compensation Act 1972 in New Zealand, which instituted a no-fault compensation scheme for various accidents involving personal injury.[17] In particular defamation[18] is often governed (partly) by specific acts.

There are also quite often specific acts that regulate various issues that are general to tort law, such as contributory negligence, joint and several liability. Examples are the Wrongs (Miscellaneous Provisions) Act of Papua New Guinea which covers these issues along with regulating a few specific torts, the Malaysian Civil Law Act 1956, the Singapore Civil Law Act, the Jamaican Law Reform (Tort-Feasors) Act of 1946.

A complication is that common law countries may recognize similar torts under slightly different names. This goes in particular for the economic torts. For instance, in Canada the tort of interference with trade by unlawful means is called *unlawful interference with economic relations.*[19]

A further complication is that local law may require you to refer to local precedents for rules that are familiar in English law by English precedents. In Ireland, for example, in *Glencar Exploration plc and Andaman Resources plc v Mayo County Council*[20] the Irish Supreme Court formulated a rule for negligence similar to the (now abolished) 'Caparo-test' in English law.

If you need to ascertain the exact state of the law, you will need to verify whether there are specific statutes that change and codify parts of tort law, and whether there are local precedents that deviate from English common law. You should furthermore realize that you cannot assume that recent developments of English common law are also accepted after the independence of the country. Your knowledge of English law helps to comprehend a description of tort law in a specific common law country, but does not provide you with definite knowledge about the precise state of local tort law. Even if the same torts are available, they may have different requirements. Two examples may suffice. In Australia the tort of trespass to the person does not require intention; there is the possibility of negligent trespass.[21] In Singapore the courts

---

[15] Supreme Court of India: *M.C. Mehta v Union of India (UOI) and Ors.* 1987 SCR (1) 819, AIR 1987 965, on which further Badrinarayana 2017 and Raj, Mookherjee and Borthakur 2021.

[16] [1983] 1 SCR 205. Incidentally, it is argued that Canadian courts still take statutory rules into account when deciding a cause of action based on negligence (Forster 2011). This is in line with the way in which in French law the general rule of fault-liability includes violations of statutory rules.

[17] Brown 1985.

[18] Defamation Act 2005 in Australia, Defamation Act 1957 in Malaysia, or simply Defamation Act in countries like Jamaica, Kenya, Zambia, Singapore.

[19] *A.I. Enterprises Ltd., et al. v Bram Enterprises Ltd., et al.* 2014 SCC 12.

[20] [2002] 1 I.R. 84.

[21] *Williams v Milotin* (1957) 97 CLR 465.

have – diverging from the earlier reading of *Caparo v Dickman* in English law – developed a two-stage negligence test that also applies in cases of pure economic loss.[22]

16.4   CIVIL LAW SYSTEMS

The French civil code and German BGB have had an enormous influence on later codifications, directly and indirectly. Many countries outside the European legal tradition have in recent years taken over the model of a civil law codification, taking into account the experiences and examples from the earlier codifications. Here I will provide a bird's eye overview of the main trends in civil law systems. I will discuss a few examples as illustration of the difficulties you may encounter. The focus here is on codified provisions. As we have seen, the provisions of a civil code may be reinterpreted by later case law, and may also require additional knowledge about the way they are interpreted by national lawyers. To substantiate your interpretation you should therefore check with national doctrinal literature and/or local experts. Here I will only point out what can be gleaned from the provisions themselves, being aware that the actual state of the law may differ from the impression obtained from the text of the code.

16.4.1   The spread of civil law

Civil law systems exhibit a greater variety than common law. The French *Code civil* of 1804[23] was one of the first codifications of private law, including tort law, and served as a model for later codifications. Several countries still have a code that – as far as tort law is concerned – is almost identical to the original French *Code civil*.[24] The countries that still have a code close to the Code civil are usually former colonies, or in the case of Belgium[25] and Luxemburg, countries that were invaded by Napoleon (or colonies of such countries).[26] The French Code civil was usually imposed on the former French colonies, although France also allowed local modifications to the code to suit the specific conditions or pre-existing law of the country. After independence, most colonies retained their code, but quite a few countries have since updated their civil code. In those countries the codes, as far as tort law is concerned, usually still follow the French system quite closely, in particular in having a general norm similar to art. 1240 Cc.

---

[22]   *Spandeck Engineering (S) Pte Ltd v Defence Science & Technology Agency* [2007] 4 SLR (R) 100; [2007] SGCA 37. See further Tan 2010.

[23]   While the French civil code has been modified in 2016, the provisions on tort law were mostly left intact (they were merely renumbered). A project for material change of these provisions is underway, although it is uncertain whether its suggested modifications will be adopted in the end.

[24]   For example, Belgium, Indonesia, Ivory Coast, Haiti, Burkina Faso, Burundi, Togo, Democratic Republic Congo, Mauritania, Mauritius.

[25]   Belgium is at the time of writing (2021) in the process of recodification.

[26]   As in the case of Indonesia, which used to be a Dutch colony and thereby received a modified copy of the old Dutch civil code which was a revised version of the modified copy of the French Code civil that had been implemented in The Netherlands when Napoleon's brother was king.

The specific delicts are often updated and extended, by adding rules on topics like defamation, state liability, product liability.

The Spanish and Portuguese civil code have also been derived from the French model, although they have been modified later. Former Spanish and Portuguese colonies clearly show the influence of the French Code civil but contain also several innovations of their own.

The current Spanish *Código Civil* dates from 1889. In art. 1902 it contains a general rule of liability in art. 1902, essentially the same as the French rule of arts. 1240 and 1241 Cc.[27] The articles following this provision contain rules on strict liability for persons, animals, and buildings in a style very similar to the French Code civil. The Chilean *Código Civil* of 1855 (entry in force 1857) was drafted by Professor Bello, influenced by the French Code civil and Spanish law,[28] and this code served as a model for other former Spanish colonies in the Americas.[29] These codifications regularly contain provisions for several specific wrongful acts besides a general rule for fault liability (and rules for strict liability). For instance, art. 1912 of the Mexican *Código Civil Federal* establishes liability for abuse of right, which in most jurisdictions is not a specific tort (rather recognized elsewhere in the code, or left to case law).

In Portugal the original *Código Civil* of 1868, which took after the French model, was replaced by a new code in 1967 that followed the German layered structure of the BGB, although not the specific German approach to torts. The Portuguese code deals with torts in art. 483-510, providing a general norm, specific grounds of liability, and strict liability provisions including liability for land-based vehicles. Most former Portuguese colonies, part of the *Comunidade dos Países de Língua Portuguesa* (Community of Portuguese Language Countries),[30] have retained a code based on the new Portuguese Código Civil of 1967.[31] Although many modifications have been made later on, the tort law provisions are usually left intact. Brazil has developed its own code, as it was already independent at the time of enactment of the new Portuguese code in 1967.[32]

The *Codice civile* of Italy was, again, inspired by the French Code civil. In its most recent iteration of 1942, arts. 2043–2059 deal with delicts (*Dei Fatti Illeciti*). Its origins are still recognizable, although there are also differences such as the explicitly listed defences of legitimate defense (*Legittima difesa*) and necessity (*Stato di necessità*) in arts. 2044 and 2045, liability for vehicles (art. 2054), and several provisions on damages (arts. 2056–2059). Some former Italian colonies[33] have adopted the Italian code or have their own code modeled on the Italian code.

---

[27] An English translation provided by the Spanish government can be found at http://derechocivil-ugr.es/attachments/article/45/spanish-civil-code.pdf:

[28] Matus Valencia 1958.

[29] De Morpurgo and Peñailillo Arévalo 2021.

[30] Particularly Angola, Cabo Verde, Guinea Bissau, Mozambique, and São Tomé and Príncipe; Timor-Leste (East Timor).

[31] Moura Vicente 2013.

[32] Celli 2021.

[33] Such as Eritrea, Ethiopia, Somalia. See also Bussani 1996. Bussani and Infantino 2021, p. 12 point out that the code is actually not followed in Ethiopia, but that customary law still is applied. Similarly in Somalia there is Xeer law besides the Somali Civil Code of 1973,

Other countries do not fit neatly into the aforementioned families. Starting with Austria (1812), Japan (1898)[34] and Switzerland (1912), and continuing at a steady pace in the twentieth century, many states on all continents (except Antarctica) have enacted codes.[35] Since the 1990s this process has accelerated: many new codifications or recodification projects have been completed all over the world.[36] A few examples in Europe from the last decade are Hungary (2014),[37] the Czech Republic (2014)[38] and Turkey (2012). Outside Europe we can point to new codes in Vietnam (2017), Argentina (2015) and China (2010).

Those codifications have profited from the wealth of comparative materials that have become available. Because of this, these codes usually cannot be simply categorized as following a single model, rather they exhibit multiple influences and ideas. Nonetheless the terminology, doctrines and approaches discussed in the previous chapters are usually recognized and help to understand these systems.

Most codifications have a general rule of fault liability, possibly with a few specific delicts such as breach of statutory duty. Several former Soviet republics have more or less followed the Russian civil code.[39] Other codifications in the last 20 years (in particular in many East-Asian and Middle-European countries) do not have a clear model, rather are a mix of the more systematic approach of German law and the general norm of French law. In some instances (particular east-Asian codifications) the German approach of protected interests is imported.[40] However, the specific German list of three general norms and several rather particular delicts is not followed. The codes show various approaches to organizing strict liability. Product liability and liability for motorized vehicles are also frequently regulated in the code itself instead of a separate act. General rules such as defences, damages, contributory negligence, prescription, joint and several liability are sometimes placed in the title on tort law, but may also be found in more general part of the code (following the German approach).

16.4.2 The material norms

The French use of a general norm can be found in many different codes, such as in Estonia[41] or Brazil.[42] The German system has been quite influential as well. The complicated structure

---

[34] The first code was from 1890, but the tort law provisions were modified in 1898. See Matsumoto 2021.

[35] A comparative description of European countries can be found in Von Bar 1998, part. 3, pp. 13–258.

[36] Some of those projects are described in Rivera 2013.

[37] Menyhárd 2014.

[38] Hrádek 2013.

[39] Lee 2014 points out influences regarding the burden of proof of fault and a general clause of strict liability, which can be found in Kazakhstan, Uzbekistan, Estonia, Armenia, Lithuania, Belarus, Tajikistan, Ukraine, Kyrgyzstan, while the Czech code also exhibits the influence of the Russian codification.

[40] For instance, the Japanese Civil code, art. 709, on which Matsumoto 2021, and art. 584 Bộ Luật (Civil Code of Vietnam), a translation of which can be found at https://wipolex-res.wipo.int/edocs/lexdocs/laws/en/vn/vn079en.pdf.

[41] § 1043 Võlaõigusseadus (Law of Obligations Act 2002), a translation can be found at www.riigiteataja.ee/en/eli/ee/Riigikogu/act/507032019001/consolide.

[42] Art. 927 Código Civil Brasileiro (2002), cited in Celli 2021, p. 544.

of three general and several specific grounds of liability has not found widespread adoption, but the use of 'protected interests' for regulating behaviour,[43] and the detailed logic of the BGB has been a model for many later codifications. For instance, the Czech civil code operates with several general norms in §§ 2900–2902 of the *Zákon občanský zákoník* (Civil code).[44] If you examine these, you will recognize one rule for infringement of certain interests, another for creation of dangerous situations, and a third rule for breach of a legal duty (which may either mean breach of statutory duty, or in the French manner, breach of any official written rule).

As always, you need to be careful not to go by first impressions. The Russian code, for example, contains a general clause which seems to refer to protected interests in the German style.[45] However, in later case law it was decided that this provision should not be understood as a list of protected interests in the manner of § 823 BGB. Rather it is simply a general norm in the French style.[46] This example serves to show that you cannot rely solely on consulting the code, you need to verify your interpretation with local experts and doctrinal literature.

Besides one or more general rules, civil law systems may have provisions for specific delicts or torts. These are comparable to the specific grounds of liability in German law. Some codes recognize abuse of right as a distinct ground of liability.[47]

You should also bear in mind that specific delicts may be found in statutes besides the code. An example is defamation in French law (§ 7.5). While such specific delicts are comparable to some extent to English torts, they differ from English tort law in that the general rules on tort law will normally also apply to specific delicts if there are no explicit deviations.

16.5   TORT LAW IN THE NORDIC COUNTRIES

Tort law in the Nordic countries is historically based on customary law. The rules have, however, mostly been codified in the twentieth century. The most relevant acts are as follows.[48]

- Norway: *Skadeserstatningsloven* (Compensation for Damage Act) 1969
- Sweden: *Skadeståndslagen* (Tort Liability Act) 1972
- Finland: *Vahingonkorvauslaki* (Tort Liability Act) 1974
- Denmark: There is no codification of general tort law,[49] but there is an act regulating damages, the *Erstatningsansvarloven* (Liability for Damages Act) 1984

---

[43]   Some codes have adopted a general provision and/or list of protected interests similar to § 823 BGB. For example see China (on which Jiang 2021), Thailand, Japan, Vietnam.

[44]   A translation can be found at http://obcanskyzakonik.justice.cz/images/pdf/Civil-Code.pdf.

[45]   Art. 1064 Russian Civil Code.

[46]   Yagelnitskiy 2021, at p. 357.

[47]   For instance, s. 421 of the Thai Civil and Commercial Code (1925), art. 1.353 Romanian Noul Cod Civil.

[48]   See also www.casebooks.eu/documents/tortLaw/heading1.4.4.pdf (online addition to the Ius Commune casebook on tort), and Von Bar 1998, part 3, pp. 259–81.

[49]   Gomard 2001, also Ulfbeck, Ehlers and Siig 2018.

These systems are based on the customary law of these countries, and are not like many European civil law systems indirectly derived from Roman law. Despite this distinct background, the tort law provisions and rules in Nordic countries are fairly easy to understand in outline. Hence you may be able to obtain a footing in Nordic tort law, all the while being aware that further research is required to ascertain the precise legal picture.

As an example we can look at a brief excerpt from the Swedish Tort Liability Act:[50]

---

2 kap. Skadeståndsansvar på grund av eget vållande
1 § Den som uppsåtligen eller av vårdslöshet vållar personskada eller sakskada skall ersätta skadan.
2 § Den som vållar ren förmögenhetsskada genom brott skall ersätta skadan.
3 § Den som allvarligt kränker någon annan genom brott som innefattar ett angrepp mot dennes person, frihet, frid eller ära skall ersätta den skada som kränkningen innebär.
...
3 kap. Skadeståndsansvar för annans vållande och för det allmänna
...
5 § En förälder som har vårdnaden om ett barn ska ersätta
1. personskada eller sakskada som barnet vållar genom brott, och
2. skada på grund av att barnet kränker någon annan på sätt som anges i 2 kap. 3 §.

Chapter 2. Liability on the basis of personal fault
§ 1 He who intentionally or through negligence causes personal injury or property damage shall compensate the damage.
§ 2 He who causes pure economic damage by a criminal act shall compensate the damage.
§ 3 He who seriously violates someone else by a criminal act involving an attack on his person, freedom, peace or honor shall compensate the damage caused by the violation.
...

Chapter 3 Liability for another's fault and for the public
...
Section 5 A parent who has custody of a child shall compensate
1. personal injury or property damage caused by the child by a criminal act, and
2. damage due to the child violating someone else in the manner stated in chapter 2, § 3.

These provisions seem quite clear and use categories that we are familiar with, such as pure economic loss, violation of certain interests. Note that compensation of pure economic loss is apparently restricted to crimes. Of course further research would be required to ascertain what Swedish law really understands by crime (*brott*), and whether this provision has nonetheless found broader application.[51] But the general outline can be readily understood.

---

[50] On the Act see Hellner 1974.

[51] Kadner Graziano 2018, p. 92 refers to Schulz 2007 as confirming that this provision is only applied to criminal acts.

16.6   ROMAN-DUTCH LAW

A peculiar legal system is Roman-Dutch law.[52] In these jurisdictions Roman law is still a source of law, in the form as received in the Netherlands in the sixteenth century and exported to Dutch colonies. It has survived principally in South Africa and several neighbouring countries (Namibia, Lesotho, Swaziland, Botswana and Zimbabwe), but mixed with common law. In Sri Lanka Roman-Dutch law is valid law, besides common law.[53] The main developments and scholarship are found in South Africa where there is a large and active legal community.

The approach of Roman-Dutch law is at first sight rather different from the systems we have discussed up to now. The principal source consists of the classic Roman texts, in particular the Digests. Present-day lawyers may debate about the precise meaning of texts of which the authors have been dead for centuries, and try to apply those texts to situations that these authors didn't dream of. However, the notion of authoritative texts that have to be interpreted in order to apply them is not fundamentally different, whether you are reading provisions that were enacted last year or texts that have been drafted centuries ago. Furthermore, Roman-Dutch law is a living law which is developed continually by new case law and statutes, and through the writings of legal scholars who are very much aware of the developments in common law and civil law countries.

The outlines of the law of delict, as it is called in South Africa, can be reconstructed with the help of the general principles we discussed.[54] Delictual liability is analysed similar to the model of fault liability presented in Chapter 2 and the extensions to strict liability, but with the complication that many Latin terms and concepts are used. In particular, the law distinguishes between three actions, the *Actio legis aquiliae* (which refers back to the Roman *Lex Aquilia*), *Actio iniuriarum* and what is called the 'Germanic action' for pain and suffering, which is not based on Roman law. These actions correspond broadly to negligence (for patrimonial loss), injury to personality, and actions causing immaterial harm.

Due to these unfamiliar categories, it is harder to gain an understanding of the law of delict in Roman-Dutch law, but the distinctions and concepts we have discussed should give you a starting point from where to approach this system.

16.7   ISLAMIC TORT LAW

Tort law in Islamic countries is principally based on Islamic religious texts. There is not a single uniform interpretation of Islamic law or Shari'a law, as there are several competing schools of interpretation. Nonetheless there appears to be consensus about the broad outlines.[55] Several Islamic countries have a code that follows Islamic law. Some codes contain provisions follow-

---

[52]   An excellent study of Roman law, with relevance to South African law, is Zimmermann 1996.

[53]   Cooray 1974.

[54]   Loubser 2018, Neethling, Potgieter and Knobel 2021.

[55]   Basir Bin Mohamed 2021.

ing the civil law approach, but have distinct Islamic influences.[56] Others take a fundamentally different approach to tort law than usual in civil codes. Consider the code of Afghanistan,[57] which provides the following categorization of torts:

- destruction of property,
- usurpation,
- harmful acts to persons.

This categorization is unlike other codes, and follows the outlines of Islamic law for non-contractual liability. However, you may also see similarities to several common law torts such as trespass to goods, conversion, trespass to the person. Even though the exact contours of these torts may differ, the knowledge gained from this text may hopefully help you to familiarize yourself with a different classification. Indeed, it is possible to describe the Islamic law of non-contractual liability in a way that is relatable for lawyers coming from a civil law or common law background.[58] A proper appreciation of the system will, of course, require thorough study.

16.8   TORT LAW IN MIXED AND OTHER LEGAL SYSTEMS

In comparative legal research we also distinguish a category of so-called mixed legal systems.[59] These are jurisdictions that mingle several different kinds of legal systems, such as common law and customary law. Some authors consider mixed legal systems as countries where both common law and civil law applies.[60] However, it is also pointed out that 'mixed' should not be limited and could equally well apply to all countries that do not have a complete uniform legal system.[61] An example is Somalia, which has a mixture of various sources of law, including customary law for specific groups. Roman-Dutch law is also considered to be a mixed legal system, but given its particular background was discussed separately above.

If the differences are between regions, we do not consider the system to be a mixed legal system (hence the UK as such does not have a mixed legal system). However, certain regions

---

[56]   An example is the UAE Civil code (Federal Law No. 5 of 1985 regarding civil transactions). Art. 282 provides a general norm for liability, but later provisions are clearly derived from Shari'a law. On Shari'a influences on the UAE code see Ballantyne 1986.

[57]   Civil Law of the Republic of Afghanistan (Civil Code) – Official Gazette No. 353, published 1977/01/05 (1355/10/15 A.P.), Arts. 759–799. Another example is the Civil code of Iran (1928/1935), arts. 301–337, also arts. 950–955.

[58]   Basir Bin Mohamad 2021, and references therein. See for strict liability Basir Bin Mohamad 2000 on vicarious liability and Basir Bin Mohamad 2001 on liability for animals.

[59]   Palmer 2007, Palmer 2012.

[60]   E.g. Palmer 2007, 2012.

[61]   Siems 2014, pp. 85–93.

are considered to have a mixed legal system, such as Scotland, Quebec, Louisiana which all have common law and civil law elements.

If you are confronted with such a jurisdiction, you will have to ascertain how those different systems are mixed, whether one takes precedence over the other or whether they have restricted spheres or areas in which they apply. It may be, for example, that family matters are regulated by religious law or customary law, while tort law is exclusively based on common law. When concentrating on tort law, we merely need to consider whether tort law itself is based on a single kind of legal system, and classify the jurisdiction accordingly. In other words, the issue here is whether there is a mixed *tort law*, not whether the entire legal system is mixed.

Even if tort law itself is mixed in its origins, the modern day understanding of such systems tends to be influenced by comparative scholarship. Systems such as South Africa, Islamic law and Nordic law can be presented in terms of the structures we discussed in the previous chapters. The complicated history of those systems need not be an obstacle towards understanding the outlines of tort law.

Hence, from a more practical point of view, in particular given the recent flood of codifications, it is not necessary for a first impression to focus on the historical background of legal systems. Rather the actual content of tort law is what matters. Even if the system allows influences from traditional custom, a recent codification tends to overshadow other influences which subsequently appear as corrections to the outlines of the code. We will discuss how to deal with such influences later on.

Only a few remaining countries do not fit into one of the earlier categories. Bhutan is fairly unique in having retained its traditional law, albeit nowadays in codified form. Bhutan tort law is codified in the Penal Code. For some countries the actual legal situation is difficult to ascertain because of social or military unrest, as in Sudan and South Sudan, or because of its lack of public sources, as in the case of North Korea.

16.9   COMPLETING THE RECONSTRUCTION OF NATIONAL TORT LAW

The basic understanding of tort law that you may obtain from reconstructing the national tort law system may need to be complemented with additional research. In order to be able to provide a complete reconstruction, you will need to take into account other sources and phenomena.[62] The difference between the legal rules from statute and case law, and the law as actually applies in practice, is also referred to as the difference between law in the books and law in action.

There are several influences which you need to take into account when trying to construct a complete overview of relevant rules. First of all, you need to look at international and supranational influences. Secondly, you may need to look into rules that elaborate or slightly modify

---

[62]   Such other factors have been called 'legal formants' by Sacco 1991.

national law: regional law and customary law[63] and private regulation. The best source for finding relevant rules are doctrinal works.[64]

A few brief notes on the sources mentioned just now may help you on your way to become a comparative tort law researcher.

16.9.1   International and supranational influences

There are several influences to discuss.

1.   International treaties

First of all, there are several rules in *international treaties* (also called conventions) concerning tort law.[65] See in particular:

- Warsaw convention (1929): Convention for the Unification of certain rules relating to international carriage by air, updated by the Montreal convention (1999)
- Convention on damage caused by foreign aircraft to third parties on the surface (1952)
- Paris Convention on Third Party Liability in the Field of Nuclear Energy (1960)
- International Convention on Civil Liability for Oil Pollution Damage (CLC) (1969)
- Convention on International Liability for Damage Caused by Space Objects (1972)
- Convention on Limitation of Liability for Maritime Claims (1976)

As is clear from their titles, these treaties mostly address new risks.[66] They only regulate a few aspects of tort law for these risks. These treaties may also be implemented in national acts.

These treaties contain rules about who is liable, how cases of multiple tortfeasors are to be decided, which country has jurisdiction, and limitations as to the amount of damages that may be awarded.[67] In the following chapters these concepts will be explained.

The ratio of these rules is that the convening states were anxious to stimulate certain (new) types of business that could easily lead to cross-border accidents, and wanted to remove the uncertainty as to the state of the law for such accidents.[68] The Oil Pollution Convention (1969)

---

[63]   This would in practice be approached through doctrine or a local expert.

[64]   It should be noted that doctrine is, generally speaking, more influential in the 'older' larger Western jurisdictions than elsewhere. For example, De Morpurgo and Peñailillo Arévalo 2021 note on pp. 535–6 that scholarship in Latin American countries tends to be fairly positivistic, staying close to the text of the code and case law, and paying little attention to law in practice, while lawyers look to Western Europe and the USA for new developments. However, López-Medina 2012 forcefully argues for the richness of the Latin American and Caribbean tradition as legal cultures of their own.

[65]   Treaties like these still have to be implemented in national law, but the effect is that all signatory states (states that have accepted the treaty) have identical rules on the issues regulated in the treaty.

[66]   An exception is the Convention on Limitation of Liability for Maritime Claims (1976).

[67]   Not all of these treaties contain all of these kinds of rules.

[68]   A similar justification underlies the rules on liability of Internet Service Providers in the European Union, see § 7.5.

is different: it contains an intricate set of rules for setting up a fund to provide compensation to victims.

Incidentally, there are also several fundamental rights treaties. These have been discussed in § 6.5.

2.   Supranational legislation

Secondly, there is supranational law. The most prominent example is the law of the European Union, which has led to various rules that influenced tort law. An example is the Product Liability Directive 85/374 which has led to effective harmonization of a contested area of law. Other forays into the field of tort law are the liability of Internet Service Providers[69] and the liability for unfair trading practices.[70] However, the actual influence of the European Union on tort law in Member States has been fairly limited.

The European Union may also, more indirectly, influence tort law. This may occur through the case law of the European Court of Justice.

3.   Academic principles

Thirdly, there have been various academic projects to create a relatively abstract set of principles that would describe the common rules underlying most national tort law systems. However, such principles are not binding law as such, although they may influence court decisions.

An example of a significant influence on the law is the Restatement of Torts in the USA (§ 16.3). Restatements have been drafted not as rules of positive law, but as a description of the broad outlines of the commonalities in various US states.

In Europe a similar approach was taken, through a practice of drafting what are called 'principles'. These are not principles in the sense of Dworkin's philosophy of law, where principles are distinguished from rules, such as the principle that no-one should benefit from his own wrongful conduct.[71] Rather the 'principle projects' are model laws, that look very much like civil codes. Two European examples in the area of tort law are the Principles of European Tort Law (PETL) and the Draft Common Frame of Reference (DCFR).

The Principles of European Tort Law (PETL) have been drafted by an independent group of academic researchers, the European Group on Tort Law, also called the Spier/Koziol-group or the Tilburg-group.[72] Their work has led to a number of books on separate topics of tort law, and finally resulted in the publication of a complete set of principles.[73]

An alternative set of principles for tort law can be found in Book VI of the Draft Common Frame of Reference (DCFR). The DCFR is the result of an EU-funded research project to

---

[69]   Art. 12-15 E-commerce Directive 2000/31/EC.

[70]   Directive 2005/29/EC.

[71]   Rules provide a clear outcome when their conditions are fulfilled, while principles only point in the direction of a desirable outcome without requiring that this *must* be the outcome.

[72]   Professors Spier (Tilburg) and Koziol (Vienna) were the two leaders of the research. See also www.egtl.org.

[73]   Published as *Principles of European Tort law, Text and Commentary*, Vienna/New York: Springer 2005. See www.egtl.org/Principles/index.htm.

set up a 'Frame of Reference' for EU legislation and legal development. The final output was something that looks like a civil code. At the time of its conclusion (2009) it was hoped that the EU would indeed adopt this as a basic civil code, or at least would use it to drive developments to complete harmonization of private law in the EU. These hopes were quickly dashed as the EU made it quite clear that it would not consider a full harmonization of private law.

The direct legal influence of these principles is limited, as they have no legal authority. However, indirectly they have proven to influence the law. Courts in various European countries have on occasion cited these principles in their decisions. Furthermore, in academic discussions on the future development of tort law these principles figure fairly often, as providing a handy summary of the broad consensus in different European countries. Arguably several new codifications of tort law are influenced by these principles.

16.9.2   Regional law

A significant number of nation-states have conferred considerable autonomy on inter-state regions.[74] Examples are the USA, Germany, Australia, Canada,[75] Mexico[76] and the UK.[77] Such regions may thereby formally have their own sovereignty over issues of tort law, while the nation-state may only interfere for specific issues. Or the region is allowed to deviate from the rules of the state. One reason for regional divergence is that the nation-state is actually a federation of formerly independent states. That is not the only option. Several countries have uniform national law but have granted more or less autonomy to specific regions, such as islands[78] or particular provinces[79] or (former) colonies.[80] These may therefore deviate from the legislation in the majority of the country or even have their own laws.[81]

If you need to know the precise legal state of affairs in such countries, you will therefore need to check whether there is relevant regional law. An example is Canada, where provinces have a large degree of autonomy over tort law, which can be illustrated by the treatment of privacy. In the province British Columbia the Supreme Court has ruled that there is no common law tort of invasion of privacy,[82] only a statutory right (Privacy Act [RSBC 1996] Chapter 373),

---

[74]   Such regions may also be called 'state', which is confusing. In this section I use 'nation-state' to refer to what we commonly call state or country, i.e. the member of the United Nations.

[75]   Quebec has a civil law system, while the other provinces of Canada have a common law system.

[76]   In Mexico there is a Federal Civil Code of Mexico, but individual states have their own codes as well.

[77]   Scotland formally has its own law and does not have tort law but a law of delict. However, the content of the law may share many traits with English tort law; in particular the case *Donoghue v Stevenson* [1932] AC 562 was a case in Scots law of delict, which however has served as a landmark case for both Scots and English law.

[78]   Such as the Isle of Man or Guernsey, which are part of the United Kingdom.

[79]   For instance, the Italian autonomous province of South Tyrol (Alto Adige).

[80]   As in the case of the Caribbean Islands (Aruba, Curaçao and Sint Maarten) that are part of the Kingdom of The Netherlands,

[81]   An example is Curaçao, which has its own civil code.

[82]   *Ari v Insurance Corporation of British Columbia*, 2013 BCSC 1308.

while in Ontario the Court of Appeal on the contrary did recognize a common law tort of invasion of privacy.[83] Quebec, as mentioned above, is a civil law jurisdiction.[84]

The local autonomy in regulating tort law must not be confused with the possibility that an inter-state region may have instituted local rules that influence the application of specific torts. For instance, a city may have a local ordinance that prohibits serving alcoholic drinks without a license. Violation of that rule may also be a tort for breach of a statutory duty. That does not mean that the city hereby has the power to create new torts.

Sometimes the region may not have full autonomy over the issues it can create tort law rules about. Also, in many cases a region is not interested in creating specific rules. In Germany the local regions, 'countries' (*Länder*), only deviate from the BGB in a few instances.[85] In the USA, on the contrary, the various states do have their own tort law rules which, although exhibiting some uniformity, may deviate in many places. State courts and lawyers practising in such a state refer primarily to the case law from their own state, although they may on occasion also mention precedents from other states.

You should at the very least always check whether the nation-state that you are investigating does have regions with independent legislative power over tort law. If the answer is in the affirmative, you may need to check subsequently whether there are indeed regionally specific rules for the topic and location that you are researching.

16.9.3   Customary law

Customary law poses a particular challenge in reconstructing the law.[86] Even though customary law may nominally have a role in most jurisdictions,[87] it can usually be disregarded unless it is relevant to a specific case or area. Formally speaking, customary law is a third source of law in those jurisdictions that recognize it, on an equal footing with legislation (and case law). Western jurisdictions used to recognize the role of custom quite openly.[88] For instance, the Louisiana Civil code starts with art. 1: 'The sources of law are legislation and custom.' However, over time customary law has seen a steady decline in status.[89] Nowadays rules in Western states

---

[83]   *Jones v Tsige*, 2012 ONCA 32.

[84]   Quebec also has a Privacy Act (Act Respecting the Protection of Personal Information in the Private Sector, chapter P-39.1).

[85]   An example of a difference is Saarland Neighbour law (*Saarländisches Nachbarrechtsgesetz*) of 1973 which contains specific rules on neighbour relations. These can apply concurrently with general tort law of the BGB, and have different prescription rules. Regional law can furthermore lead to liability on the basis of § 823 II BGB. See for a list of potentially relevant rules Bamberger Kommentar 2019, § 823, para 291, mentioning rules regarding buildings, environment, and animals.

[86]   Polánski 2007, pp. 99–141 provides an overview of the history and present status of customary law.

[87]   Possibly in the guise of ethical or moral rules, general notions of justice, and so on.

[88]   Glenn 1997 describes how custom was marginalized in Western law. Mayali and Mousseron 2018 discuss customary law more broadly.

[89]   Typical is the approach in § 10 ABGB: custom can only be taken into account in cases where a law refers to it (*Auf Gewohnheiten kann nur in den Fällen, in welchen sich ein Gesetz darauf beruft, Rücksicht genommen werden*).

that in the past would have been called customary law tend to be discussed rather as forms of private regulation. Business practices are an example.

In jurisdictions where customary law is still a major influence, one has to take this into account from the outset. In several countries in Sub-Saharan Africa, customary law is explicitly recognized as a source of law and relevant to tort law.[90] In many other countries customary law is mentioned as a corrective to or part of received common law;[91] customary law may refer particularly to the laws of particular communities and not to customs shared in the whole nation. In that respect it is not very different from regional law (§ 16.9.2), except that it may be related to persons instead of territory,[92] and it is usually not codified.

Given the nature of customary law, it requires specific research into the local customs. Very generally speaking, customary law is particularly important in torts that involve family matters or interpersonal conflicts. Dagbanja helpfully suggests (for Sub-Saharan Africa) to look at the protected interests: torts involved are for example insults, adultery and enticement.[93] Other examples of customary law can be found in Somalia, Laos[94] and in Andorra.[95] In the USA, Native Americans may for certain issues be subject to tribal law instead of state and federal law.

A practical problem is that the enforcement of customary law may involve customary dispute settlement institutions that deviate from the Western court system and may operate outside and next to the official courts. Hence when customary law is involved, you will have to tread carefully to familiarize yourself with the legal system, not focus only on the official law, rather look at how the law is applied in practice.

Incidentally, uncodified Shari'a law (§ 16.7) may be treated to a certain extent like customary law, except that it is easier to determine as it is still based on written sources.

16.10 TOWARDS TORT LAW IN PRACTICE

By now you should understand that tort law is a lot more complicated than the bare overview that you might obtain from solely consulting national statutes and case law. There is still a further step to take. Although we already discussed the way in which statutes and case law may take outside influences into account (§ 6.2), there are also other influences that can determine the outcome of court cases or the practice of settlement of disputes. We already

---

Custom is thereby accorded a subsidiary status to the code.

[90]   Dagbanja 2021.

[91]   This is found in former English colonies in Africa, where the rules regarding validity of common law after independence often contain a reference to customary law. For example, see arts. 11(2) and 11(3) Constitution 1992 of Ghana, in Uganda the Judicature Act, Cap. 13, s. 14 and 15, in Sierra Leone the Constitution 1991, ss. 170(2) and (3).

[92]   I.e. only members of the community may be subject to such customs regardless of the place, whereas regional law applies to each person on the territory of that region.

[93]   Dagbanja 2021.

[94]   Customary Law and Practice in Lao PDR, (report from Laotian Ministry of Justice, July 2011), at www.undp .org/content/dam/laopdr/docs/Reports%20and%20publications/Customary_Law_Laos2011_english_master1.pdf.

[95]   Angelo 1970.

encountered an example in the discussion on vicarious liability (§ 14.3). The common law rule whereby an employer could recover damages for vicarious liability from his employee is in practice rendered mostly ineffective by a gentleman's agreement between insurance companies. If you really wish to understand how tort law works in practice, you would ideally need to submerge yourself entirely in the legal practice that you are studying. This, in effect, is the message of what is called legal pluralism: the law is far more varied and extensive than the sources of statute and case law might lead you to believe.

Indeed, although we started with a simple structure of only two sources of law, we have gradually worked towards a more nuanced view of the law. When studying new jurisdictions, it is nonetheless wise to start off with the outlines provided by statute and case law. This is the approach of a tourist or newcomer into a town: to orient yourself you focus on a few easily recognizable buildings or streets. Only once you have familiarized yourself with the outlines will you be able to find your way around in the narrow alleys, the nooks and crannies of the town. There is no shame in starting off as a tourist, as long as you don't mistake this with the familiarity of a resident that can only be acquired over time.

This analogy leads us to a further remark. The perspective of this text is the viewpoint of Western jurisdictions, which have a tendency to consider other jurisdictions merely as recipients of Western law. The perspective of the countries themselves is rather the opposite: they may perceive the new codifications as foreign impositions that supplant their time-honoured traditions.[96] Indeed, it is possible that the code remains only an official text that does not find practical application.[97] This is an important warning to overreliance on the official presentation of law ('law in the books'). Again, you should realize that all legal systems, including Western systems, are characterized by continuous minute struggles and discussions between courts at all levels, advocates, legal scholars, politicians and citizens. These discussions are what keeps the law alive. The hierarchical idea of a law that emanates from the top and is blindly obeyed by lower courts and citizens is in that respect false.

The political side of the 'post-colonial' invasion of local systems by Western ideas of law is a topic that is outside the purpose of this introduction, where we concentrate on the law as it is. That is not to deny the importance of considering cultural and political critique of the implicit tendencies in the approach taken here. This critique may serve as a sobering reminder of the broader debate in law, and a call to more sensitivity towards competing opinions and positions that do not fit your preconceptions. It is important to keep your eyes peeled for anything out of the ordinary, and not being too quick to impose your own preconceptions. The structure and doctrines that we discussed in this text are intended as a heuristic device to help you understand, not as a straitjacket into which every system should be forced.

This text hopefully prepared you for future encounters with tort law systems over the world. It should make you more humble by not presuming too much about specific systems, while

---

[96] See also the critical discussion in Siems 2014, pp. 260–82.

[97] E.g. Bussani and Infantino 2021 on Eritrea, O'Neill 2009 on India and China. But see Siems 2014, pp. 80–85, warning against oversimplifying differences and similarities.

simultaneously allowing you to have fruitful discussions with the local experts. If you take away this attitude, the present introduction has succeeded in its aim.

17
Bibliography

Al-Qasem, Anis (1989), 'The Injurious Acts under the Jordanian Civil Code', 4 *Arab Law Quarterly*, pp. 183–98

Althammer, Christoph and Tolani, Madeleine (2019), 'Proof of Causation in German Tort Law', in Tichý 2019, pp. 109–22

Angelo, A.H. (1970), 'Andorra: Introduction to a Customary Legal System', 14 *American Journal of Legal History*, pp. 95–111

Badrinarayana, Deepa (2017), 'The Jewel in the Crown: Can India's Strict Liability Doctrine Deepen Our Understanding of Tort Law Theory?', 55 *University of Louisville Law Review*, pp. 25–56

Ballantyne, W.M. (1986), 'The New Civil Code of the United Arab Emirates: A Further Reassertion of the Shari'a', 1 *Arab Law Quarterly*, pp. 245–64

Bamberger, Heinz Georg, and others (eds) (2019), *Bürgerliches Gesetzbuch: Kommentar*, volume 3, 4th ed., München: C.H. Beck

Bamberger Kommentar (2019), alternative for Bamberger (2019)

Barak, Aharoa (1990), 'The Codification of Civil Law and the Law of Torts', 24 *Israel Law Review*, pp. 628–50

Basir Bin Mohamad, Abdul (2000), 'Vicarious Liability: A Study of the Liability of Employer and Employee in the Islamic Law of Tort', 15 *Arab Law Quarterly*, pp. 197–205

Basir Bin Mohamad, Abdul (2001), 'The Islamic Law of Tort: A Study of the Owner and Possessor of Animals with Special Reference to the Civil Codes of the United Arabian Emirates, Lebanon, Tunisia, Morocco, Sudan and Iraq', 16 *Arab Law Quarterly*, pp. 333–45

Basir Bin Mohamad, Abdul (2021), 'Islamic Tort Law', in Bussani and Sebok, pp. 469–516

Beuermann, Christine (2019), *Reconceptualising Strict Liability for the Tort of Another*, Oxford: Hart Publishing

Borghetti, Jean-Sébastien and Whittaker, Simon (eds) (2019), *French Civil Liability in Comparative Perspective*, Oxford: Hart Publishing

Brown, Craig (1985), 'Deterrence in Tort and No-Fault: The New Zealand Experience', 73 *California Law Review*, pp. 976–1002

Bussani, Mauro (1996), 'Tort Law and Development: Insights into the Case of Ethiopia and Eritrea', 40 *Journal of African Law*, pp. 43–52

Bussani, Mauro and Infantino, Marta (2021), 'The Many Cultures of Tort Liability', in Bussani and Sebok 2021, pp. 9–34

Bussani, Mauro and Mattei, Ugo (2012), *The Cambridge Companion to Comparative Law*, Cambridge, Cambridge University Press

Bussani, Mauro and Sebok, Anthony J. (2021), *Comparative Tort Law: Global Perspectives*, 2nd ed., Cheltenham, UK and Northampton, MA, USA: Edward Elgar Publishing

Büyüksagis, Erdem and Van Boom, Willem H. (2013), 'Strict Liability in Contemporary European Codification: Torn Between Objects, Activities, and Their Risks', 44 *Georgetown Journal of International Law*, pp. 609–40

Cafaggi, Fabrizio (2016), 'Transnational Private Regulation. Regulating Private Regulators', in Cassese, S., *Research Handbook on Global Administrative Law*, Cheltenham, UK and Northampton, MA, USA: Edward Elgar Publishing

Cane, Peter (2000), 'Mens Rea in Tort Law', 20 *Oxford Journal of Legal Studies*, pp. 533–56

Cane, Peter (2017), *Key Ideas in Tort Law*, Oxford: Hart Publishing

Celli, Umberto (2021), 'Tort Law in Brazil', in Bussani and Sebok 2021, pp. 539–52

Clerk and Lindsell (2020): alternative for Jones, Dugdale and Simpson 2020.

Cooray, L.J.M. (1974), 'The Reception of Roman-Dutch Law in Sri Lanka', 7 *Comparative and International Law Journal of Southern Africa*, pp. 295–320

Dagbanja, Dominic Npoanlari (2021), 'The Customary Law of Tort in Sub-Saharan Africa', in Bussani and Sebok, pp. 443–68

Dannemann, Gerhard (2009), *The German Law of Unjustified Enrichment and Restitution*, Oxford: Oxford University Press

Dari-Mattiacci, G. and Parisi, F. (2021), 'Liability Rules: An Economic Taxonomy', in Bussani and Sebok, pp. 112–32

De Morpurgo, Marco, and Peñailillo Arévalo, Daniel (2021), 'Tort Law in Hispanic America', in Bussani and Sebok, pp. 517–38

Deutsch, Erwin and Ahrens, Hans-Jürgen (2014), *Deliktsrecht*, 6th ed., Cologne: Vahlen

Ebert, Ina (2021), 'Tort Law and Insurance', in Bussani and Sebok 2021, pp. 133–9

Emaus, Jessey M. (2013), *Handhaving van EVRM-rechten via het aansprakelijkheidsrecht (Enforcing ECHR rights by means of liability law)*, The Hague: Boom Juridische uitgevers

Fabre-Magnan, Muriel (2021), *Droit des obligations, 2. Responsabilité civili et quasi-contrats*, 5th ed., Paris: PUF.

Ferreira, Nuno (2011), *Fundamental Rights and Private Law in Europe*, London/New York: Routledge

Forster, Neil (2011), 'The Merits of the Civil Action for Breach of Statutory Duty', 33 *Sydney Law Review*, pp. 67–93

Geigel (2020): see Haag 2020

Giliker, Paula (2010), *Vicarious Liability in Tort. A Comparative Perspective*, Cambridge: Cambridge University Press

Giliker, Paula (2020), *Tort*, 7th ed., London: Sweet & Maxwell

Gilleri, Giovanna (2021), 'Compensation at the Intersection of Tort Law and International Human Rights Law', in Bussani and Sebok 2021, pp. 63–83

Glenn, H. Patrick (1997), 'The Capture, Reconstruction and Marginalization of "Custom"', 45 *American Journal of Comparative Law*, pp. 613–20.

Glenn, H. Patrick (2010), *Legal Traditions of the World*, 4th ed., Oxford: Oxford University Press

Goldberg, John C.P. and Zipursky, Benjamin C. (2010), *The Oxford Introductions to U.S. Law: Torts*, Oxford, Oxford University Press

Gomard, Bernhard (2001), 'Recent Developments in the Danish Law of Tort', 41 *Scandinavian Studies in Law*, pp. 233–48

Gordley, James (2021), 'The Architecture of the Common and Civil Law of Torts: An Historical Survey', in Bussani and Sebok 2021, pp. 160–85

Goudkamp, James (2004), 'Negligence and Especially Capable Defendants: Does the Objective Standard of Care Cut Both Ways?', 12 *Tort Law Review*, pp. 111–13

Goudkamp, James (2013), *Tort Law Defences*, Oxford: Hart Publishing

Goudkamp, James and Nolan, Donal (2020), *Winfield & Jolowicz on Tort*, 20th ed., London: Sweet & Maxwell

Haag, Kurt ed. (2020), *Der Haftpflichtprozess*, 28th ed., München: Beck

Heinze, Christian (2017), *Schadenersatz im Unionsprivatrecht*, Tübingen: Mohr Siebeck

Hellner, Jan (1974), 'The New Swedish Tort Liability Act', 22 *American Journal of Comparative Law*, pp. 1–16

Helms, Tobias (2015), 'Disgorgement of Profits in German Law', in Hondius and Janssen, pp. 219–30

Hondius, Ewout ed. (2007), *Precedent and the Law*, Reports to the XVIIth Congress International Academy of Comparative Law, Utrecht, 16–22 July 2006, Brussels: Bruylant

Hondius, Ewout and Janssen, André (eds) (2015), *Disgorgement of Profits*, Vienna: Springer

Horsey, Kirsty and Rackley, Erika (2019), *Tort Law*, 6th ed., Oxford: Oxford University Press

Hrádek, Jiří (2013), 'V. The Czech Republic', in 3 *European Tort Law Yearbook* pp. 119–50

Infantino, Marta (2021), 'Causation Theories and Causation Rules', in Bussani and Sebok, pp. 264–83

Jeuland, Emmanuel (2019), 'The Standard of Proof in France', in Tichý 2019, pp. 183–95

Jiang, Hao (2021), 'Chinese Tort Law: Tradition, Transplants and Some Difficulties', in Bussani and Sebok, pp. 397–426

Jones, Michael A., Dugdale, Anthony M. and Simpson, Mark (eds) (2020), *Clerk & Lindsell on Torts*, 23rd ed., London: Sweet & Maxwell

Jutras, Daniel (2021), 'Alternative Compensation Schemes from a Comparative Perspective', in Bussani and Sebok, pp. 140–58

Kadner Graziano, Thomas (2018), *Comparative Tort Law: Cases, Materials, and Exercises*, London: Routledge

Kötz, Hein, and Wagner, Gerhard (2016), *Deliktsrecht*, 13th ed., Cologne: Vahlen

Koziol, Helmut and Wilcox, Vanessa (eds) (2009), *Punitive Damages: Common Law and Civil Law Perspectives*, Vienna/New York: Springer

Koziol, Helmut, Green, Michael D., Lunney, Mark, Oliphant, Ken, and Yang, Lixin (eds) (2017), *Product Liability: Fundamental Questions in a Comparative Perspective*, Berlin/Boston: De Gruyter

Lange, Hermann and Schiemann, Gottfried (2021), *Schadensersatz*, 4th ed., Tübingen: Mohr Siebeck

Le Morvan, Pierre (2018), 'Information, Privacy, and False Light', in Cudd, Ann E. and Navin, Mark C., *Core Concepts and Contemporary Issues in Privacy*, Cham: Springer, pp. 79–90

Le Tourneau, Philippe ed. (2020), *Droit de la responsabilité et des contrats regimes d'indemnisation*, 12th ed., Paris: Dalloz

Lee, Jewoo (2014), 'Two Defining Features of Russian Tort Law: Their Rationale and Legal Effect', 39 *Review of Central and East European Law*, pp. 109–43

Liew, Ying Kai (2015), 'The Rule in Wilkinson v Downton: Conduct, Intention, and Justifiability', 78 *Modern Law Review*, pp. 349–60

López-Medina, Diego (2012), 'The Latin American and Caribbean Legal Traditions', in Bussani and Mattei, pp. 344–68

Loubser, M., et al. (eds) (2018), *Law of Delict in South Africa*, 3rd ed., Cape Town: OUP South Africa

Magnus, Urich and Busnelli, Francesco Donato (eds) (2001), *Unification of Tort Law: Damages*, The Hague/Boston: Kluwer Law International

Markesinis, Basil S., Bell, John and Janssen, André (2019), *Markesinis' German Law of Torts*, 5th ed., Oxford: Hart Publishing

Matsumoto, Emi (2021), 'Tort Law in Japan', in Bussani and Sebok, pp. 373–96.

Matus Valencia, Juan G. (1958), 'The Centenary of the Chilean Civil Code', 7 *American Journal of Comparative Law*, pp. 71–83

Mayali, Laurent and Mousseron, Pierre (eds) (2018), *Customary Law Today*, Cham: Springer

McGregor, Harvey (2018), *McGregor on Damages*, 20th ed., London: Sweet & Maxwell

Menyhárd, Attilla (2014) 'XIII. Hungary', in 4 *European Tort Law Yearbook*, pp. 305–17

Merryman, John Henry and Pérez-Perdomo, Rogelio (2019), *The Civil Law Tradition*, 4th ed., Stanford: Stanford University Press

Moura Vicente, Dário (2013), 'The Scope and Structure of the Portuguese Civil Code', in Julio César Rivera ed., *The Scope and Structure of Civil Codes*, Dordrecht: Springer, pp. 319–31

Murphy, John (2019), 'Malice as an Ingredient of Tort Liability', 78 *Cambridge Law Journal*, pp. 355–82

Neethling, Johann, Potgieter, J. and Knobel J.C. (2021), *Law of Delict*, 8th ed., Johannesburg: LexisNexis SA

Nolan, Donal (2017), 'Rights, Damage and Loss', 37 *Oxford Journal of Legal Studies*, pp. 255–75

Oertel, Christoph (2010), *Objektive Haftung in Europa*, Tübingen: Mohr Siebeck

O'Neill, Timothy J. (2009), 'Through Glass Darkly: Western Tort Law from South and East Asian Perspective', 11 *Rutgers Race the Law Review*, pp. 1–30.

Palmer, Vernon Valentine (2007), 'Two Rival Theories of Mixed Legal Systems', 3 *Journal of Comparative Law*

Palmer, Vernon Valentine (2012), 'Mixed Jurisdictions', in Smits, Jan ed., *Elgar Encyclopedia of Comparative Law*, 2nd ed., Cheltenham, UK and Northampton, MA, USA: Edward Elgar Publishing, pp. 590–99

Palmer, Vernon Valentine (2021), 'A Comparative Law Sketch of Pure Economic Loss', in Bussani and Sebok 2021, pp. 284–304

Perry, Ronen (2019), 'Law of Torts' in Walter, Chr., et al. (eds), *The Israeli Legal System: An Introduction*, Baden-Baden: Nomos, pp. 87–111

Polański, P.P. (2007), *Customary Law of the Internet, in the Search for a Supranational Cyberspace Law*. Information Technology & Law Series, T.M.C. Asser Press, The Hague

Posner, Richard A. (1972), 'A Theory of Negligence', 1 *Journal of Legal Studies*, pp. 29–96

Raj, Manjeri Subin Sunder, Mookherjee, Ujal Kumar and Borthakur, Aman Deep (2021), 'Tort Law in India', in Bussani and Sebok 2021, pp. 427–42

Reimann, Mathias (2003), 'Product Liability in a Global Context: the Hollow Victory of the European Model' 11 *European Review of Private Law*, pp. 128–54

Reimann, Mathias (2021), 'Product Liability', in Bussani and Sebok 2021, pp. 236–63

Rivera, Julio César ed. (2013), *The Scope and Structure of Civil Codes*, Dordrecht: Springer

Sacco, Rodolfo (1991), 'Legal Formants: A Dynamic Approach to Comparative Law', parts I and II, 39 *American Journal of Comparative Law*, pp. 1–34 and pp. 343–401

Samuel, Geoffrey (2013), *A Short Introduction to the Common Law*, Cheltenham, UK and Northampton, MA, USA: Edward Elgar Publishing

Schulz, Marten (2007), 'Disharmonization: Reflections on the Principles of European Tort Law', 18 *European Business Law Review*, pp. 1305–26

Sejean, Michel (2015), 'The Disgorgement of Illicit Profits in French Law', in Hondius and Jansen, pp. 121–37

Senden, Linda A.J. (2005), 'Soft Law, Self-Regulation and Co-Regulation in European Law: Where Do They Meet?', 9 *Electronic Journal of Comparative Law*, at https://ssrn.com/abstract=943063

Siems, Matthias (2014), *Comparative Law*, Cambridge: Cambridge University Press

Sirena, Pietro (2019), 'The Concepts of "Harm" in the French and Italian Laws of Civil Liability', in Borghetti and Whittaker, pp. 205–22

Sorabji, John (2019), 'The English Approach to the Standard of Proof in Civil Proceedings', in Tichý 2019, pp. 249–69

Steiner, Eva (2018), *French Law*, 2nd ed, Oxford: Oxford University Press.

Tan, David (2010), 'The Salient Features of Proximity: Examining the Spandeck Formulation for Establishing a Duty of Care', *Singapore Journal of Legal Studies*, pp. 459–83

Tichý, Luboš (2019), *Standard of Proof in Europe*, Tübingen: Mohr Siebeck

Tilbury, Michael (2018), 'Aggravated Damages', 71 *Current Legal Problems*, pp. 215–44

Tjong Tjin Tai, T.F. Eric (2018), 'Liability for (Semi-)Autonomous Systems', in Mak, V., Tjong Tjin Tai, T.F.E. and Berlee, A. (eds), *Research Handbook in Data Science and Law*, Cheltenham, UK and Northampton, MA, USA: Edward Elgar Publishing, pp. 55–82

Ulfbeck, Vibe, Ehlers, Andreas and Siig, Kristina (2018), 'Denmark', in Winiger, Benedict, Karner, Ernst and Oliphant, Ken, *Digest of European Tort Law: Essential Cases on Misconduct*, Berlin: De Gruyter, pp. 58–60

Van Dam, Cees C (2013), *European Tort Law*, 2nd ed., Oxford: Oxford University Press

Van Gerven, Walter, Lever, Jeremy and Larouche, Pierre (2000), *Tort Law*, Oxford: Oxford University Press

Verbruggen, Paul and Paiement, Philippe (2017), 'Transnational Private Regulation' at www.oxfordbibliographies.com/view/document/obo-9780199756223/obo-9780199756223-0226.xml

Viney, Geneviève, Jourdain, Patrice and Carval, Suzanne (2013), *Les conditions de la responsabilité*, 4th ed., Paris: LGDJ

Viney, Geneviève, Jourdain, Patrice and Carval, Suzanne (2017), *Les effets de la responsabilité*, 4th ed., Paris: LGDJ

Von Bar, Christian (1998), *The Common European Law of Torts*, vol. 1, Oxford: Clarendon

Von Bar, Christian (2000), *The Common European Law of Torts*, vol. 2, Oxford: Clarendon

Von Bar, Christian (2011), 'The Notion of Damage', in Hartkamp, A.S., et al (eds.), *Towards a European Civil Code*, 4th ed., Alphen a/d Rijn: Kluwer Law International, pp. 387–99

Wagner, Gerhard (2021), *Deliktsrecht*, 14th ed., Cologne: Vahlen

Weinrib, E.J. (2012), *The Idea of Private Law*, revised ed., Oxford: Oxford University Press

Wendehorst, Christiane (2020), 'Strict Liability for AI and other Emerging Technologies', 11 *Journal of European Tort Law*, pp. 150–80

Werro, Franz and Büyüksagis, Erdem (2021), 'The Bounds between Negligence and Strict Liability', in Bussani and Sebok 2021, pp. 186–213

Winfield and Jolowicz (2020): alternative for Goudkamp and Nolan 2020

Wolf, Manfred and Neuner, Jörg (2012), *Allgemeiner Teil des Bürgerlichen Rechts*, 10th ed., München: Beck

Wright, Richard W. (2002), 'Justice and Reasonable Care in Negligence Law', 47 *American Journal of Jurisprudence*, pp. 143–96

Wright, Richard W. (2003), 'Hand, Posner, and the Myth of the "Hand Formula"', 4 *Theoretical Inquiries in Law*, pp. 145–274

Wright, Jane (2017), *Tort Law and Human Rights*, 2nd ed., Oxford: Hart Publishing

Yagelnitskiy, Alexander (2021), 'Basics of Russian Tort Law', in Bussani and Sebok, pp. 355–72

Youngs, Raymond (2014), *English, French & German Comparative Law*, 3rd ed., Abingdon and New York: Routledge

Zimmermann, Reinhard (1996), *The Law of Obligations*, Oxford: Clarendon Press

Zweigert, Konrad and Kötz, Hein (1998), *An Introduction to Comparative Law*, 3rd ed., Oxford: Clarendon

INDEX